Mistaken identification

Mistaken identification
The eyewitness, psychology, and the law

BRIAN L. CUTLER
Florida International University

STEVEN D. PENROD
University of Nebraska-Lincoln

Published by the Press Syndicate of the University of Cambridge
The Pitt Building, Trumpington Street, Cambridge CB2 1RP
40 West 20th Street, New York, NY 10011-4211, USA
10 Stamford Road, Oakleigh, Melbourne 3166, Australia

First published 1995

Library of Congress Cataloging-in-Publication Data
Cutler, Brian L.
Mistaken identification : the eyewitness, psychology, and the law
/ Brian L. Cutler, and Steven D. Penrod.
p.   ca.
Includes bibliographical references and index.
ISBN 0-521-44553-1 (hc). – ISBN 0-521-44572-8 (pbk.)
1. Eyewitness identification – United States.   2. Criminals – United
States – Identification.   3. Psychology, Forensic.   I. Penrod,
Steven.   II. Title.
KF9672.C87   1995
363.2'58 – dc20   94-45187
                                                    CIP

A catalog record for this book is available from the British Library.

ISBN 0-521-44553-1 Hardback
ISBN 0-521-44572-8 Paperback

Transferred to digital printing 2001

Contents

The authors

Brian L. Cutler is Associate Dean and Associate Professor of Psychology, Florida International University. He earned his Ph.D. from the University of Wisconsin in 1987 and joined the faculty at Florida International University later that year. He was awarded the 1988 dissertation award from the American Psychology-Law Society for his research on jury decision making in eyewitness identification cases. He has published over 35 articles on eyewitness testimony and jury decision making in psychology and law journals and has presented his research at regional, national, and international conferences.

Steven D. Penrod is Professor of Psychology and Professor of Law, University of Nebraska-Lincoln. He earned his J.D. from Harvard Law School in 1974 and his Ph.D. in psychology from Harvard University in 1979. He joined the faculty of the psychology department of the University of Wisconsin in 1979, became a professor of law at the University of Minnesota Law School in 1988, and in 1995 joined the faculty at the University of Nebraska-Lincoln as director of the Psychology-Law Program. He received an early-career award in applied psychology from the American Psychological Association in 1986 and has published over 50 articles on eyewitness reliability and jury decision making. He is an author of a book on juries and two textbooks.

Preface

The day on which this preface is written marks, almost to the day, the beginning of a collaboration between graduate student and mentor that can be described as a research roller coaster that shows little sign of slowing and no sign of ending. At the outset of our collaboration our mission was, and remains, to advance the academic and legal communities' understanding of the factors that influence eyewitness identification and how best to protect suspects and defendants from the consequences of mistaken eyewitness identification. This monograph represents our attempt to summarize and integrate the research we and others have conducted on these topics.

Most of the research described in this book has been published in psychology and interdisciplinary scientific journals. A substantial portion has also been reviewed in other volumes. Whereas our journal articles are primarily written for scholars of law-psychology, this volume is meant for consumption by a wider audience, including lawyers, judges, professors of law, academic psychologists who do not follow law-psychology research, and graduate and undergraduate students in the social sciences and law. Our goal is not to provide a comprehensive summary of eyewitness research or even of research on eyewitness identification. Rather, we focus on the specific questions that have served as the unifying themes in our collaborative research program: eyewitness identification and the effectiveness of legal safeguards in eyewitness cases. For a more general review of eyewitness research, interested readers may wish to consult Ross, Read, and Toglia (1994).

In reviewing research on eyewitness identification and legal safeguards, we have tried to provide readers with the gist of the research findings as well as to acquaint readers with the methodology commonly employed in law-psychology research, for understanding the methodology is critical to evaluating the research conclusions. Where possible, we give detailed examples of specific studies. These studies were not chosen because they represent the best quality or most accurate research. They were chosen because they well illustrate the approaches adopted by law-psychology researchers.

It is our hope that the research reviewed in this book will be useful for a variety of purposes: advancing our scientific understanding of eyewitness identification; informing policymakers, judges, lawyers, and police officers about policy considerations and practical aspects of eyewitness identification; and stimulating more research on these important topics. We will not be surprised if readers are sometimes frustrated with our inability to reach firm conclusions. As with any young academic enterprise, research on some of the topics we consider is sparse, the methodology is sometimes imprecise, and much research work remains to be done. Thus, we will be satisfied if this book acquaints practitioners and students with the enterprise of law-psychology research and whets their appetites for more.

Our research has benefited from the valuable contributions of our colleagues, including fellow professors, graduate students, and undergraduate students. Particularly helpful were Peter Shapiro, Carol Krafka, James Coward, Hedy Red Dexter, Todd Martens, Thomas O'Rourke, Ronald Fisher, and Douglas Narby. Many additional graduate and undergraduate students provided important assistance and we thank them sincerely. Preparation of this volume was greatly aided by the services of WESTLAW of West Publishing Company. Funding for our research was provided by the National Science Foundation (SES-8411721 to Steven Penrod; SBR-9320960 and SES-8911146 to Brian Cutler) and the National Institute of Justice (84-IJ-CX-0010 to Steven Penrod). We thank the Minneapolis Star Tribune for permission to reproduce materials in Chapter 1. We are also indebted to Florida International University and the Universities of Wisconsin and Minnesota for their support for this research.

Finally, we wish to dedicate this volume to Reuben and Elaine Cutler and Rachel Penrod.

Part I

Introduction

1 Eyewitness identification errors

Convicted burglar Jerome Thomas Clepper had tried to go straight. But his rural Pine City body shop was failing. He needed cash, one way or another. His solution pulled Shaun Deckinga into a nightmare. On December 15, 1992, at the Forest Lake State Bank, Clepper opened a brown accordion folder wide enough for the teller to see that it contained a black semiautomatic pistol. After she stuffed $13,370 into the folder, he walked casually from the bank and vanished. One month later, using the same method, Clepper robbed Norwest Bank in Two Harbors of $2,395. "I want to make a withdrawal," he told the teller as he showed her the gun. He struck again two weeks later, on Jan. 29, this time at the Lakeside branch of St. Louis Bank for Savings, in Duluth, where he got $3,545.

That night, Duluth TV stations ran blurry bank pictures from the robberies. At 10:20 p.m., as news turned to weather, someone called the Duluth Police Department anonymously and told the desk sergeant that the robber on the news looked like Shaun Deckinga. In that moment, Deckinga went from being an obscure Duluth carpenter to a suspect in major federal crimes.

His resemblance to Jerome Clepper may have put Shaun Deckinga in the sights of the FBI, but cruel coincidents put him behind bars. Men who recently worked with Deckinga told agents they'd seen him in a black leather jacket, dark knit hat and gold-rimmed sunglasses like the robber's. One man said Deckinga mentioned buying a handgun. On Feb. 4, investigators questioned Deckinga and his girlfriend, Jill Puglisi, in their home in West Duluth. Both he and Puglisi said they were home together, with Shaun nursing a cold, at the time of the Lakeside robbery, and they couldn't remember where they were during the other robberies. A police officer said that during the interviews he saw a black leather jacket on a hook and a dark knit hat on the floor. Investigators noted that Deckinga had a discolored front tooth, a characteristic that one teller said the robber had. They left, but continued to investigate.

Tellers in Two Harbors and Duluth picked Deckinga's photo out of a lineup. Acquaintances and even a homeowner who'd hired Deckinga to work on her house said the man in the bank photos appeared to be him. A Duluth man told the FBI he'd shopped for snowmobile parts with Deckinga the afternoon of Jan. 29, contradicting the alibi that he had stayed home sick. Several people told detectives that Deckinga was a bad businessman who sometimes shortchanged people, and records showed he

3

had filed for bankruptcy that year. And he'd worked at construction jobs near two of the banks before each was robbed.

On Feb. 17, U. Magistrate Raymond L. Erickson ordered Deckinga detained without bail pending trial. Among other things, he cited Deckinga's alleged use of a firearm and his apparent disdain for the legal system; he'd registered vehicles in Wisconsin illegally and used a fake address to get a Wisconsin driver's license after his Minnesota license was suspended for traffic violations. Other than that, he had no criminal record. For the next five months, Deckinga's home would be the St. Louis County jail.

On May 18, 1993, a bank in Grantsburg, Wisconsin – a town about 30 minutes from Pine City, Minnesota, – was robbed. David Malban, Deckinga's attorney, was shown an unusually clear photo of the bank robber produced by the bank officers together with a brown accordian file in which the robber carried his gun.

The bearded robber looked like Deckinga, and he looked like the robber in the photos from all the other banks. But this one could not be Deckinga, and suddenly, finally, Malban knew that the others weren't either. They were all one man, this man.

In the trial before Judge Paul A. Magnuson, three tellers from Two Harbors and Duluth identified Deckinga, one remembering the set of his eyes, another a front tooth that stood out somehow. They all said they were either positive or sure. Jurors told the Star Tribune they convicted Deckinga because the tellers seemed so sure. But what jurors didn't know hurt Deckinga badly. Magnuson denied the defense's request to call University of Minnesota Law School Prof. Steven Penrod, who has devoted his career to studying the reliability of eyewitness identifications. . . Penrod, who has conducted 15 studies on the subject and has testified in 100 cases nationwide, said he would have told the jury that an eyewitness "could be 100 percent confident and still be 100 percent wrong." Factors that inhibit accuracy include stress, the presence of a weapon, and especially whether the subject was wearing a hat. "A hat proves to be a very effective disguise," said Penrod. "It covers one of the critical cues in differentiating faces – the hairline." But Magnuson, relying on higher court precedent, ruled that Penrod's testimony would have invaded the "province of the jury."

The Deckinga jury thus had no reason to question the eyewitness accounts. Said juror Diana Freese of Kent, Minnesota: "He was identified; that's what made the biggest impression on most of us. The tellers said he did it."

The loss of Penrod's testimony was a blow, but Malban reassured himself that Grantsburg would blow the case wide open. The Duluth News-Tribune likened the testimony on Grantsburg to a scene out of Perry Mason. Suddenly, it seemed possible that the government had made a serious mistake.

Despite Malban's optimism, Deckinga was convicted on two of the three robberies. On June 17, Clepper struck again, this time robbing the First Federal Bank of Eau

Claire in St. Croix Falls, Wisconsin. Again he used a folder, and again he covered his left arm.

Authorities sent a photo of the [St. Croix Falls] robber to nearby law enforcement agencies. On June 23, jailers Brent Jahnz and Rick Boland saw the photo where they work in the Pine County Jail, and both said the same thing: "I should know this guy." After a minute, one of them said it: Jerry Clepper, a former inmate, owner of a local body shop. On June 29, the FBI and local authorities searched Clepper's mobile home, shop, and cars. Among other things they seized a black leather jacket, black pellet gun made to look like a semiautomatic pistol, brown accordion file folder and red jacket, all of which fit the cases. Clepper arrived home during the search and was arrested. He admitting robbing banks in Forest lake, Two Harbors, Duluth, Grantsburg, and St. Croix Falls. He identified himself in bank pictures and described his method. He revealed that for one of the robberies he'd placed aluminum foil over one of his front teeth to make it stand out. He said he tried to save his business with some of the money, and gambled away the rest.

FBI agent Harvey, along with assistant U.S. attorneys Dunne and Magill, quickly attended to their next move: getting Shaun Deckinga out of jail. The sun shone brightly on July 1 as Deckinga walked lightly down the front courthouse steps a free man.

The case of Shaun Deckinga was reported in the Minneapolis *Star Tribune* (Oakes, October 17, 1993, p. 1). Lest you think that mistaken eyewitness identification is a freakish phenomenon consider the story of Elmer P. Jacobs. During August the Los Angeles police received a series of reports from taxi drivers who had been the victims of robberies by two male passengers. On August 16 E.A. Stocks reported his cab and $7.00 had been stolen. On August 17, Newt Troelson reported a similar crime, with the loss of $12.00. On the 18th, E. M. Shaw, and on the 20th, E. I. McDonald, reported similar experiences. Each time the taxi driver was asked to drive to a remote location where he was robbed. Similar crimes were being reported elsewhere in the Los Angeles vicinity.

Early in September the four victims attended police department lineups where groups of arrested persons were marched before victims of many types of crimes for possible identification. All four of the taxi drivers identified a prisoner, Elmer P. Jacobs, as one of the robbers. Jacobs had been arrested for stealing an automobile for a joy ride on August 18, 1928. He eventually pleaded guilty to grand larceny for the car theft and was sentenced to Folsom prison due to his record as a second offender. In the meantime, he was indicted for the four taxi robberies and was tried on October 30 in Los Angeles County Superior Court. Each victim appeared, described the holdup, and identified Jacobs as one of the robbers. Jacobs had wavy hair, almond-shaped eyes, a crooked nose, and tight, thin lips (as viewed from the side). He was easily recognized. Jacobs offered some imprecise alibi evidence intended to show that he was elsewhere at the time each crime occurred, but the jury returned a guilty verdict for each of the robberies. On November 5, Jacobs was sentenced to serve from fifteen years to life on each count.

During the week Jacobs was sentenced, Harvey Hossafrasse, Fredell Nicholson, John Shelby Hobbs, and William Schmittroth were arrested on an assortment of charges. Hossafrasse and Nicholson soon confessed to robbing Newt Troelson and the confessions were corroborated with fingerprints. Further confessions linked these two with the Stocks and Shaw robberies, and implicated Hobbs and Schmittroth in the McDonald robbery. None of these gang members knew Jacobs. The four men were placed in lineups for the victims to view. All the confessed robbers were positively identified and it was clear to the victims that their identifications of Jacobs were in error.

These events all took place in 1928 and the Jacobs story became one of many reported by Edwin M. Borchard, former Professor of Law at Yale University, in *Convicting the Innocent* (1932, pp. 340–341), a collection of cases in which people were erroneously convicted.

Eyewitnesses in the criminal justice system

The criminal justice system recognizes that eyewitness testimony in general and eyewitness identification in particular play profoundly important roles in the apprehension, prosecution, and adjudication of criminal offenders. Police investigators rely heavily on eyewitness testimony in their initial investigation of a crime (Fisher & Geiselman, 1992). Eyewitness identifications from photospreads and lineups are frequent occurrences (Brigham & Bothwell, 1983; Goldstein, Chance, & Schneller, 1991). And the eyewitness is probably the single most common form of witness in many criminal trials. The criminal justice system also acknowledges the influence that eyewitnesses have on trial outcomes.

Prosecutors typically do not debate whether or not to put the eyewitness on the stand; they do so reflexively. Defense attorneys do not equivocate when establishing strategies for cross-examining eyewitnesses; they make every attempt to discredit eyewitnesses. The criminal justice system also recognizes the fallibility of eyewitness identification. Cases of mistaken identification are amply documented in the legal and popular literature, as are the cases already described. Eyewitnesses may be mistaken for a variety of reasons: because they have weak memories for the event or because they have been deliberately or accidentally subjected to investigation procedures that compromise the quality of eyewitness identification or some degree of both.

The accuracy of eyewitness identification

One of the fundamental concerns that motivates psychologists' interest in the factors that affect eyewitness reliability is a recognition that eyewitness identification evidence is frequently the source of erroneous convictions. How often does eyewitness evidence result in erroneous convictions? The compelling instances of mistaken identification described in the beginning of this chapter illustrate the problem but they do not speak to the overall accuracy rate of eyewitness identification.

Huff (1987) notes that there is no known method for authoritatively determining how many erroneous convictions occur each year, but the estimates in the literature range from only a few cases per year to as many as 20% of all convictions. There are several possible methods one might employ to make such estimates. For example, one can survey criminal justice officials and secure their estimates of false conviction rates. One can even use these officials and other sources to identify cases of erroneous conviction. Huff (1987) used both tactics: He conducted a national survey of state attorneys general ($N = 54$) and in-depth surveys of criminal justice officials from Ohio (including judges, public defenders, and prosecutors). The overall response rate was 65% ($N = 229$). Over 70% of these respondents believed that erroneous convictions comprise less than 1% of all felony convictions, and another 20 percent of the estimates fell into the 1 – 5% range. In addition to this survey, Huff undertook a search of major newspapers and 1,100 magazines and journals. These methods produced a total of 500 known cases of erroneous conviction.

Even if one assumes, as did Huff, that the error rate is only .5%, the number of erroneous convictions could be staggering: In 1991 there were an estimated 14.1 million arrests in the United States (including drunken driving, but not other traffic offenses). Nearly 3 million of these arrests were for serious FBI "index crimes" such as murder, rape, robbery, burglary, and larceny. Department of Justice data (1983) suggest that over half of these index crime arrests result in convictions. The 50% conviction rate appears reasonable: In 1990 there were nearly 830,000 felony convictions in the state courts and this does not include misdemeanor convictions that followed from arrests for more serious offenses. In addition, in 1992 there were over 42,000 convictions in federal courts (BJS, 1992). These numbers indicate that there could easily have been 1.5 million convictions per year for serious offenses in recent years and if only .5% are erroneous, that yields 7,500 erroneous convictions per year for serious offenses! As Huff noted based on similar computations: "This level of accuracy is at once both reassuring and frightening – reassuring in the aggregate, but frightening to contemplate individual cases of injustice, even if they constitute a very small proportion of all convictions" (p. 103).

Sources of conviction errors

What produces these erroneous convictions? Several legal scholars, beginning with Borchard (1932), have studied the causes of erroneous conviction in over 1,000 criminal cases (see also Brandon & Davies, 1973; Frank & Frank, 1957; Huff, 1987; Huff, Rattner, & Sagarin, 1986). Huff (1987) readily concludes, on the basis of the 500 cases of erroneous conviction that he identified, that the single leading cause of mistaken conviction was erroneous eyewitness identification of the defendants. He states that eyewitness error was involved in nearly 60% of the cases he studied. This rate is all the more remarkable given that eyewitness cases probably constitute a small proportion of all cases: Loh (1981) estimates that eyewitness identifications are a prominent feature in only 5% of trials (Loh, 1981) and a survey of prosecutors in 30 states produced an estimate that 3% of felony cases are based on eyewitness identifications (Goldstein, Chance, & Schneller, 1989).

Such archival data are indeed compelling evidence that mistaken eyewitness identifications occur. Based on the estimate of 7,500 cases of erroneous conviction just mentioned, the archival data suggest there may be as many as 4,500 erroneous convictions each year arising from mistaken identifications. If these erroneous convictions follow the pattern of other cases, in 85 – 90% of them the defendant has pleaded guilty in exchange for a lightened, plea-bargained sentence. Of course it is also entirely plausible that truly innocent defendants such as Elmer Jacobs and Shaun Deckinga, when confronted by mistaken identifications, are less likely to plea bargain and more likely to proceed to trial in an effort to reveal the error. Thus, a disproportionate number of erroneous convictions may arise from trials before juries and judges.

The cases reviewed by Borchard, Huff, and the others are unique in that there was some basis for confidently concluding that the identifications were mistaken. However, there is no way to know how representative those cases are of all cases of erroneous conviction – it may, for instance, be easier or more difficult to establish innocence in an eyewitness case than in cases of erroneous conviction that arise from other sources such as unethical prosecutorial behavior, false accusations, or false confessions. As a result of these problems it is hazardous to use the computations above to estimate the likelihood that the average identification is mistaken.

Error rates in eyewitness identifications

Experimental studies of eyewitness identification performance provide another source of information on the plausible rates of mistaken identifications. In experiments, crimes are simulated in various ways. In some experiments (e.g., Cutler, Penrod, & Martens, 1987a) subjects view videotaped enactments of crimes and later attempt to identify the perpetrators. In others (e.g., Cutler & Fisher, 1990), innocuous thefts are staged in classrooms in view of a large number of students. In still others (e.g., Lindsay, Wells, & Rumpel, 1981), thefts are staged for individual subjects who visit the laboratory believing they are there to participate in an unrelated experiment. In a more realistic but unusual laboratory experiment conducted by Hosch and Cooper (1982), the experimenters staged a theft of subjects' watches, leading them to believe they were victims of an actual crime.

Many of these experiments test the accuracy of identification performance by having some eyewitnesses attempt identifications from lineups (or photoarrays) in which the perpetrator is present and others attempt identifications from lineups in which the perpetrator is absent. The purpose of using perpetrator-present lineups is to assess eyewitnesses' abilities to identify crime perpetrators correctly. The purpose of using perpetrator-absent lineups is to assess the extent to which eyewitnesses falsely identify lineup members as crime perpetrators. In other words, the perpetrator-present lineups resemble the situation in which the suspect is guilty, and the perpetrator-absent lineups resemble the situation in which the suspect is innocent.

Wells (1993) notes that across the many laboratory experiments on eyewitness identification, the false identification rates varied from nearly 0% to nearly 100%. Moreover, Wells notes that, in many of these studies, false identifications are made with expressions of high levels of certainty. Although the laboratory evidence clearly demonstrates that false identifications can occur with some regularity and that many eyewitnesses are capable of persuading themselves that their false identifications are correct, this evidence falls short of addressing the question of how accurate are identifications in actual cases. The problem with generalizing the accuracy rates from these experiments is that the crime simulations can depart in many ways from actual crimes. Hence, even if we were to average the rates across experiments and find that false identification rates occur, say, 40% of the time, we would have to be cautious in generalizing this rate to actual crimes involving eyewitness identification.

Indeed, estimating the identification accuracy rates in actual crimes is not the purpose of most eyewitness identification experiments. The purpose of most experiments is to isolate some factor, such as viewing conditions or the manner in which a lineup test is conducted, and examine its influence while holding all other factors constant. Thus, the investigator is primarily interested in the accuracy rates in one experimental condition (e.g., when eyewitnesses receive one set of instructions prior to a lineup test) as compared to accuracy rates in an alternative experimental condition (e.g., when eyewitnesses receive another set of instructions prior to the lineup test). In attempting to test the effect of a factor on eyewitness identification accuracy, the investigator typically devises a methodology that will yield an average accuracy rate of about 50%. By doing so, the investigator maximizes the sensitivity of the experimental test so that the effect of some potentially important factor, such as lineup instructions, can be detected. This point can be illustrated with an example.

Imagine attempting to test the influence of suggestive lineup instructions on identification accuracy in a situation in which 100% of eyewitness are likely to make an accurate identification, such as if they are asked to identify a family member they saw engaging in a crime. All of the eyewitnesses would be expected to correctly identify their brothers and not falsely identify innocent suspects as their brothers, regardless of how suggestive the lineup instructions were. Thus, suggestive instructions would appear to have no effect on identification accuracy. The lack of an effect would probably be due to insensitivity of the test situation rather than to a resistance to suggestion on the part of all eyewitnesses. Identification tests and the data they produce are more sensitive to the effects of experimental factors if they are equally distributed over the possible range of performance accuracy. The fact that most investigators deliberately aim for identification accuracy rates of around 50% in their experiments is powerful reason to question the generalizability of the accuracy rates in experiments to those in actual cases. Of course, the fact that these levels of error can readily be attained in experiments tells us something about the general unreliability of eyewitness identifications.

Field experiments with eyewitnesses

With these caveats in mind, perhaps the most relevant source of data pertaining to accuracy rates of actual eyewitness identifications emerges from field studies of eyewitness identification. Some researchers (Brigham, Maass, Snyder, & Spaulding, 1982; Krafka & Penrod, 1985; Pigott, Brigham, & Bothwell, 1990; Platz & Hosch, 1988) have attempted to reap the benefits of both laboratory experiments and realistic crime conditions by conducting well-controlled experiments in more realistic field settings. The primary purpose of this research is, like laboratory experiments, to estimate the effects of an isolated factor on identification accuracy. Two of the experiments (Brigham et al., 1982; Platz & Hosch, 1988) were primarily interested in the influences of witness and perpetrator race on identification accuracy. One (Krafka & Penrod, 1985) was primarily concerned with the influence of procedures designed to improve the accuracy of eyewitness identifications. Pigott et al.'s (1990) study examined the relation between accuracy of eyewitnesses' descriptions and identifications. Because these studies were conducted in more realistic settings, their identification accuracy rates might be a better indication of those that are likely in actual crimes, at least as compared to archival studies and laboratory experiments.

Brigham et al. (1982) conducted the first of these experiments. Their procedure required two casually dressed males independently to enter a Tallahassee, Florida, convenience store, 5 minutes apart. Each engaged in an unusual (but safe) transaction with the convenience store clerk. One "customer" paid for a pack of cigarettes entirely with pennies, and either the customer or clerk had to count them (70 to 90 cents). That customer then asked for directions to a local airport, bus station, hospital, or shopping mall. The other customer carried a product to the counter as if he were going to purchase it, discovered that he did not have enough money, started for the door, found enough change, and returned to the counter to purchase the item. He then asked directions to one of the aforementioned locations. Each transaction lasted 3 to 4 minutes. Clerks were later asked to identify the customers from photoarrays.

In their pilot work for this experiment, Brigham et al. tested the clerks 24 hours later and found that only 7.8% were able to identify the customers correctly. This accuracy rate was comparable to what one would observe just from guessing. They then modified the procedure to test for identification accuracy after only 2 hours. In all, 73 clerks participated as eyewitnesses, each providing two identifications, one of each customer. With the 2-hour time delay, 50 out of 146 total identifications (34.2%) were correct. Customer-absent photoarrays were not used in this experiment, so false identification rates could not be estimated.

In Krafka and Penrod's (1985) experiment, a "customer" entered convenience stores in Madison, Wisconsin, and purchased a small item with a traveler's check. Either 2 or 24 hours later, a researcher, posing as a law intern, asked the clerks to identify the customer. Eighty-five clerks were shown either customer-present or customer-absent photoarrays. When the customer was present in the photoarray, 41% of the clerks correctly identified him. When the customer was absent from the photoarray, 34% falsely identified a photograph as that of the customer.

Platz and Hosch (1988) used the same convenience store scenario as did Brigham et al. (1982) except that three accomplices entered the store rather than two. The convenience stores were in El Paso, Texas. The first two accomplices engaged in the same routines carried out in Brigham et al.'s experiment. The third attempted to pay for a purchase with a combination of dollars and pesos. Upon being informed that the store did not accept pesos, the customer asked the clerk if the store carried a particular sports magazine. Identifications were tested using customer-present photoarrays

2 hours after the customers entered the stores. Each of 86 clerks attempted to identify all three customers. In all, 44.2% of the identifications were correct. The false identification rate could not be assessed as customer-absent photoarrays were not used.

Apparently having exhausted all of the convenience stores in Tallahassee, Florida, Brigham and colleagues (Pigott et al., 1990) turned to local banks for their next field study. In each scenario, one of two accomplices entered the bank through its main entrance, walked to the center island, and pretended to fill out a deposit slip. The accomplice then approached a teller and attempted to cash a check. The check was a "crudely altered United States Postal Service money order" in which the amount of $10 was altered to $110. All tellers refused to cash the money order. Each time the accomplice argued with the teller, claiming that the alteration was made by post office personnel. After repeated refusals from the clerk, the accomplice became irate, took the money order, and hurried out of the bank. The interaction lasted approximately 90 seconds. Four to five hours later an experimenter, posing as a law officer, showed the teller a customer-present or customer-absent photoarray. In all, 47 bank tellers participated as eyewitnesses. Among tellers shown a customer-present photoarray, 47.8% made a correct identification. Among tellers shown a customer-absent photoarray, 37.5% made a false identification.

In summary, data were gathered in these experiments from 291 mock-eyewitnesses who were administered 536 separate identification tests. The correct and false identification rates in these experiments are summarized in Table 1.1. The average percentage correct is 41.8% for correct identifications and 35.8% for false identifications. What we learn from these experiments is that identifications for persons seen briefly, in nonstressful conditions, and attempted after brief delays, are frequently inaccurate. In customer-present photoarrays that resemble the situation in which the suspect is guilty, only two out of five guilty persons were correctly identified. In customer-absent photoarrays that represent the situation in which the suspect is innocent, one out of three innocent persons was falsely identified. In one of these studies (Pigott et al., 1990), the mock-eyewitnesses were bank tellers, 77% of whom reported that they had received training for eyewitness situations.

Although the scenarios used in these four studies do not resemble the events in many crimes such as armed robbery or murder, the results are still relevant. More important, the scenarios do resemble many eyewitness situations. Eyewitnesses do not always experience violent and heinous crimes. Sometimes eyewitnesses are asked to identify persons whom they did not know were perpetrators at the time an interaction occurred. At other times eyewitnesses are asked to identify persons whom they viewed fleeing a scene.

Table 1.1. *Identification accuracy rates in field experiments*

	Sample study size	Percentage correct identifications	Percentage false identifications
Brigham et al. (1992)	146	34.2	
Krafka & Penrod (1985)	85	41. 0	34. 0
Platz & Hosch (1988)	258	44.2	
Pigott et al. (1990)	47	47.8	37.5
Total/Unweighted Average	536	41.8	35.8

In comparing the methodologies used in these studies with what does happen in violent crimes, some potentially important differences can be identified. The time during which the to-be-recognized person was available for viewing was substantial and comparable to many crimes. The time between the crime and identification was relatively brief and we know that longer retention intervals generally lead to less accurate identifications (see Chapter 5 below).

The largest deficiency in the field research is that the scenarios employed do not simulate the emotional duress experienced by an eyewitness to a violent crime. The effects of emotional duress on eyewitness memory in general, and identification accuracy in particular, are less clear (Christiaanson, 1992). Thus, the factors that distinguish the field studies from real-life violent crimes lead us to believe that if there is any bias, the field studies overestimate the accuracy of eyewitness identifications.

The data from laboratory experiments and field studies complement the archival studies, which demonstrate compellingly that mistaken identification have, on numerous occasions, led to miscarriages of justice. The laboratory experiments clearly demonstrate that combinations of factors can produce eyewitness identification accuracy rates that span the full range of possibilities: from nearly 0% accuracy to nearly 100% accuracy. And field studies demonstrate that, in some realistic crimelike situations, eyewitness identifications are often inaccurate.

But what accounts for these inaccuracies? Are human beings simply poor at recognizing other people? As social animals, such a state of affairs would serve us poorly. Do we frequently mistakenly identify persons such as our family members, friends, and fellow employees? Hardly. Many psychologists have argued that certain factors predictably influence identification accuracy at the perception, encoding, storage, and retrieval stages of memory. This research is summarized in the following chapters.

The response of the criminal justice system to identification errors

In an effort to reconcile the conflict produced by the powerful need for eyewitness testimony and the dangers of mistaken identification, the criminal justice system has designed safeguards that, in theory, protect the defendant from erroneous conviction due to mistaken identification. The courts have established pretrial criteria designed to encourage the use of fair identification procedures. During trial the most common safeguards are cross-examination of witnesses and judicial instructions delivered to the jury at the conclusion of the trial. These instructions advise the jury on how to evaluate the credibility of the witnesses they have heard testify. Sometimes these instructions are supplemented with special instructions concerning the evaluation of eyewitnesses who have made an identification of the defendant.

A less common safeguard is the use of expert testimony on the psychology of eyewitness memory, as was attempted in the Deckinga case. Psychologists have been studying memory for over 100 years. The foci of these investigations include theoretical and applied aspects of memory processes. Examples of theoretical questions include: How is memory organized? How do we update memory? Do we have different types of memory systems for different types of information? How does aging influence memory processes? Examples of applied questions include: Which mnemonic techniques are most effective for memorizing information for later retrieval from memory? How can we improve memory for critical events? If aging has a detrimental effect on memory, how can we counteract it?

Why has the criminal justice system become interested in what psychologists have to say about eyewitness memory? Traditionally the criminal justice system has been receptive to new technologies. The role of forensic science has grown exponentially over the past century. Anyone who has observed a contemporary crime scene investigation can attest to its rigor. Within the shortest possible time of notification (usually within 1 hour), the police can dispatch a mobile laboratory to the crime scene. While a nosy public is kept behind the familiar yellow tape, a large group of dispassionate forensic experts engage in a well-planned routine of evidence gathering with the use of scientifically sophisticated equipment. Evidence of all shapes and sizes (including barely visible particles) is kept sterile for less rushed and more thorough analyses. These forensic investigations provide not only clues for detectives but their results are frequently used in court to buttress one or the other side's theories. Judges and juries have heard expert testimony about scientific analyses of hair, soil, fibers, and various kinds of body fluids. They have heard the testimony of pathologists who describe the manner and time of death. And increasingly they are hearing about DNA matching – a process that has the potential to revolutionize criminal justice proceedings.

Inviting (or tolerating) the testimony of psychologists who are experts in human memory processes is merely an extension of the criminal justice system's invitation to forensic science. Psychologists have learned a great deal about memory in general and eyewitness memory in particular. Why not use the information learned from their investigations to improve the quality of judges' or juries' appraisals of eyewitness identification? If the information is accurate and relevant to a specific case, wouldn't it help the judge and jury more accurately to discriminate between accurate and inaccurate eyewitnesses? Wouldn't the defendant be better protected from the legal consequences of mistaken identification?

Some courts have admitted expert psychological testimony on eyewitness memory and do so with some regularity. These courts, however, are a minority. At this point in time, admission of expert psychological testimony on eyewitness memory is the exception rather than the rule. Nonetheless, the courts have grown dramatically more receptive to eyewitness expert testimony in recent years. In the next two chapters we examine the state of the law with respect to expert witness testimony concerning eyewitness identification issues. The following four chapters concern the scientific psychology of eyewitness identification. Chapter 4 considers what it means for research to be "scientific" and Chapter 5 considers the problems one encounters when trying to provide a summary of scientific research findings. Chapters 6 and 7 review the scientific literature on the accuracy of eyewitness identification and the various factors that affect accuracy. Also reviewed in Chapters 6 and 7 are the factors that are sometimes believed to affect, but show little relation to, identification accuracy. Chapter 8 examines the roles of specific factors affecting the suggestiveness of eyewitness identification tests. The next two chapters review the effectiveness of traditional safeguards believed to protect the defendant from the consequences of mistaken eyewitness identification: Chapter 9 considers the problems attorneys have in developing information that would be useful for cross-examination of eyewitnesses and Chapter 10 reviews research on the effectiveness of cross-examination. Chapter 11 reviews research surveying laypersons about their knowledge of the factors that contribute to eyewitness unreliability and Chapters 12 and 13 examine research on juror decision making in eyewitness cases. Chapters 14, 15, and 16 focus on research studying the impact of expert psychological testimony in eyewitness cases. Chapter 17 summarizes research on the effects of instructions to juries as a safeguard against mistaken convictions.

Part II

Eyewitnesses, expert psychologists, and the law

2 The admissibility of expert testimony on the psychology of eyewitness identification

Fulero (1993) identifies *Criglow v. State* (1931), an Arkansas case, as the first recorded instance in which a psychologist was proffered as an eyewitness expert. The defendant was charged with robbery and wanted the expert to testify about the "powers of observation and recollection of two eyewitnesses." The trial court rejected the expert testimony and the Arkansas Supreme Court upheld the lower court's decision. The basis for the Supreme Court's ruling was that the expert testimony would "invade the province of the jury." Twenty one years later, in *People v. Collier* (1952), the defense offered a psychologist as an expert witness to testify about the contention that "an individual under emotional stress would be less likely than at other times to make correct observations." The California trial court did not admit the expert testimony, noting, as in *Criglow*, that the expert testimony would invade the province of the jury. The *Criglow* court also considered the content of the testimony was "within the field of common knowledge and experience."

Fulero observes that the testimony offered in these early cases differs in important ways from the testimony offered in contemporary cases. In the early cases there was no attempt by the expert to discuss the factors that influence eyewitness identification accuracy nor the empirical literature bearing on those factors. The content of the proffered testimony was the expert's opinion about the reliability of a particular eyewitness in a particular situation, given in response to a hypothetical question. In the modern approach, notes Fulero, the expert typically does not offer an opinion as to the reliability of a particular identification, but instead provides general background information about the factors that may influence eyewitness performance. The jury is also typically instructed that it is free to accept or reject the expert's testimony and any opinions, in whole or in part – thus it is, at least in theory, much more difficult to "invade the province of the jury."

Attempts to introduce expert psychological testimony on eyewitness memory began to flourish in the early 1970s. Evidence of these efforts can be found in appellate court decisions. In the state courts of appeal, two states, Kentucky (*Pankey v. Commonwealth*, 1972) and Massachusetts (*Commonwealth v. Jones*, 1972), upheld their trial courts' decisions to exclude such expert testimony. Trial court exclusion of expert testimony was also upheld in an early and important decision by the United States Court of Appeals for the Ninth Circuit (*United States v. Amaral*, 1973).

Fulero reports that by 1988, 111 state and 29 federal case opinions pertaining to the admissibility of expert testimony on eyewitness memory had been published. This, of course, is an underestimate of the number of cases in which such testimony was offered, for when expert testimony is admitted, there is no appeal on the admissibility issue, and no opinion is issued. Similarly, when the defendant is acquitted there is no appeal of a decision to exclude expert testimony. In addition, even when the defendant is convicted and expert testimony has been excluded, most appeals will not proceed on the basis of such exclusions – particularly in states where the appellate courts have recently and/or pointedly upheld the discretion of trial judges to exclude such testimony.

It is difficult to specify how many times experts have testified about problems or eyewitness reliability, but a survey conducted in the mid-1980s by Kassin, Ellsworth, and Smith (1989) provides some useful information. After conducting a search of research writings on eyewitness reliability, these researchers identified and surveyed 119 experts on eyewitness memory. Of the 63 experts who responded to the survey, 34 reported that they had testified at least once, and all together these experts had testified in 478 cases. Because only half of the experts responded, it is entirely plausible that the full set of experts has testified over 900 times. Furthermore, because the survey respondents were primarily research scientists and it is possible for individuals to qualify as experts solely on the basis of their familiarity with the research (e.g., through teaching or simply reading the literature), these numbers may substantially underestimate the number of expert witness appearances by psychologists.

Of course, the growing number of cases in which a party – typically the defendant in a criminal case – has proposed to present eyewitness expert testimony is the principal factor that has prompted state and federal courts to address, more systematically, the question of admissibility of eyewitness expert testimony. A trial judge generally turns to two sources for guidance on the question of whether or not expert testimony should be admitted at trial: appellate court opinions and rules of evidence. What do these opinions and rules have to say about the admissibility of expert testimony? There is no single answer to this question, for the rules and standards vary across jurisdictions and change over time. Nonetheless, it is possible to discern some general patterns in the rules and opinions.

Criteria for admitting expert testimony

As a starting point, the opinion of the Ninth Circuit Federal Court of Appeals in *United States v. Amaral* (1973) provides some insight into the criteria courts initially applied when determining whether or not to admit eyewitness expert testimony. The *Amaral* court drew upon the classic *Frye* test developed in *United States v. Frye* (1923) in which the trial court confronted the question of whether or not to admit evidence produced by a crude precursor to the polygraph. The Ninth Circuit decided that in order for expert testimony to be admissible, the expert must provide the jury with "appreciable help." In making this determination the following admissibility criteria were advanced:

1. The expert must be qualified to testify about the subject matter.
2. The expert must testify about a proper subject.
3. The testimony must conform to a generally accepted explanatory theory.
4. The probative value of the testimony must outweigh its prejudicial effect.

The *Amaral* court rejected the testimony of the expert (social psychologist Bertram Raven), apparently on the grounds that the testimony was not a proper subject matter:

it would not be appropriate to take from the jury their own determination as to what weight or effect to give to the evidence of the eye-witness and identifying witnesses and to have that determination put before them on the basis of the expert witness testimony as proffered. (p. 1153)

Fulero (1993) notes that although the *Amaral* test applied only to federal courts in the Ninth Circuit (California, Oregon, Hawaii, Washington, Alaska, Arizona, Guam, Idaho, Montana, and Nevada), it has been influential in many other courts as well.

To some extent, admissibility analyses such as those reflected in the *Amaral* decision began to change when the U. S. courts began using the new Federal Rules of Evidence (FRE) in 1975. Rules 702 and 403 are relevant to the issue of admissibility. Rule 702 states that expert testimony is admissible if:

1. The expert is qualified.
2. The testimony assists the trier of fact.
3. The expert's testimony is sufficiently reliable.

It should be noted that the federal rule adopted a standard that requires the expert testimony "assist" the jury – this stands in contrast to the higher *Amaral* standard that required "appreciable help."

Rule 403 states that the probative value of the expert testimony must outweigh its prejudicial impact.

Most states now use similar language in their rules governing the admissibility of expert testimony and even those states that have not explicitly adopted the federal language have been influenced by the reforms introduced by those rules. Compared to the traditional common law rules governing the admissibility of expert testimony, the Federal Rules and their progeny are fairly lax. The rules emphasize that the testimony be of some assistance to the jury and, consistent with this view, since the mid-1980s appellate courts have been more receptive to expert testimony on eyewitness memory (e.g., *People v. McDonald*, 1984; *State v. Chapple*, 1983; *State v. Moon*, 1986).

The more liberal standards for admissibility of expert testimony under the Federal Rules of Evidence are clearly articulated in the decision in *United States v. Downing* (1985), in which the Third Circuit of the Federal Court of Appeals (which covers Pennsylvania, Delaware, New Jersey, and the Virgin Islands) adopted an alternative test for the admissibility of eyewitness expert testimony based on proposals advanced by leading evidence scholar and federal judge, Jack Weinstein. The *Downing* court acknowledged that the new federal rules usually favor admissibility, including testimony about matters that are simply difficult, even if not beyond the ken of ordinary jurors, and favor admissibility even over an objection that the testimony might "invade the province of the jury." The *Downing* court explicitly rejected the traditional "general acceptance" standard of the *Frye* test and also expressed its doubts that the *Amaral* criteria conform with the more liberal Federal Rules. Under the *Downing* analysis trial judges were instructed to evaluate:

(a) the soundness and reliability of the process or technique used in generating the evidence,
(b) the possibility that admitting the evidence would overwhelm, confuse or mislead the jury, and
(c) the proffered connection between the scientific research or test result to be presented and particular disputed factual issues in the case. (p. 1237)

The Weinstein-inspired *Downing* analysis has proven quite prescient, as both the general approach and the *Downing* criteria were cited quite favorably by the United States Supreme Court in a 1993 decision that is certain to be the most important "scientific evidence" and "expert witness" decision for many years.

Although the 1993 case, *Daubert et al. v. Merrell Dow Pharmaceuticals*, involved purported expert testimony on the question of whether the antinausea drug Bendectin caused birth defects, it is likely to have profound implications for the admissibility of many forms of expert testimony, including eyewitness testimony. In considering the admissibility of the expert evidence offered in the trial court, the Supreme Court, like the *Downing* court, explicitly rejected the *Frye* test, noting, in a unanimous decision written by Justice Blackmun that:

a rigid "general acceptance" requirement would be at odds with the "liberal" thrust of the Federal Rules and their general approach of relaxing the traditional barriers to "opinion testimony." ([citing Beech Aircraft Corp. v. Rainey, 488 U.S., at 169] p. 2794)

The Court also articulated a perspective on scientific knowledge that most scientists would resonate to:

The subject of an expert's testimony must be "scientific . . . knowledge." . . . Of course, it would be unreasonable to conclude that the subject of scientific testimony must be "known" to a certainty; arguably, there are no certainties in science. . . . But, in order to qualify as "scientific knowledge," an inference or assertion must be derived by the scientific method. Proposed testimony must be supported by appropriate validation – i.e., "good grounds," based on what is known. In short, the requirement that an expert's testimony pertain to "scientific knowledge" establishes a standard of evidentiary reliability. (p. 2795)

The Court identified two general criteria to be applied by trial judges:

Faced with a proffer of expert scientific testimony, then, the trial judge must determine at the outset, pursuant to Rule 104(a), whether the expert is proposing to testify to (1) scientific knowledge that (2) will assist the trier of fact to understand or determine a fact in issue. This entails a preliminary assessment of whether the reasoning or methodology underlying the testimony is scientifically valid and of whether that reasoning or methodology properly can be applied to the facts in issue. (p. 2796)

As to the question of whether or not the proffered testimony does, in fact, constitute scientific knowledge, the Court offered the following guidance:

Ordinarily, a key question to be answered in determining whether a theory or technique is scientific knowledge that will assist the trier of fact will be whether it can be (and has been) tested. "Scientific methodology today is based on generating hypotheses and testing them to see if they can be falsified; indeed, this methodology is what distinguishes science from other fields of human inquiry." Green, at 645. See also C. Hempel, *Philosophy of Natural Science* 49 (1966) ("[T]he statements constituting a scientific explanation must be capable of empirical test"); K. Popper, *Conjectures and Refutations: The Growth of Scientific Knowledge* 37 (5th ed. 1989) ("[T]he criterion of the scientific status of a theory is its falsifiability, or refutability, or testability").... Another pertinent consideration is whether the theory or technique has been subjected to peer review and publication. (pp. 2796–7)

The inquiry envisioned by Rule 702 is, we emphasize, a flexible one. Its overarching subject is the scientific validity – and thus the evidentiary relevance and reliability – of the principles that underlie a proposed submission. The focus, of course, must be solely on principles and methodology, not on the conclusions that they generate. (p. 2797)

[The abuse of] trial court discretion

The decision to admit expert testimony is within the discretion of the trial court judge and appeals focus on whether or not the trial judge abused her or his discretion in excluding the expert testimony. Judges are given considerable latitude in applying their decisions; therefore, such appeals are rarely successful. However, admission of expert testimony on eyewitness memory gained momentum in 1983 when the Arizona Supreme Court ruled that exclusion of such testimony resulted in reversible error in *State v. Chapple*. The court, in the first decision of its kind, ruled that a trial judge abused his discretion in excluding expert testimony. The expert in *Chapple* was prepared to discuss the effects of unconscious transference, postevent information, the weak relationship between confidence and accuracy, and several other related factors. Unlike previous courts (for example, the court in the *Amaral* case), the *Chapple* court was unwilling to assume that knowledge of such factors was within the ken of the jury.

The *Chapple* decision set the stage for another oft-cited decision (*People v. McDonald*, 1984), which even more forcefully argued for the admission of expert psychological testimony on eyewitness memory. In *McDonald* the California Supreme Court also ruled that a trial judge abused his discretion in excluding an expert's testimony. The Court went so far as to specify the circumstances under which exclusion may constitute an abuse of discretion:

When an eyewitness identification of the defendant is a key element of the prosecution's case but is not substantially corroborated by evidence giving it independent reliability, and the defendant offers qualified expert testimony on specific psychological factors shown by the record that could have affected the accuracy of the identification but are not likely to be fully known to or understood by the jury, it will ordinarily be error to exclude that testimony. (p. 254)

Few courts have been so explicit about the circumstances under which a trial court will be judged to have abused its discretion with regard to an eyewitness expert. However, another example can be found in language from *State v. Moon* (1986), in which the Washington Court of Appeals decided that exclusion will be an abuse of discretion when: (a) the identification of the defendant is the principal issue at trial; (b) the defendant presents an alibi defense; and (c) there is little or no evidence linking the defendant to the crime. The *Moon* test was further refined by the Washington court in *State v. Johnson* (1987) in which the court held that expert testimony would be admitted only in close fact patterns that "cry out for explanation." The court in the *Downing* decision discussed earlier also identified a standard that trial judges might apply in assessing the admissibility of expert testimony: The court suggested a requirement that the expert testify on matters that "fit" the facts of the particular case being decided by the jury – this assures that the evidence is relevant to the jury's fact-finding.

The *Chapple*, *McDonald*, and *Downing* decisions have been instrumental in facilitating the admission of expert testimony on eyewitness memory. Several additional appellate courts have rendered opinions favorably inclined to admission of expert testimony on eyewitness memory, including the Third Circuit (*United States v. Sebetich*, 1985, and *United States v. Stevens*, 1991), the Seventh Circuit (*United States v. Curry*, 1992), the Ninth Circuit (*United States v. Langford*, 1986), Ohio (*State v. Buell*, 1986), Alaska (*Skamarocius v. State*, 1987), New York (*People v. Brooks*, 1985; *People v. Lewis*, 1987), Colorado (*People v. Campbell*, 1993), Connecticut (*State v. Johnson*, 1992), Florida (*State v. Malarney*, 1993), Indiana (*Farrell v. State*, 1993), Nevada (*Echavarria v. State*, 1992), South Dakota (*State v. McCord*, 1993 – in which a police officer testified for the prosecution concerning witness memory and the preparation of a composite), and Texas (*Rousseau v. State*, 1993).

Other appellate courts have noted that experts have testified in cases that are under appeal for other reasons, including the Northern District of California (*Easter v. Stainer*, 1994 – court upholds admission of identification evidence), California (*People v. Contreras*, 1993 – presence of the expert used to support trial judge's admission of a lineup that the defendant argued was suggestive), Ohio (*State v. Dillon*, 1994 – expert's presence cited as evidence of counsel's effective assistance of the defendant), Michigan (*People v. Kurylczyk*, 1993 – court upholds admission of a lineup identification), Texas (*Jordan v. State*, 1994), and Wisconsin (*State v. Miller*, 1994).

Despite these generally favorable recent developments, the overall position of the courts is still somewhat negative with respect to admitting eyewitness expert testimony. Recent opinions from the federal courts illustrate the unresolved nature of admissibility practices and highlight some of the impediments to admissibility that are not necessarily addressed in the general rules governing admissibility of expert testimony.

In the following pages we review some of the major federal and state appellate opinions concerning the admissibility of eyewitness expert evidence (the U.S. Supreme Court has not directly addressed the issue of eyewitness expert testimony in many years) . As will become evident in later chapters, we believe that the concerns expressed by state and federal courts of appeal about the admissibility of eyewitness expert testimony are essentially empirical questions. And, although the issues are multifaceted, we will focus, in the following discussion and in subsequent chapters, on three basic issues raised by the courts:

1. What is the state of scientific findings regarding eyewitness performance? Are the findings reliable/do they rest on an adequate scientific foundation?
2. Do traditional trial safeguards – cross-examination and cautionary instructions to jurors – afford adequate protection to defendants identified and prosecuted on the basis of eyewitness evidence?
3. Can eyewitness expert evidence assist jurors in their assessment of eyewitness evidence?

We have quoted liberally from a number of the leading opinions on eyewitness experts and annotated them to underscore the ways in which the courts have approached these three basic issues, which, for shorthand use we will refer to as the eyewitness expert evidence triad:

1. scientific reliability,
2. traditional safeguards, and
3. jury assistance.

3   Eyewitness experts in the courts of appeal

The Third Circuit of the Federal Court of Appeals

The Third Circuit is one of the most advanced of the federal circuits insofar as receptivity to eyewitness expert testimony is concerned. Three notable opinions on the issue have appeared since the Circuit's ground-breaking 1985 decision in *Downing*. As noted earlier, the court in *Downing* both foreshadowed the Supreme Court's recent decision in *Daubert* on the bases for assessing the admissibility of scientific evidence and vacated the defendant's conviction and remanded the case to the trial court for a new determination on the question of whether the trial court should have admitted the expert testimony proffered at trial.

Judge Becker, who wrote the opinion in *Downing*, made a number of significant observations about eyewitness expert testimony that bear on the triad issues: the scientific reliability of eyewitness research findings, the effectiveness of traditional safeguards against mistaken identifications, and the extent to which expert testimony about eyewitness research may assist the jury. (Note: Emphasis has been added throughout this chapter in order to highlight language bearing on these three issues.) Judge Becker:

The district court refused to admit the testimony of a psychologist offered by the defendant, apparently because the court believed that such testimony can never meet the "helpfulness" standard of Fed. R. Evid. 702. We hold that the district court erred. We also hold that the admission of such expert testimony is not automatic but conditional. First, the evidence must survive preliminary scrutiny in the course of an in limine proceeding conducted by the district judge. *This threshold inquiry, which we derive from the helpfulness standard of Rule 702, is essentially a balancing test, centering on two factors: (1) the reliability of the scientific principles upon which the expert testimony rests, hence the potential of the testimony to aid the jury in reaching an accurate resolution of a disputed issue; and (2) the likelihood that introduction of the testimony may in some way overwhelm or mislead the jury.* (emphasis added)

Second, admission depends upon the "fit," i.e., upon a specific proffer showing that scientific research has established that particular features of the eyewitness identifications involved may have impaired the accuracy of those identifications. (p. 1226)

In reaching this conclusion the court considered the relationship between the expert testimony and the role of the jury and tersely rejected one traditional argument against expert testimony:

Initially, it would appear that the court was concerned that the expert witness would testify as to the "ultimate issue of fact," Fed. R. Evid. 704. Were this so, the first ground of decision would also be erroneous. As the advisory committee's note on Rule 704 points out, the basic approach to opinion testimony in the Federal Rules is one of helpfulness. "In order to render this approach fully effective and to allay any doubt on the subject, the so-called 'ultimate issue' rule is specifically abolished by [Rule 704]." Notes of Advisory Committee on Proposed Rule 704. . . . The rule rejects as "empty rhetoric" the notion that some testimony is inadmissible because it usurps the "province of the jury." . . .

In light of this clear mandate of Fed. R. Evid. 704, it appears rather that the district court based its ruling on an interpretation of Fed. R. Evid. 702, in effect concluding that expert testimony concerning the reliability of eyewitness identifications is never admissible in federal court because such testimony concerns a matter of common experience that the jury is itself presumed to possess. (p. 1229)

The court considered a number of cases in a variety of jurisdictions where appellate courts had declined to overturn convictions in cases where expert testimony was excluded and underscored all three elements of the critical triad (scientific reliability, traditional safeguards, and jury assistance). The court observed:

several courts of appeals have upheld the exclusion of expert testimony on eyewitness perception and memory because the testimony would involve questions that "can be adequately addressed in cross-examination and that the jury can adequately weigh . . . through common-sense evaluation. . . . some courts have upheld the exclusion of evidence of this type on the ground that no reliable scientific basis exists for it. . . . Other courts have concluded that the introduction of such testimony would lead to an unduly confusing or time-consuming "battle of the experts" which, in the context of the particular case, would have added little of probative value, but would have increased the risk of unfair prejudice. (emphasis added) (p. 1229)

We have serious doubts about whether the conclusion reached by these courts is consistent with the liberal standard of admissibility mandated by Rule 702. . . . Instead, we find persuasive more recent cases in which courts have found that, under certain circumstances, this type of expert testimony can satisfy the helpfulness test of Rule 702.... (emphasis added) (p. 1230)

After delineating its analysis of the criteria to be used when determining whether or not proposed testimony meets scientific standards of reliability (see the previous discussion), the court considered the question of whether the eyewitness expert testimony offered in *Downing* met its standards:

Unfortunately the district court never addressed the reliability question because it essentially – and erroneously – concluded that expert evidence of this type could never assist the trier of fact. *From the facts available on the record and otherwise, it would appear that the scientific basis for the expert evidence in question is sufficiently reliable to satisfy Rule 702. In a recent case approving the use of expert testimony on eyewitness perception and memory in certain circumstances, the California Supreme Court noted the proliferation of empirical research demonstrating the pitfalls of eyewitness identification and concluded that "the consistency of the results of these studies is impressive." People v. McDonald* (emphasis added) (pp. 1241–1242) [Author's note: Additional supporting citations were offered in footnote 23 of the opinion]

We agree with the courts in Chapple, Smith, and McDonald that under certain circumstances expert testimony on the reliability of eyewitness identifications can assist the jury in reaching a correct decision and therefore may meet the helpfulness requirement of Rule 702. (emphasis added) (p. 1231)

On remand the District Court conducted a new hearing on the admissibility issue. At that hearing the defense offered the testimony of psychologist Robert Buckhout in support of its effort to secure expert testimony at a new trial. The prosecution offered the testimony of psychologist Michael McCloskey who critiqued Dr. Buckhout's conclusions and noted inconsistencies in the research findings on which Buckhout relied. In his opinion (*United States v. Downing*, 609 F. Supp. 784, 1985) the trial judge observed:

In view of the inconsistent results produced by the studies and the lack of testimony regarding either the methodology of those studies or the underlying data on which the test results are based, the court finds that the proffered testimony of Dr. Buckhout does not carry with it a sufficient degree of reliability to warrant its admission. . . .

Absent such information, a jury has little basis for evaluating the testimony they hear. Accordingly, the court finds that even if the evidence offered by defendant was reliable, it could not be admitted due to its risk of misleading the jury. (emphasis added) (p. 791)

The court also noted that the studies relied upon by the defense did not "fit" the particular facts of the case insofar as the studies used fact patterns or circumstances unlike those offered at trial. With respect to our triad of fundamental issues: The trial court concluded that scientific reliability had not been established and that the testimony would not help the jury. One must presume that the court regarded traditional safeguards such as cross-examination and instructions on eyewitness identifications as adequate to protect the defendant against eyewitness mistakes, though no explicit mention was made of these safeguards. On these bases the court reaffirmed its earlier decision to exclude the expert testimony and reinstated the defendant's conviction.

Very shortly after the *Downing* decision the Third Circuit considered *United States v. Sebetich* (1985), a case that was tried just before the *Downing* opinion was published. The eyewitness expert's testimony on the effects of stress and a long delay between the witnessing of the crime and the subsequent identification had been excluded at the Sebetich trial. The Third Circuit (in another opinion written by Judge Becker) noted that the case against the defendant rested solely on the identification in question and remanded the case to the trial judge for an evidentiary hearing on the aptness of the expert testimony. In doing so the court reiterated its three-pronged *Downing* analysis: Is the evidence reliable? Will it overwhelm, confuse, or mislead the jury? Does the evidence "fit" particular disputed factual issues in the case? The court noted features of the case that suggested the lower court should perhaps view the requested testimony favorably:

> The facts of this case illustrate the potential utility of testimony such as that proposed to be given by Dr. Buckhout. Filoni testified that he saw the passenger in the pickup truck during a number of brief intervals amounting to only forty-nine seconds. These sightings occurred while Filoni was pursuing the truck at speeds of up to seventy-five miles an hour and while his life was threatened by gun fire. Filoni thus saw his assailant under highly stressful circumstances. . . . *There is evidence that stress decreases the reliability of eyewitness identifications, contrary to common understanding.* . . . (emphasis added)

> According to the proffer, Dr. Buckhout would also have given evidence regarding the vagaries of identifications made long after an event. A similar proffer was part of the basis for our decision in Downing. (p. 419)

The trial court nonetheless determined that the expert testimony was not admissible and reinstated the conviction (*United States v. Sebetich*, 841 F.2d 1120, 1988) – there is no published opinion that would reveal the grounds for this judgment.

Several years after *Downing* and *Sebetich*, the Third Circuit upheld the exclusion of an eyewitness expert (*United States v. Dowling*, 1988) on two primary grounds. The court (in an opinion written by Sloviter and joined by Judges Becker and Seitz) indicated that it was first disturbed that the defense gave the prosecution only five days' notice of its intent to offer the expert:

> In *Downing*, we stated that the trial court could consider "[t]he extent to which the adverse party has had notice of the evidence and an opportunity to conduct its own

tests or produce opposing experts." 753 F.2d at 1241. The late proffer substantially prejudiced the government because, on such short notice, it could not reasonably be expected to search for its own expert and find one available to come to the Virgin Islands in time to be given the available facts and the opportunity to assimilate them. We therefore cannot hold that the district court abused its discretion in declining to admit the testimony on this ground alone. (p. 118)

The trial judge had also determined that there was a poor fit between the matters the expert was prepared to testify about and the facts of the case. Thus, the expert's testimony about the effects of stress applied to one witness but perhaps not to another; testimony about opportunity to view the perpetrator was not linked to the particular viewing times in the case; testimony about "weapon focus" was not linked to any evidence about the presence of weapons while the witnesses observed the perpetrator; and there were no witnesses who fit the testimony about impaired performance among children and older eyewitnesses. In addition, the expert acknowledged that many of his observations were consistent with common sense.

Thus, the primary basis for rejecting the testimony was that it would not assist the jury. It appears that scientific reliability (a second component of our triad) was not an issue, although a comment by the court of appeals on this issue is a bit ambiguous:

Having reached the issue of "fit," the court had necessarily found there to be a sufficient scientific basis for Krop's testimony, and the court's statement that "there was simply no proffered proof reflecting treatises, reports, workshop results, research data or the like, as to the possible misidentifications in this case," . . . went to the lack of a connection between Krop's acknowledged expertise and the particular facts presented. (emphasis added) (p. 119)

Once again, one must presume, with respect to the third aspect of the expert triad, that the court believed traditional safeguards against eyewitness error were adequate.

More recently, in *United States v. Stevens* (1991), the Third Circuit scrutinized the fit between proffered testimony facts in great detail. The case and the opinion (written by Judge Becker) are most notable in light of the background facts of the case. The defendant in this case was ultimately tried three times. The first trial ended in a hung jury, the second trial resulted in a conviction and produced the appellate opinion discussed here. This conviction was overturned, in part, because portions of eyewitness expert testimony were excluded at trial. The defendant was convicted at his third trial (which included testimony by the expert), but just prior to his sentencing the charges were dropped in light of newly discovered evidence produced following the arrest of another individual on unrelated charges (*Star-Ledger* [Trenton, New Jersey], October 20, 1992, p. 21).

At the defendant's second trial, the expert was permitted to testify about several matters (including problems associated with cross-racial identifications, weapon focus, and stress) but the court excluded testimony about other matters (suggestiveness in the identification procedure, the lack of independence of multiple identification procedures, and the modest correlation between eyewitness confidence and accuracy). Thus, at least with respect to the issues admitted at trial, the trial court believed the testimony was scientifically reliable, would be of assistance to the jury, and would supplement the traditional safeguards against mistaken identification. With respect to the excluded testimony the appellate court concurred in all but one of the trial court's judgments, concluding that the trial judge had misapplied the *Downing* "fit" test with respect to the proffered testimony on confidence and accuracy and based, in part, on this error, overturned the conviction. The court undertakes a careful analysis of the proffered testimony that emphasizes two points: the "fit" of the testimony to the facts of the case and the extent to which the testimony goes beyond ordinary lay knowledge and would therefore assist the jury:

Stevens hoped to have Dr. Penrod testify that, if there are features in an array that draw the witness's attention to a particular person, the witness is more likely to identify that person as the perpetrator. Given these facts, there was, we think, a sufficient "fit" between Dr. Penrod's tendered testimony and the victims' identifications of Stevens from the assertedly suggestive wanted board.

That Dr. Penrod's proposed testimony derived from studies involving "non-eureka type" arrays does not undermine the "fit." The "eureka"/"non-eureka" distinction is, in our view, a red herring: a suggestive feature may induce a witness to misidentify a particular individual regardless of whether the array was constructed for the express purpose of allowing that witness to identify that individual. We instead think that this distinction simply reflects a limitation inherent in this type of scientific research. Dr. Penrod testified that "the only way a psychologist [can] study [the] suggestiveness of an array is to assemble an array[,] so . . . it's implicit in our methodology that we can't study eureka type arrays." This strikes us as a matter of common sense. A psychologist cannot analyze suggestive arrays without first arranging an array with some subtly suggestive features. *We therefore are satisfied that there is an ample connection between Dr. Penrod's tentative testimony and the facts of this case.* Had the district court permitted him to do so, Dr. Penrod would have testified that the wanted board's suggestive attributes could have induced Smith and McCormack to scrutinize Stevens's photographs more carefully and thus could have resulted in a mistaken identification. (emphasis added)

We believe, nonetheless, that the district court's exclusion of Dr. Penrod's testimony on this point did not amount to an abuse of discretion. "The touchstone of Rule 702 . . . is the helpfulness of the expert testimony, i.e., whether it 'will assist the trier of fact to understand the evidence or to determine a fact in issue.' " *Downing,* 753 F.2d at 1235 (quoting Fed. R. Evid. 702). As we noted supra at 1390, the wanted board was potentially suggestive for several obvious reasons. Stevens was the only person on the display whose picture appeared twice and was the only person whose photograph was in color. Also, most of the other pictures on the wanted board were sketches, not photographs; and those that were photographs were significantly smaller than Stevens's. *That these features quite possibly drew the victims' attention to Stevens is, in our view, a rather intuitive proposition. Indeed, we are confident that Stevens persuasively could have argued this point to the jury without adducing expert testimony.* (emphasis added)

Stevens also sought to elicit from Dr. Penrod testimony concerning the pitfalls of multiple identifications. At the preliminary *Downing* hearing, Dr. Penrod explained that, once a witness makes an identification, he or she will tend to stick with that initial choice at subsequent photographic arrays or lineups, even if it was erroneous. The reason for this phenomenon, Dr. Penrod submits, is that "information acquired at an initial identification [often] influence[s] identifications made later on." That is, witnesses sometimes base subsequent identifications on their vague recollection of a face viewed in a prior array or lineup, not on their memory of the crime itself.

Once again, we do not think that there is a "fit" problem with this aspect of Dr. Penrod's testimony. Stevens was the only individual from the wanted board who also appeared in either the photographic array or the lineup. According to Dr. Penrod, this factor, together with the alleged suggestiveness of the wanted board, could have brought about successive misidentifications. If the victims erroneously identified Stevens from the wanted board, the scientific studies cited by Dr. Penrod suggest that the victims would tend to remain faithful to that choice at later identifications, because they would recognize Stevens's face from the wanted board. There is, in short, a nexus between Dr. Penrod's tendered testimony and the facts of this case.

But, as we noted supra, *Downing* demands more than just a "fit." Stevens asserts that the introduction of Dr. Penrod's testimony on the "relation-back" issue would have prompted the jury to discount the corroborative value of the victims' identifications of him from the photographic array and lineup. *We think, however, that this point, like Dr. Penrod's comments on the suggestiveness of the wanted board, is rather pedestrian. It is, we believe, susceptible of elucidation without specialized scientific knowledge and thus could have been fleshed out adequately by counsel through probing cross- examination and arguments pitched to the common sense of the jury.* (emphasis added) (1398 – 1400)

Dr. Penrod also testified at the in limine hearing about scientific studies that seek to measure the relationship between the degree of confidence a witness purports to have in his or her identification and the accuracy of that identification. In these studies, subjects either are exposed to a live staging of some highly unusual event or are shown a videotape of a reenacted crime. The subjects then are requested to make an identification and to rate how confident they are in that identification. According to Dr. Penrod, these studies have revealed "a fairly weak relationship" between confidence and accuracy.

At the conclusion of the in limine hearing, the district court prohibited Dr. Penrod's testimony on these confidence/accuracy studies, finding no "fit" between the proffered testimony and the facts of this case. The court based this conclusion on its belief that witnesses function differently in "real life situations" than in tests performed in a controlled environment. The district court stated that, unlike the studies that Dr. Penrod outlined, the crime in this case transpired over several minutes and placed the assailant in close proximity to the witnesses. The court further noted that Smith and McCormack, both of whom were trained in surveillance techniques, observed the assailant knowing that an offense was occurring and that they later would be called upon to identify him. In contrast, the subjects in the aforedescribed studies were unaware at the time of the staged events that they eventually would be asked to make an identification.

We think that the district court misapprehended Downing's "fit" requirement. Both Smith and McCormack expressed high confidence in their identifications of Stevens as the perpetrator. To rebut the natural assumption that such a strong expression of confidence indicates an unusually reliable identification, Stevens sought to admit Dr. Penrod's testimony that there is a low correlation between confidence and accuracy. We believe that Dr. Penrod's proposed testimony "is sufficiently tied to the facts of the case that it will aid the jury in resolving a factual dispute." (emphasis added) (p. 1400)

The factors listed by the district court as destroying the "fit" are characteristic of all studies in the field of eyewitness identifications. Scientists cannot replicate real-life violent crimes; therefore, they are forced to conduct their testing in a simulated, yet somewhat artificial, environment. This limitation, we suspect, also applies to studies concerning cross-racial identification, weapon focus, and stress; yet the district court readily admitted Dr. Penrod's testimony on these subjects. The fact that the subjects in the classroom and videotape studies observed the "assailant" under much different circumstances than did Smith and McCormack obviously constitutes a fertile ground for cross-examination. But we fail to see how these differences undo the "fit" in this case: both Smith and McCormack proclaimed that they were exceedingly confident in their identifications of Stevens, and Dr. Penrod offered to testify that such declarations do not necessarily mean that the victims' identifications were accurate.

Moreover, in contradistinction to the proffered testimony about the suggestiveness of the wanted board and the "relation-back" issue, Dr. Penrod's explication of the confidence/accuracy studies could prove helpful to the jury in assessing the reliability of Smith's and McCormack's identifications. That witnesses ofttimes profess considerable confidence in erroneous identifications is fairly counterintuitive. See id. at 1230 n. 6 ("To the extent that a mistaken witness may retain great confidence in an inaccurate identification, cross-examination can hardly be seen as an effective way to reveal the weakness in a witness' recollection of an event."). In fact, Dr. Penrod opined at the preliminary hearing that the correlation between confidence and accuracy in eyewitness identifications is far lower than people probably would expect. Given this potential for helpfulness and "the liberal standard of admissibility mandated by Rule 702," id. at 1230, we hold that the district court abused its discretion in barring Dr. Penrod's tendered testimony on the confidence/accuracy factor. (emphasis added) (pp. 1401–1402)

One might argue on the basis of the Third Circuit appellate opinions that eyewitness expert testimony has reached a stage where admissibility turns largely on the fit between the facts of the case and the proffered testimony. The court appears to be generally receptive to the notion that the testimony has a reliable scientific foundation and implicitly recognizes that such testimony may be a useful supplement to traditional safeguards against mistaken identification such as cross-examination. The stumbling points with respect to "fit" are more likely to concern the question of whether the scientific research reveals anything that is not within common knowledge or experience – as gauged by the trial courts and the court of appeals. We underscore that disparities in lay and scientific knowledge is an empirical question – one that we will turn to in later chapters.

The Fourth and Sixth Circuits

We consider these two circuits together because the recent opinions in both circuits reflect a common disposition: a general endorsement of the proposition that eyewitness expert evidence is admissible at trial, but a reluctance to overturn convictions in cases where the testimony has been excluded *and* the government offers substantial evidence of the defendant's guilt other than the challenged eyewitness identification. Thus even in situations where the appellate courts reject the traditional impediments to eyewitness expert testimony, it is still possible the jury will never hear proffered testimony. For example, in *United States v. Smith*, 736 F.2d 1103 (1984) the defendant appeared, on appeal, to have everything "going for him:"

The government conceded that Fulero was an expert, but the district court ruled that the testimony was inadmissible [*sic*] pursuant to Federal Rule of Evidence 403. The district court's decision to exclude that testimony is the subject of this appeal. . . . In *United States v. Green*, 548 F.2d 1261 (6th Cir. 1977), this Court adopted four criteria for review of trial court decisions involving expert testimony: (1) qualified expert, (2) proper subject, (3) conformity to a generally accepted explanatory theory, and (4) probative value compared to prejudicial effect. See also *United States v. Brown*, 557 F.2d 541 (6th Cir. 1977).

The district judge found that Fulero's testimony was not a "proper subject" because it "would not assist the jury in determining the facts at issue." . . . The district court. . . concluded that the "jury is fully capable of assessing the eyewitnesses' ability to perceive and remember." (emphasis added)

[however] Dr. Fulero . . . offered proof based upon the facts of this case. . . . Dr. Fulero also might have provided insight outside the jury's "ken" about the possibility of cross-racial misidentification. . . . The proffer in this case, therefore,

demonstrated that Dr. Fulero's testimony may have assisted the factfinder understand the facts of this case. (emphasis added)

The district judge concluded, in addition, that a sufficient proffer had not been made to show that Dr. Fulero's research "is a Science containing enough of a degree of exactness or exactitude to render his opinion admissible." . . . [However], Dr. Fulero's science has gained reliability. Moreover, his testimony would not only "surpass" common-sense evaluation, it would question common-sense evaluation. This Circuit has been particularly mindful of the dangers of misperception in criminal cases and has itself relied upon psychological studies of the problems of misidentification and suggestion. In *United States v. Tyler*, 714 F.2d 664, 667, this Court relied upon psychological studies for the proposition that the danger of misidentification "is inherent in every identification." Citing, *United States v. Russell*, 532 F.2d 1063 (6th Cir. 1976). We concluded that "courts should be especially vigilent [*sic*] to make certain that there is no further distortion." *Russell*, 532 F.2d at 1066. We reached that conclusion in Russell based upon the scientific research of Buckhout in "Eyewitness Testimony," 231 Scientific American 23 (Dec. 1974). In summarizing and adopting Buckhout's findings, the *Russell* Court declared: Witnesses focus on gross or salient characteristics of any sensory experience, and fill in the details, not according to the observed facts of the experience, but according to some previously internalized pattern they associate with the perceived gross characteristics. In addition, the construction of memory is greatly influenced by post-experience suggestion. Suggestions compatible with the witness' internalized sterotype [*sic*] are likely to become part of the witness' memory, not because they are in fact similar to the actual experience, but because they fit the preconceived stereotype. 532 F.2d at 1066. The day may have arrived, therefore, when Dr. Fulero's testimony can be said to conform to a generally accepted explanatory theory.

The final Green test requires the reviewing court to balance the probative value of the evidence against the prejudicial effect. This balancing is identical to the Rule 403 balancing. . . . The "relevance" of Dr. Fulero's testimony may have been established in his proffer that it would involve a "proper subject." The prejudice envisioned by Rules 403 and 702 is prejudice to a criminal defendant. (emphasis added)

In the case before us, however, we "hesitate to step in" because even if it were error to exclude the expert's testimony, such error was "harmless" to the defendant. See *Hamling v. United States*, 418 U.S. 87, 135... (1974). The government presented three eyewitnesses who identified Smith as the bank robber. The government also presented uncontroverted evidence that Smith's palmprint was found at the bank. The expert testimony would have done little to discredit the testimony of three eyewitnesses, each of whom independently identified Smith at a line-up. More significantly, however, the existence of Smith's palm print at the Arcanum bank by itself wholly discredited his alibi defense. Smith's trial defense was that he had never in his entire life been in the robbed bank. Evidence of his palm print found at the bank flies directly in the face of his alibi defense. The exclusion of Dr. Fulero's testimony under the particular facts of this case, therefore, was not "prejudicial" to the defendant. We can not conclude that "it is more probable than not the [exclusion] affected the verdict." *United States v. Rasheed*, 663 F.2d 843 (9th Cir.) cert. denied,

454 U.S. 1157, 102 S.Ct. 1031, 71 L.Ed.2d 315 (1982). *Although we find that Dr. Fulero's expert testimony may have involved a "proper subject," conformed to a "generally accepted explanatory theory" and provided "probative value," we conclude that its exclusion in this particular case, therefore, did not "prejudice" the defendant to the extent of affecting the verdict and therefore was harmless.* (emphasis added) (pp. 1106–1108)

The decision in a more recent Sixth Circuit eyewitness expert case (*United States v. Collins*, 1988) follows the Smith decision fairly closely in holding that any error in excluding the proffered expert was harmless in light of the other compelling evidence offered by the government.

In two similar Fourth Circuit cases (*United States v. Harris*, 1993 and *United States v. Little*, 1994), the court reviewed a number of recent appellate opinions and acknowledged that expert testimony is admitted by increasing numbers of courts under what it termed "narrow" circumstances. It upheld exclusion of the expert testimony in *Harris*, noting:

Even though Harris's proffer included most of the common justifications recognized as supporting the admission of such expert testimony, the facts simply do not support his argument that the identification was suspect. The commonly encountered problem in identifying a robber involves one identification, by one witness, under stress. . . . In contrast, the jury here could pick and choose from an evidentiary cornucopia. There was not one eyewitness here, but three. The identification did not result from one observation on one occasion, but from three identifications on three separate occasions. Harris even admitted that he was in the bank on two occasions on the date of the robbery. (p. 535)

In *Little* the Fourth Circuit, once again, acknowledged the increased receptivity to eyewitness expert testimony, but upheld exclusion of the expert testimony and observed:

After hearing the proffered testimony of Dr. Cole, the district court determined that, in part because the expert intended to speak in general terms of the difficulties of eyewitness identification and had not heard the witnesses testify *his testimony would not be sufficiently helpful to the jury.* JA 302. We note that Little's conviction did not rest solely on Scott and Pittman's identification testimony, and that *skillful cross-examination was of course available to emphasize some of the weaknesses of Pittman and Scott's identifications that Dr. Cole's testimony was to address.* For these reasons, the court's refusal to admit this proffered expert opinion evidence was not an abuse of discretion. (emphasis added) (p. 4)

The Seventh Circuit

The Seventh Circuit has had several occasions to consider the admissibility of eyewitness expert testimony and in the court's extensive writings on the subject it has considered a number of hurdles to admissibility. For example, in *United States v. Hudson* (1989) the court, after the passage of 12 years, revisited the question of admissibility:

At trial, defendants offered the testimony of Dr. Patricia Devine, a psychologist, to show: (1) the effect of stress upon identification; (2) the difficulty of cross-racial identification; (3) an overview of the memory process; and (4) the impact of a short viewing period upon the accuracy of an identification. Defendants argue that the district court erred in determining that this evidence would not have been helpful to the jury. Second, they maintain that this court misapplied our holding in *United States v. Watson*, 587 F.2d 365 . . . (1978) . . . by interpreting it as having established a per se rule against the admission of this type of testimony.

. . . In *United States v. Lundy*, 809 F.2d 392 (7th Cir. 1987), this court summarized the requirements in this circuit for admission of expert testimony when it said:

Because experts are given special latitude to testify based on hearsay and third-hand observations and to give opinions, . . . courts have cautioned that an expert must be qualified as an expert, provide testimony that will assist the jury and rely only on evidence on which a reasonable expert in the field would rely. . . . *Courts agree that it is improper to permit an expert to testify regarding facts that people of common understanding can easily comprehend.* . . . (emphasis added)

In *Watson*, we rejected the defendants' proffer of expert testimony on witness identification for two reasons. *First, under the circumstances of that case involving prompt and positive identification, the expert's testimony would have been of little use to the jury. Second, we noted that we believed that work in the field of witness identification still remained inadequate to justify its admission into evidence.* . . . (emphasis added) [Author's note: These criteria are, of course, two of the three components of the eyewitness expert evidence triad.]

Defendants maintain that we should join those circuits that have held that this testimony now is sufficiently reliable in general to go to the jury, but which decide on the particular facts of the case whether or not to admit the evidence. . . . We need not revisit the question whether this type of testimony is sufficiently reliable in general to go to the jury. It properly is excludable in any event under Rule 702 because it will not assist the trier of fact. *Such expert testimony will not aid the jury because it addresses an issue of which the jury already generally is aware, and it will not contribute to their understanding of the particular dispute.* . . . Thus, we do not think that the district judge abused his discretion in excluding this evidence. Because this evidence properly was excluded as unhelpful, we need not address the government's contention that Dr. Devine was not qualified as an expert witness. (emphasis added)

For the reasons discussed above, the judgment of the district court is affirmed. (pp. 1022–1023)

In short and with respect to the expert evidence triad: The Seventh Circuit rejects the expert testimony offered in *Hudson* because it believes the testimony concerns matters of common knowledge and will, therefore, not be of assistance to the jury. The court does not explicitly tackle the question of scientific reliability, and the exclusion of the expert testimony implicitly reaffirms the viability eyewitness safeguards.

Is the Seventh Circuit utterly convinced that the scientific research on factors influencing memory cannot be of assistance to juries? In 1990 Richard Posner, one of the leading scholarly members of the Seventh Circuit bench, wrote at length and rather favorably about the memory research that underlies expert testimony on eyewitness reliability. However, the case in question did not concern proffered testimony on eyewitness reliability and the case was not even a criminal matter. The relevant portions of Posner's opinion are essentially dicta but his comments are revealing.

The case, *Krist v. Eli Lilly and Company et al.*, 897 F.2D 293 (1990), was a civil suit in which the plaintiff asserted that she and her daughter had been injured by the mother's use of a drug, DES, manufactured by the defendant and a number of other companies. There was conflicting evidence from the mother on the question of whether the pills she had taken 40 years earlier had been manufactured by the defendants or another company. The mother had described the pills in question as "red," and although the defendants were able to demonstrate that they were not making red pills at the time in question, other aspects of the mother's description of the pills did match the characteristics of pills manufactured by the defendants. The case was dismissed by the trial judge because, in his view, no jury could rationally find for the plaintiff given the inconsistencies in the mother's testimony. The court upheld the trial judge, but Posner, writing for the court, noted that the plaintiff might have taken a different approach to the case. And, along the way, he commented on the Seventh Circuit's earlier opinions concerning eyewitness expert testimony.

How could the jury rationally conclude that she had gotten the color and coating wrong but the size, shape, and other features connecting the pill to Lilly right?

There may be answers to these questions, but answers that come out of a scholarly literature of which the plaintiff's counsel appears to be unaware and which he in any event made no attempt to present through the affidavit of an expert who might later testify at the trial, as in such cases as *United States v. Smith, . . .* , and *United States v. Moore, ...* An important body of psychological research undermines the lay intuition that confident memories of salient experiences (such as taking a red pill for many weeks during pregnancy in an effort to prevent a miscarriage) are accurate and do not fade with time unless a person's memory has some pathological impairment. Much of this evidence can be found in *Credibility Assessment* (Yuille Ed., 1989); *Eyewitness Testimony: Psychological Perspectives* (Wells & Loftus Eds., 1984);

Evaluating Witness Evidence (Lloyd-Bostock & Clifford Eds., 1983). A leading scholar in this field is Elizabeth F. Loftus, author of papers in each of the three volumes we have cited and co-author of one of the volumes.

The basic problem about testimony from memory is that most of our recollections are not verifiable. The only warrant for them is our certitude, and certitude is not a reliable test of certainty. Many people are certain that God exists. Many are certain that He does not exist. The believer and the nonbeliever are equally certain, but they cannot both be correct. Similarly, the mere fact that we remember something with great confidence is not a powerful warrant for thinking it true. It therefore becomes an empirical question whether and in what circumstances memory is accurate. Cognitive psychologists such as Loftus have tried to answer this question. The answers are controversial. . . . They are based for the most part on experiments with college students, and as with much experimentation in the social sciences it is uncertain how well the experimental results generalize to "real world" situations. But although the answers certainly are not definitive, they are suggestive. The basic findings are: accuracy of recollection decreases at a geometric rather than arithmetic rate (so passage of time has a highly distorting effect on recollection); accuracy of recollection is not highly correlated with the recollector's confidence; and memory is highly suggestible – people are easily "reminded" of events that never happened, and having been "reminded" may thereafter hold the false recollection as tenaciously as they would a true one.

All three of these findings could have been used in this case – how effectively we need not decide.

We do not want to be too hard on the plaintiff's counsel. In forgoing the expert-witness route he may have been concerned with language in opinions of this court that could be thought dismissive of expert testimony in the field of perception and memory. In *United States v. Watson*, . . . , speaking of psychological studies of identification evidence in which the witness and the person identified are of different races, we said that "work in that field still remains inadequate to justify its admission into evidence." That was twelve years ago, and dealt with an esoteric topic as to which the defendants' own expert acknowledged that prior work was generally considered inadequate.

Certainly in routine cases the trial judge is not required to allow wide-ranging inquiry into the mysteries of human perception and recollection. But few cases involve recollections from forty years earlier. Such cases are not routine, and psychological evidence may be helpful to the judges and jurors required to decide them.

Similarly in the present case the district judge might well have allowed expert psychological evidence on the vagaries of confident recollections of events lying decades in the past. But, again, the plaintiff's counsel did not want to take that route.

There is a tension in our decisions. *Hudson* and *Watson* evince a more skeptical view of expert evidence on perception than *Carroll* does. We need not try to reconcile the tension here. It may have more to do with the particulars of the cases in question than with any deep difference of opinion on the utilization of science in litigation; it may therefore be illusory. . . . The issue is not whether a jury composed of experts in perceptual psychology, presided over by a judge equally expert in that field, could find for the plaintiff in the absence of evidence in the usual sense. The issue is whether a normal jury could so find. It could not.

Lacking scientific knowledge that an expert might have imparted to it but did not, no rational jury could bring in a verdict for the plaintiff. . . . Rationality is not a synonym for omniscience. . . . In deciding what a rational jury could decide, we may not impute to it knowledge that it could have obtained only from expert testimony that no party was prepared to obtain. Affirmed. (pp. 296–300)

Do Posner's views reflect a generally favorable view of such evidence among the members of the Seventh Circuit Court of Appeals? A more recent case (in which Posner was not involved) indicates that the answer is a qualified no. In *United States v. Curry et al.* (1992) the Seventh Circuit considered a trial court decision to exclude expert testimony. The court offered its summary of the content of the proffered testimony:

Dr. Loftus would have testified on a number of issues relating to the accuracy of these identifications. Among the propositions discussed in her offer of proof that are arguably beyond the understanding of an average person are: 1) witnesses invariably overestimate the duration of their observation of an individual; 2) a witness' confidence in his identification bears little or no relationship to the accuracy of the identification; 3) memory fades at a geometric rather than an arithmetic rate; 4) "post-event phenomena" may distort or supplant original memory, and memory is easily distorted by leading questions or other manipulations; 5) prior photographic identifications increase the likelihood that later in-person identifications will be erroneous; and 6) social alcohol and marijuana use hinders the ability of an individual to retain information. (p. 1051)

The court also considered what the trial judge had to say about this testimony:

The district court entered a written order denying the admissibility of Dr. Loftus' testimony, concluding that:

[S]uch testimony may be properly excluded where the testimony addresses an issue of which the jury is generally aware. In the present controversy the jury was questioned during voir dire about recall and the ability to identify persons they had seen only briefly, or had not seen for a period of time.

The district court's focus on what the jury is "generally aware" of could be a finding that Dr. Loftus' testimony would not assist the trier of fact under Rule 702, or it could be considered a finding that her testimony would be unduly confusing or a waste of time under Rule 403. As has been noted, "The Rule 702 analysis. . . incorporates to some extent a consideration of the dangers, particularly the danger of unfair prejudice, enumerated in Fed. R. Evid. 403." *United States v. Downing* . . . The "helpfulness factor" under Rule 702 involves consideration whether the expert testimony would be misleading or confusing in the context of the trial. . . .

Additionally, all of the witnesses who identified defendants were thoroughly cross-examined about the reliability of their identification, the length of time they saw the defendant, the conditions under which they saw the defendant, the length of time which elapsed between the witness seeing the defendant and the photos or the defendant in person, the number of times the witness saw the photo arrays, and when the witness was shown the photo array. Thus, the jury was made aware of many of the factors which may effect [*sic*] perception, retention and recall. . . . Thus, although the jury may not understand the intricacies of perception, recall and retention, the jury is generally aware of the problems with identification. Government's Br. App. at 7. (p. 1052)

Dr. Loftus' testimony may not have been totally unhelpful; as the court noted, most persons do not understand the intricacies of perception, retention, and recall. The district court also apparently had no quarrel with her competency to testify or with the reliability of her scientific testimony. We conclude, however, that the district court's decision to exclude Dr. Loftus' testimony was a proper exercise of its discretion, whether under Rule 702 or Rule 403. The eyewitness testimony was far from the only evidence against the defendants. Indeed, as noted above, the bulk of testimony came from two government witnesses and co-conspirators, Brenton Long and Mary Lynch. The testimony of Joan Hylinski was also important. *Although the eyewitness testimony bolstered the government's theory that there was no real Rich Kelly, it can fairly be described as minor and amounted to only one day in a four-week trial. The intrusion of an expert to comment on this minor testimony was not necessary, especially when the record reveals that vigorous cross-examination by the defendants exposed the weakness of the identifications.* (Emphasis added).

Although we make no specific assertion as to its reliability or general acceptance, a number of cases indicate that Dr. Loftus' field of study is now well accepted. . . . (1051–1052)

Where does the Seventh Circuit stand with respect to the eyewitness expert triad? As was true in the Seventh Circuit's earlier decision in *Hudson*, the court does not take a position on the scientific reliability of the evidence triad (though it notes favorable rulings on this question by other courts). A partial stumbling block for the testimony offered in *Curry* is it may concern matters of common knowledge and will, therefore, not be of assistance to the jury. It is significant that the court does not conclude outright that the testimony will not be helpful; rather it rejects possibly helpful testimony on the grounds that eyewitness evidence was a minor matter in the case that could be handled effectively with the traditional safeguard or cross-examination.

In light of the *Curry* decision, Posner's musings in *Krist* clearly did not reflect a pervasive or fundamental shift in the Seventh Circuit's approach to eyewitness expert testimony; nonetheless, Posner's speculations about the use of such evidence suggest that some of the members of the Seventh Circuit bench may take a more positive view of the "helpfulness" of the research than is reflected in the *Curry* opinion.

The Ninth Circuit

The Ninth has considered more eyewitness expert cases than any other circuit. They had an early start with the *Amaral* case in 1973 where they rejected a defense argument that special instructions should be given to jurors in eyewitness cases:

Defendant's counsel . . . had a "full opportunity" to develop all facts relevant to identification. Furthermore, we concur with the Second Circuit's endorsement . . . that "it is necessary neither to instruct the jury that they should receive certain identification testimony with caution, nor to suggest to them the inherent unreliability of certain eye-witness identification." (cite omitted, p. 1151)

At trial the defense offered testimony by psychologist Bertram Raven. This testimony was rejected in deference to traditional safeguards:

The trial court excluded the proffered testimony of Dr. Raven on the ground that "it would not be appropriate to take from the jury their own determination as to what weight or effect to give to the evidence of the eye-witness and identifying witnesses and to have that determination put before them on the basis of the expert witness testimony as proffered." [R.T. 313]

Our legal system places primary reliance for the ascertainment of truth on the "test of cross-examination." . . . We need not reach the question, even assuming our competency to pass on it, whether the proffered testimony was in accordance with a generally accepted theory explaining the mechanism of perception. Furthermore, while we see the dangers of admitting such testimony in terms of confusing the jurors and undue delays, we believe that our holding makes it unnecessary to analyze those dangers in detail. (pp. 1153–1154)

In *United States v. Smith,* (1977) the defendants (not brothers) sought to introduce testimony by an expert and the court affirmed the exclusion of this testimony in one sentence citing *Amaral.*

Nine years later the court confronted another proffered expert in *United States v. Poole* (1986) and touched upon helpfulness and cross-examination:

In ruling on the motion in limine, the district court questioned the scientific basis for the proffered testimony. The district court also commented that the proffered testimony was general and suggested that Dr. Shoer could not testify about the case without dealing with the actual testimony of the witnesses, something Dr. Shoer proposed not to do. . . . Apparently, the court believed that general testimony, not tied to the specific testimony in the case, *would not be helpful to the jury*. The district court's ruling is squarely supported by Amaral. . . . In Amaral, we stated that *"effective cross-examination is adequate* to reveal any inconsistencies or deficiencies in the eyewitness testimony." (emphasis added) (p. 464)

A similar rationale was used to uphold rejection of expert testimony in *United States v. Brewer* (1986). In *United States v. Langford* (1986) the trial court did appoint an eyewitness identification expert to assist in preparation of the defense, but excluded the expert's trial testimony about the unreliability of eyewitness identification. The trial judge observed:

I rather think in all of these situations it is a balancing question. The ruling of the court (excluding the proffered testimony) is in no way predicated upon the absence of qualifications of the witness who has been identified in his professional field of psychology. The ruling, including the use of his testimony as an expert, is that it goes beyond the field of expertise to which such testimony should be directed or can be directed, and is basically argumentative and intrusive upon the jury's responsibility as triers of the facts of the case. (p. 1179)

The Court of Appeals upheld the trial court's exercise of discretion.

In 1987 in *United States v. Christophe* the court again upheld exclusion of eyewitness expert testimony, this time emphasizing a perceived lack of scientific reliability and emphasizing the effectiveness of cross-examination:

the proffered expert testimony does not conform to a generally accepted explanatory theory. *Psychologists do not generally accept the claimed dangers of eyewitness identification in a trial setting.* See McCloskey & Egeth, *Eyewitness Identification: What Can A Psychologist Tell A Jury?* 38 *Am. Psychologist* 550, 551 (May 1983) (stating that "there is virtually no empirical evidence that [jurors] are unaware of the problems with eyewitness testimony"). Consequently, this criterion set forth in Amaral for the admission of expert testimony is not met. The trial court neither abused its discretion nor prejudiced Christophe in excluding the proffered expert testimony. *We adhere to the position that skillful cross-examination of eyewitnesses, coupled with appeals to the experience and common sense of jurors, will sufficiently alert jurors to specific conditions that render a particular eyewitness identification unreliable.* Cross-examination was sufficient to bring to the jury's attention any difficulties in Williams' or Patton's identification of Christophe as the robber. (emphasis added) (pp. 1299–1300)

The Ninth Circuit revisited the issue in *United States v. George*, 975 F.2D 1431 (1992), but the essential result was the same:

George argues vigorously that study of eyewitness identification has substantially advanced since the time when this court took its position on the use of psychological experts to testify on the general unreliability of eyewitness identification. . . . Undoubtedly, there has been increased hospitality to the testimony of experts on eyewitness identification. [cites omitted] But each court has "invariably held that the district court has broad discretion" in admitting such testimony. (p. 1432)

More recently, in *United States v. Rincon*, 984 F.2d 1003 (1992), the Ninth Circuit has addressed the admissibility issue at greater length. The court first reaffirmed its reliance on the *Amaral* admissibility criteria (arguably criteria that are significantly eroded by the 1993 United States Supreme Court decision in *Daubert*). The court dispatched the expert and in doing so touched upon all three components of our eyewitness expert evidence triad – scientific reliability, traditional safeguards, and jury assistance:

In *Christophe*, this court faced the same issue presented here. . . . In affirming the district court, we stated that *"the proffered expert testimony does not conform to a generally accepted explanatory theory. Psychologists do not generally accept the claimed dangers of eyewitness identification in a trial setting."* Id. (citing McCloskey & Egeth, *Eyewitness Identification: What Can A Psychologist Tell A Jury?* 38 *Am. Psychologist* 550, 551 (May 1983) (*"there is virtually no empirical evidence that [jurors] are unaware of the problems with eyewitness testimony"*)). We also noted that psychologists warn *such expert testimony may make jurors overly skeptical of an eyewitness' testimony* as a result of the expert's testimony. Id. at 1300 n. 1. (emphasis added).

In this case, . . . [t]he judge stated: *"no offer of proof had been made to show that the expert testimony had reached that degree of science as opposed to an opinion . . . that makes it a science rather than an art."* (emphasis added).

Furthermore, this court has stated that while "[w]e are aware that other federal courts and state courts are beginning to accept expert testimony on the psychological factors affecting eyewitness identifications, at least in some circumstances. [*sic*] The reasoning behind those authorities is better directed to the district court at the time it exercises its discretion." . . . Therefore, the district court did not err in ruling that expert testimony on eyewitness identification is not a generally accepted theory. (pp. 1005–1006).

The court also believed the testimony might pose dangers for the jury:

In this case, the district court determined that the proffered expert testimony would in fact confuse and mislead the jury. The judge made a determination that the prejudicial value of this expert testimony outweighed its probative value. In so deciding, he did not abuse his discretion; rather, his ruling was consistent with Ninth Circuit precedent. (emphasis added) (p. 1006)

In the court's view, exclusion of the testimony would not hamper the defense because other tools were at its disposal:

The eyewitness expert in this case would have testified neither to anything beyond the bounds of the jurors' common knowledge nor to anything that could not be revealed during an effective cross-examination. Cross-examination was sufficient to reveal any deficiencies in the eyewitness testimony involved. After examining the record, we are satisfied that Rincon's counsel effectively elicited testimony from the eyewitnesses that revealed the inconsistencies and deficiencies in each witness' particular identification. (emphasis added)

Finally, *the district court judge instructed the jury as to the potential unreliability of eyewitness testimony: "innocent miss-recollection, like failure of recollection, is not an uncommon experience."* ... Therefore, because Rincon failed to lay a sufficient foundation for admission of the expert eyewitness testimony, the district court did not abuse its discretion in excluding it. (emphasis added) (pp. 1006–1007)

Whither the Ninth Circuit After *Daubert?*

In light of the U.S. Supreme Court's 1993 decision in *Daubert*, it is appropriate to ask whether the Ninth Circuit's approach (or any other circuit's approach) to eyewitness expert evidence is likely to undergo any changes. In fact, the Ninth Circuit is providing some of the earliest answers to this question, partly as the result of an appeal by Rincon to the Supreme Court. As a result of that appeal the Supreme Court vacated Rincon's conviction (*Rincon v. United States*, 1993) and remanded the case to the Ninth Circuit, which, in turn, remanded the case to the trial court for a new hearing on the expert witness admissibility question. The trial court held the hearing and then reaffirmed its prior decision to exclude the expert testimony and reinstated the conviction. The Ninth Circuit reviewed and upheld the trial court's decision (*United States v. Rincon*, 1994):

The first inquiry, then, under *Daubert* is whether the proposed testimony of Dr. Pezdek was on a "scientific" subject. On remand, the district court denied Rincon's motion on three grounds, one of which was that "no showing has been made that the testimony relates to an area that is recognized as a science."

In the initial motion, Rincon asserted that Dr. Pezdek held a Ph.D. in psychology from the University of Massachusetts at Amherst, and was a full professor at the Claremont Graduate School of Psychology. She would testify that there are three phases of eyewitness identification: perception and encoding; storage and retention (memory); and retrieval. In turn, the perception and encoding phase are [*sic*] affected by the factors of stress, duration of exposure, cross-racial identification, and availability of facial features (whether or not the face is partially obscured). The storage and retrieval stages are affected by time delay and suggestibility.

Dr. Pezdek would also discuss certain lay notions of eyewitness identification that are contradicted by research, such as: the certainty of the identification is a measure of the reliability of the identification; accuracy of memory is improved by stress; and memory of a face does not diminish over time.

The declaration of Rincon's counsel which accompanied the motion expanded on each of these matters, with statements such as: "There is a wealth of research supporting this point, . . ."; "The research is clear . . . "; "The research suggests . . . " However, *none of the research was submitted or described so that the district court could determine if the studies were indeed scientific on the basis the Court explained in Daubert:* "whether the reasoning or methodology underlying the testimony is scientifically valid. . . ." *Daubert,* 113 S. Ct. at 2796. (emphasis added)

On remand, Rincon supplemented the record with a copy of an article entitled, The "General Acceptance" of Psychological Research on Eyewitness Testimony. . . . The article described a survey of sixty-three experts on eyewitness testimony relating to their views of the scientific acceptance of research on a number of topics, including those that Dr. Pezdek would testify to. As the article said: The results are discussed in relation to the "general acceptance" provision of the Frye test and the limitations of this test for determining the admissibility of expert testimony. Id. at 1089.

However, while the article identified the research on some of the topics, it did not discuss the research in sufficient detail that the district court could determine if the research was scientifically valid. In the argument before the district court, counsel for Rincon told the court that Dr. Pezdek could testify about the studies that had been done on the various topics. However, he again did not offer or describe the studies themselves. The district court's determination that Rincon had not shown the proposed testimony related to a scientific subject is supported by the record. (emphasis added)

B. Assist Trier of Fact

Even when a theory or methodology satisfies the "scientific knowledge" requirement, in order to be admissible, expert testimony must also "assist the trier of fact to understand or to determine a fact in issue." *Daubert,* 113 S. Ct. at 2796. This second requirement relates primarily to relevance. Id. at 2795. It requires the district court to make a preliminary determination as to whether the scientific knowledge can be applied to facts of the case at hand. Id. at 2796.

The expert testimony Rincon offered was no doubt relevant to his defense. See *Amador-Galvan,* 9 F.3d at 1418 (evidence attacking reliability of eyewitness testimony was relevant to defendant's defense, but because it was not clear whether expert testimony was scientifically valid, reliable, and helpful to jury, we remanded for such determinations in light of *Daubert*). A determination that evidence is relevant does not end the inquiry. Rather, *Daubert* reiterates that the district court may nonetheless exclude relevant expert evidence pursuant to Rule 403 "if its probative value is substantially outweighed by the danger of unfair prejudice, confusion of the issues, or misleading the jury." *Daubert,* 113 S. Ct. at 2798 (emphasis added) (internal quotations omitted). "Expert evidence can be both powerful and quite misleading because of the difficulty in evaluating it. Because of that risk, the judge in weighing possible prejudice against probative force under Rule 403 of the present rules exercises more control over experts than over lay witnesses." Id. at 2798 (internal quotations omitted). Thus, Daubert in no way altered the discretion that resides with the district court judge to determine whether such evidence is properly admitted. See id. at 2798-99.

In this case, the district court found that Dr. Pezdek's testimony would not assist the trier of fact and that it would likely confuse or mislead the jury. Rincon argues that the district court erred in excluding the evidence because Dr. Pezdek's testimony was relevant evidence which would have helped the jury arrive at informed decision. Her testimony would have addressed factors that effect eyewitness identifications, such as passage of time, stress, identification from the lower half of the face, the relationship between certainty and accuracy, and cross-ethnic identifications. We decline to disturb the district court's ruling. (emphasis added)

Even though the factors about which Dr. Pezdek was to testify may have been informative, the district court conveyed that same information by providing a comprehensive jury instruction to guide the jury's deliberations. As Rincon's own article on such expert eyewitness testimony suggests, alternative solutions exist. [O]ur results should not be taken to imply that using psychological experts is the best possible solution for the problems arising from eyewitness testimony. . . . [B]ecause expert testimony is costly, an alternative would be to educate jurors through cautionary instructions. . . . (emphasis added)

The district court gave the jury in this case a comprehensive instruction on eyewitness identifications. The instruction addressed many of the factors about which Dr. Pezdek would have testified. The district court instructed the jury to consider whether: (1) the eyewitness had the capacity and adequate opportunity to observe the offender based upon the length of time for observation as well as the conditions of observation; (2) the identification was the product of the eyewitness's own recollection or was the result of subsequent influence or suggestiveness; (3) the eyewitness has made inconsistent identifications; and (4) the eyewitness was credible. The instruction also pointed out the danger of a showup versus the reliability of a lineup with similar individuals from which the eyewitness must choose. Finally, it permitted the jury to consider, as a factor bearing upon the reliability of the eyewitness testimony, the length of time which may have elapsed between the occurrence of the crime and the eyewitness's identification. . . .

As Rincon's article indicates, "it remains to be seen whether experts can enhance jurors' ability to distinguish accurate from inaccurate eyewitnesses, or whether the dangers of such testimony outweigh its probative value; e.g., whether jurors become not more or less skeptical, but more or less accurate in their judgments of eyewitness testimony." . . . In any event, the article is inconclusive as to the effect such evidence has on a jury. Given the powerful nature of expert testimony, coupled with its potential to mislead the jury, we cannot say that the district court erred in concluding that the proffered evidence would not assist the trier of fact and that it was likely to mislead the jury. (emphasis added)

Notwithstanding our conclusion, we emphasize that the result we reach in this case is based upon an individualized inquiry, rather than strict application of the past rule concerning expert testimony on the reliability of eyewitness identification. See Amador-Galvan, 9 F.3d at 1418. *Our conclusion does not preclude the admission of such testimony when the proffering party satisfies the standard established in Daubert by showing that the expert opinion is based upon "scientific knowledge" which is both reliable and helpful to the jury in any given case. See Daubert, 113 S. Ct. at 2796. District courts must strike the appropriate balance between admitting reliable, helpful expert testimony and excluding misleading or confusing testimony to achieve the flexible approach outlined in Daubert.* See id. at 2798-2799. The district court struck such a balance in this case. (emphasis added) (pp. 3-5).

Whether the defense in another case will, in fact, persuade the Ninth Circuit that eyewitness expert evidence does meet their scientific standards and will be helpful to the jury is an open question. It is an interesting issue that may be settled in the very near future insofar as there are presently two other cases that have been remanded by the Ninth Circuit for new hearings under *Daubert*. In the first of these, *United States v. Amador-Galvin* (November 1993), the Ninth Circuit remand noted:

Under the Daubert rule, the district court should decide whether such testimony is relevant, and if so, whether the theory propounded is trustworthy and scientifically valid. Testimony attacking the reliability of eyewitness testimony is clearly relevant to Amador-Galvan's defense; it is his main line of defense. Less clear is whether the theories on eyewitness identification are "scientifically valid," helpful, and of sufficient "evidentiary reliability" and trustworthiness. *Daubert . . .*

The district court did not consider whether Amador-Galvan's proffered expert testimony met *Daubert's* requirements. Thus, we remand to the district court for it to consider whether, under *Daubert*, the testimony should have been admitted. (p. 1418)

Similar language was used in the second remanded case, *United States v. Minnis* (June, 1994):

The district court, however, excluded the expert testimony on the reliability of eyewitness identification because it was a "relatively new area" and "might be confusing to the jury." Examination of the record indicates that the district court failed to consider the *Daubert* factors in assessing the validity of the eyewitness identification theory but, instead, based its decision upon the overruled Frye test. See *Daubert, . . . ;* see also *Amador-Galvan, . . .* Moreover, the district court apparently relied upon past decisions from this court concerning eyewitness identification to determine whether the theory had gained general acceptance rather than make its own independent assessment as required.

Because the district court did not consider the scientific validity and trustworthiness of the reliability of eyewitness testimony, we remand to the district court for it to consider whether, under Daubert, the testimony should have been admitted. (emphasis added) (pp. 4–5)

The Eleventh Circuit

In addition to the Ninth Circuit post-*Daubert* remands that are yet to be decided as this volume goes to press, the Eleventh Circuit also has a case under remand, *United States v. Gates (*1994). The decision in *Gates* could mark a major turning point in the Eleventh Circuit's approach to eyewitness expert testimony, for as recently as 1992 in *United States v. Holloway* the court disposed of an expert exclusion case with ease:

Rudder and Holloway argue that the trial court abused its discretion by denying their motion in limine to admit the testimony of an expert in eyewitness identification. This argument is without merit. The established rule of this circuit is that such testimony is not admissible. See *United States v. Benitez*, 741 F.2d 1312, 1315 (11th Cir. 1984), cert. denied, 471 U.S. 1137, 105 S.Ct. 2679, 86 L.Ed.2d 698 (1985); *United States v. Thevis*, 665 F.2d 616, 641 (5th Cir. Unit B), cert. denied, 456 U.S. 1008, 102 S.Ct. 2300, 73 L.Ed.2d 1303 (1982). We see no reason to depart from our precedent in this case. (p. 679)

The decision in *Benitez* was similarly expansive. The court was more prolix in the 1982 decision in *Thevis* (*Thevis* was decided by the Fifth Circuit prior to the division of that circuit into the Fifth and Eleventh Circuits – the Eleventh Circuit adopted the Fifth Circuit decision as Eleventh Circuit precedent).

Buckhout did not comment specifically on the identification made by the two government witnesses, but instead testified generally as to problems with eyewitness identification and that pilots as a group were not better equipped than ordinary witnesses to make identifications. To admit such testimony in effect would permit the proponent's witness to comment on the weight and credibility of opponents' witnesses and open the door to a barrage of marginally relevant psychological evidence. Moreover, *we conclude, as did the trial judge, that the problems of perception and memory can be adequately addressed in cross-examination and that the jury can adequately weigh these problems through common-sense evaluation.* (emphasis added) (p. 461)

Impediments to eyewitness expert testimony

Despite the momentum gained in some federal and state courts, expert testimony is frequently not admitted. As the examples have illustrated, three general grounds are typically advanced for excluding the testimony. One common basis for excluding eyewitness expert testimony pertains to doubts as to the scientific basis underlying the proposed expert testimony. The specific concerns include a lack of explanatory theory, unreliability of research findings, questions about the methodology of existing research and lack of agreement among experts. Indeed, although we earlier noted that the *Downing* court clearly anticipated the stance of the United States Supreme Court in its recent scientific expert witness decision (*Daubert*), the *Downing* decision was significant for another reason: *Downing* was one of the first cases in which opposing experts testified about eyewitness memory. In *Downing* the defense hired an expert witness to educate the jury about the fallibility of and factors that influence eyewitness memory. The prosecution hired several experts to rebut the defense's testimony. Rather than offering a different conclusion from that of the defense-hired expert, the prosecution-hired experts argued that the defense-hired expert's conclusions were not supported by the extant psychological literature and that the body of literature on human memory was therefore not relevant to crime situations. This viewpoint has found expression in cases such as *Watson*, cited earlier.

The second common basis for excluding eyewitness expert testimony pertains to the courts' concerns about the effects of expert testimony on jury decisions. Some argue that the expert testimony is a matter of "common sense," "ordinary experience," or "common knowledge" and the expert testimony is therefore superfluous. Some claim that the exclusion of expert testimony is harmless, even when in error and would not have affected the trial outcome. And some claim that the prejudicial effect of the testimony outweighs its probative value. Some courts continue to argue that the testimony invades the province of the jury.

The third common basis for excluding eyewitness expert testimony pertains to the effectiveness of traditional safeguards. Some courts argue that the issues addressed in expert testimony are more adequately addressed in cross-examination and/or in judges' instructions to the jury

Some courts have explicitly rejected these arguments. For example, the California Supreme Court in *McDonald* criticized an earlier precedent on the grounds that:

The expert testimony in question does *not* seek to take over the jury's task of judging credibility: as explained above, it does not tell the jury that any particular witness is or is not truthful or accurate in his identification of the defendant. . . . The jurors retain both the power and the duty to judge the credibility and weight of all testimony in the case as they are told by a standard instruction. (emphasis in original) (p. 249)

We should note a fourth basis for excluding eyewitness expert testimony that reflects some court confusion about the nature of this form of testimony. Some courts have struggled to distinguish fully the intended function of the expert in eyewitness identification cases from the function of other types of psychological experts. Unlike the expert psychiatrist or clinical psychologist who typically offer opinions about the state of mind or the credibility of a witness, the eyewitness expert's goal is to educate the jury about memory and thereby improve the jury's ability to assess the credibility of a witness.

Given that the eyewitness expert generally does not comment on the reliability of a particular witness but merely discusses the factors in the case that might have affected the witness's memory, Walters (1985) argues that it is unlikely that the expert testimony would usurp the function of the jury with respect to assessment of a witness's credibility.

We believe that most, if not all, of the major concerns about the admissibility of expert testimony on eyewitness memory are essentially empirical questions:

1. What is the state of scientific findings regarding eyewitness performance? Do the findings rest on an adequate scientific foundation?
2. Do the traditional trial safeguards – cross-examination and cautionary instructions to jurors – afford adequate protection to defendants identified and prosecuted on the basis of eyewitness evidence?
3. Can eyewitness expert evidence assist jurors in their assessment of eyewitness evidence?

The purpose of this book is to review systematically the empirical literature pertaining to each of these questions. In so doing we hope to cast light on the policy questions pertaining to admissibility and provide some guidance to the courts on addressing these difficult questions. Many of the questions raised in this review of the legal background on expert testimony are addressed empirically in the research described in the following chapters.

Part III

Sources of identification error: The scientific research

4   The scientific psychology of eyewitness identifications

It is clear from the appellate case law reviewed in Chapter 3 that one of the most fundamental questions courts have asked in the past – and are even more likely to ask in the future as a result of the *Daubert* decision – is whether eyewitness research is based on the scientific method. We are confident that the answer is an unequivocal "YES." Virtually all of the empirical eyewitness research conducted by psychologists makes use of standard methods employed in the experimental sciences.

Is it science?

It is sometimes argued that psychologists – perhaps especially psychologists who are called to testify about the problems of eyewitness reliability – know nothing that is not already part of common knowledge based on everyday experience. However, it is important to note that in contrast to laypersons psychologists collect their data using systematic observation. One problem with commonsense efforts to understand the world is that they lack the rigor that a science requires. All scientists, psychologists included, generally share certain assumptions about the world and about the way in which research ought to be conducted. The following is a list of assumptions that distinguish psychology and other sciences from nonscientific approaches to understanding.

Scientific assumptions

Determinism. Psychologists and other scientists assume that the world proceeds in an orderly and systematic fashion and that by employing the proper methods, humans can come to understand that order. As a basic assumption, determinism posits that events in the world are caused by other events. By studying those events' interrelationships, scientists maintain that they can establish laws that govern behavior. Psychologists further assume that if the causal laws underlying human behavior can be understood, it is possible to predict all human behavior. It is worth emphasizing, however, that psychology is far from being able to account for (let alone predict) all human actions.

Empiricism. Like any other science, psychology is grounded in direct observation of the world. This means that psychologists, like other scientists, assume that the world is best understood by experiencing phenomena directly – an approach known as empiricism. Empiricism can be contrasted with other methods of studying the world that do not involve direct observation or actual testing of theories: speculation, reasoning, imagination, and intuition, for example.

There is a constant interplay between theories and empirical findings in all scientific endeavors. Empirically derived data often spark new theories that are in turn subjected to the test of empiricism – and added to or eliminated from the canon of scientific "truths" that are generally accepted as valid representations of how the world actually works.

Invariance. The assumption of invariance is linked to that of determinism. Scientists assume that the causal relationships studied by scientists are invariant: that is, they are orderly and do not change with the passage of time or with changes in location. You can readily see the importance of invariance in the operation of our senses; clearly, our ability to function in the world depends on our ability to share generally similar experiences when confronted by similar events and objects – and also depends on our repeated and reliable recognition of familiar events and objects. For example, in a natural science such as chemistry and in a behavioral science, say, social psychology, causal laws are presumed to remain constant. If the chemicals or social settings remain the same, changes in any given variable should always produce the same chemical or social reactions if all other conditions remain the same. As you will see later, psychologists use certain research methods in order to control conditions and then predict and identify invariant causal relationships.

Operationism. Operationism refers to the assumption that concepts can be observed and measured. Some psychologists are interested in abstract concepts such as stress, attention, attractiveness; these concepts can mean different things to different people. One of the major tasks confronting a research psychologist is to find definitions that are not only widely acceptable to others, but that also allow reliable scientific observation and measurement.

"Operational definitions" specify how a concept is to be measured. If, for example, we are interested in assessing whether a face is attractive, we might define attractiveness operationally in terms of the amount of time people spend looking at a face, the extent to which people rate the face as attractive, the strength of their desire to spend time with another person, and so on. Psychologists *can* measure all of these factors. Part of the creativity of psychology rests in the imaginative ways in which psychologists have devised operational definitions that allow for systematic study of complex human behaviors.

Objectivity. All scientists, including psychologists, seek to maintain an objective approach to their work. As a practical matter objectivity is less an assumption than a goal; it means that psychologists attempt to devise theories, make predictions, and collect, analyze, and interpret data in a fair and impartial manner. Most scientists make concerted efforts to ensure that their preconceptions about human behavior and their personal beliefs and experiences do not shape their work. Ideally, psychology should proceed in a manner that is understood by and acceptable to all other scientists regardless of their personal beliefs and expectations.

Of course, not all of psychology proceeds along an objective path. All psychologists have had personal experiences that cause them to be interested in some problems and not others. All psychologists find some theories more credible than other theories, and some psychologists propose theories in which they have personal investments (at least investments of pride). Psychologists' training and experiences influence the types of questions they pose, the methods they use to seek answers, and the interpretations they give to findings. Despite these obstacles, all psychologists strive for objectivity. Training to be a psychologist includes learning to formulate operational definitions; learning methods of data collection, measurement, and analysis; and studying how to develop and test theories in ways that help psychologists maintain an objectivity toward their work.

The scientific goals of psychology

Almost all psychologists would readily acknowledge that they study behavior because they find it intrinsically interesting, but as scientists, psychologists are directed to a set of goals that are more important than the satisfaction of their personal interests. The scientific apparatus of psychology that we have been discussing is directed toward four basic goals: description, explanation, prediction, and control.

Description. A basic task confronting the psychologist who is interested in a new problem or phenomenon is to describe the problem or phenomenon. The importance of accurate description can be illustrated through the physical sciences, in which some of the most important early advances consisted of systematic descriptions or taxonomies. Physics and chemistry were significantly advanced by the insights provided by the periodic table of elements. Biology and paleontology were advanced by the development of classification systems for plants and animals. Medicine was advanced dramatically by the descriptive work of early anatomists.

Similarly, within psychology major advances come with systematic observation and data collection. The objective of the descriptive phase of any psychological research is to observe a phenomenon systematically and to identify, collect, and organize the data that characterize the phenomenon.

Explanation. Once a phenomenon has been described systematically, researchers can tackle the problem of explaining it. They begin by observing a pattern of relationships inherent in the phenomenon; that is, certain behaviors or characteristics occurring together, from which certain causal connections can be inferred. The scientific researcher's main objective is to establish the causes of observed patterns.

Prediction. A theory must also be falsifiable: In other words, it must be *possible* to test the theory and determine whether its predictions are correct or incorrect. If theories did not provide for testable predictions, it would be impossible for researchers to prove that defective or inadequate theories are wrong.

A psychological theory must allow specific predictions to be made about which behaviors will occur under a specific set of conditions. Furthermore, those conditions and behaviors must be observable and measurable. If a test of predictions has been conducted properly and the predicted behavior occurs, confidence in the theory is increased. If a test has been conducted properly but the predicted behavior does *not* occur, confidence in the theory is shaken; it may then be time to go back to the explanation stage and reformulate the theory. The healthy growth of psychology is fostered by the ability to test, retest, and generate new hypotheses.

In some areas of psychology, predictive accuracy is still limited. For instance, psychologists cannot often predict accurately the social or emotional behavior of individuals in particular situations. However, there are many areas of psychology – for example, certain domains of physiology, cognition, learning, and clinical psychology – where theories are sufficiently well developed to allow for reasonably accurate predictions. Indeed, in some areas of psychology – including eyewitness research – our knowledge is sufficiently deep and our theories sufficiently mature that it can be argued that in those areas, psychologists are realizing the fourth goal of science: control.

Control. At first glance the notion of scientists in control of behavior may seem rather menacing; but psychologists' interests in controlling behavior are actually benign. Just as meteorologists work to develop detailed theories of weather that allow them to make accurate, long-term forecasts and ultimately help them exercise control over the weather, so are psychologists working to find ways to control human behaviors constructively. Just as it would help humankind for meteorologists to find ways to relieve droughts and predict devastating storms, it would help if psychologists could find ways to improve the identification accuracy of eyewitnesses and minimize the errors witnesses commit, and find ways to assist the police, prosecutors, judges, and juries in differentiating between accurate and inaccurate identifications.

How do psychologists realize these lofty goals? How do they avoid the pitfalls of commonsense reasoning? By adopting scientific methods of theory building, they can describe, explain, predict, and in some cases exercise a degree of control over remarkably diverse human behaviors and responses to experience.

The research methods of psychology

Because psychologists study such a wide range of phenomena – everything from the biochemistry of learning to eyewitness performance – they have developed a broad set of methodological approaches that are of interest and relevance to all psychologists. Just as psychologists share a general agreement about the assumptions and goals of scientific research, they also agree on the value of a broad set of scientific methods for conducting their research.

Theory and hypothesis. Theories of human behavior are among the most important accomplishments of psychology. Theories are important first because they help psychologists organize their knowledge about human behavior and provide coherent accounts of the causal relationships governing that behavior. Theories also are important because they allow psychologists to make testable predictions about human behavior.

The process of theory development is in some ways circular. A good theory generates testable predictions. In turn, the results of tests of these predictions help psychologists reevaluate their theories. If predictions are shown (by research) to be in error, then researchers go back to the theory and consider ways in which the theory can be reformulated to account for the error. If research results show predictions are correct, then confidence in the theory is increased, and researchers then work to formulate additional tests of the theory.

Psychological research, like other scientific research, proceeds through a process of hypothesis testing. Hypotheses are predictions that can be tested. Not all hypotheses are derived from theories. Sometimes psychologists are confronted with new phenomena that they do not really understand and therefore formulate some hypotheses as starting points for systematic research. Sometimes hypotheses are suggested by everyday experiences, popular knowledge and beliefs, and even by appellate court opinions about such matters as eyewitness behavior. Whatever their source, hypotheses must be subjected to systematic testing.

The null hypothesis. Suppose that we, as researchers, have formulated the hypothesis that people who are attractive have more recognizable faces than people who are average in attractiveness. To test this hypothesis we might identify two friends, one we think is very attractive and one who is average in attractiveness, and ask a number of people to rate how memorable their faces are (as we shall soon see, there are problems with this method). We could then compare the ratings of the person with the "attractive" face with the ratings of the person with the "average" face.

Our comparison of these ratings will allow us to evaluate two distinct hypotheses. The first hypothesis is termed the null hypothesis (*null* meaning "not any"). It states that any differences that we observe in the memorability ratings of the two faces are not actual differences but are due to chance or luck. In other words, according to the null hypothesis any differences in ratings do not reflect actual, systematic differences in people's ratings of memorability. Perhaps the differences reflect the raters' feelings about something in the acquaintances' behavior other than their appearance, or perhaps they reflect feelings in the raters and had nothing to do with the appearances of the two faces. Extraneous, even random events are always at play in people's behavior, and thus researchers must always distinguish between results that may have occurred by chance or through the influence of extraneous factors and those that may have occurred as a result of the behavior under study.

The second, or research hypothesis, states that the differences in the attractiveness of the two faces has influenced people's ratings and the differences we have observed are not merely due to chance.

Statistical significance. The research hypothesis is supported only if we can rule out the null hypothesis. To rule out the null hypothesis, we must obtain a difference in ratings large enough so that it cannot be attributed to chance events. For example, because we know that there are normally variations in people's reactions to others (whether or not the others are attractive), we must find out whether the differences in ratings that we have observed might be due to the fact that we happened to question people about the "attractive" face on a bright sunny day when most of them happened to have especially warm feelings about other people and found everyone "memorable." In contrast, if we asked for ratings of the average face on an overcast and gloomy day, this might have prompted the somewhat grumpy raters to regard any face as unmemorable. Thus, ratings of both the attractive and average faces might have had nothing to do with their appearance and everything to do with the weather! In this case, weather conditions and attractiveness are fully "confounded" in the sense that all the ratings of the attractive face were taken under good weather conditions and all ratings of the average face under poor weather conditions – even if we observe differences in ratings we cannot be sure what caused the difference.

Psychologists design their studies carefully so that they do not inadvertently contaminate their results with chance factors such as weather conditions. They also rely on tests of statistical significance. These are tests of probability designed to answer how likely it is that an observed difference between groups could be produced by chance factors when there is no actual difference between the groups. Only when a difference is so large that it is unlikely to have been produced by chance will a researcher be prepared to reject the null hypothesis and conclude a real difference between the two groups. In testing differences, most psychologists adopt the conventional level of statistical significance of $p < .05$. What this means is that the null hypothesis is rejected if the observed difference would appear fewer than 5 out of 100 times if the null hypothesis were true. In other words, psychologists reject the null hypothesis of "no difference" only when it is very unlikely to be true.

Of course, because behavior is complex, even if psychologists find that the differences are large enough to warrant rejection of the null hypothesis, they still cannot automatically assume that the research hypothesis is true. The differences might have been produced by a factor other than the one specified in the hypothesis.

Independent and dependent variables. In our study we were interested in the effects of attractiveness on memorability and, in essence, we hypothesized that attractiveness causes memorability. In most instances researchers examine variables such as attractiveness and memorability because they are interested in the causal relationships between those variables. But unless researchers can control or manipulate their causal or independent variable (attractiveness) and then examine the effects of these manipulations on the outcome or dependent variables (memorability), they can never be certain that causal variables are producing the hypothesized effects on the outcome variables.

Researchers may be able to observe correlations or simultaneous changes in the two types of variables, but that does not prove one variable caused the other. Indeed, we might repeat our little study with a hundred pairs of attractive and average faces and observe that attractiveness and ratings of memorability are almost invariably linked. But – and this is an important but – we could never really be certain, using the method just described, that we did not have the causal relation reversed: Maybe people who are memorable are perceived as more attractive. Even if we have avoided the pitfall of confounding attractiveness with weather conditions, it is still possible that some third variable (such as smiling) causes people to be both memorable and attractive. As it turns out, experimental methods give us a way to resolve such problems. Before we examine how they do so, we will look briefly at validity and reliability: two important traits of any variable.

Validity and reliability of variables. Sometimes it is difficult to devise an effective operational definition which specifies the operations (actions) that embody the independent variable and the measures that embody the dependent variables. This is especially true when researchers are working with highly abstract concepts. How, for instance, should researchers operationalize "stress"? How can and should "intelligence" be measured? When is behavior "aggressive"? What is "happiness"?

Psychologists often try a variety of operational definitions. Subjects are, for instance, "stressed" in a variety of ways. Sometimes they are subjected to loud and unpredictable noises; sometimes they are confronted with inoculations from syringes; sometimes they are crowded together in small, overheated rooms; sometimes they are confronted with parachute jumps; sometimes they are asked to drink lots of coffee (caffeine is a stimulant); sometimes they are told that they are going to be making a public presentation to a large audience – a very stressful prospect for most people.

All of these operational definitions of stress possess some face validity. That is, most of us recognize that we would be stressed under the conditions described. Yet maybe these operations represent different states (arousal? discomfort?). Only by employing a number of alternative operational definitions can psychologists determine that some or all of these operational definitions produce similar effects on subjects.

If the variables seem related in terms of their effects, psychologists talk in terms of construct validity. This means that researchers have reached some agreement about what the underlying concept or construct ("stress") is and some agreement on how it should be operationalized and measured.

One other characteristic of variables ought to be mentioned. Have you ever had a bathroom scale that registered a different weight each time you stepped on it (even over a period of a few seconds)? That scale was probably a valid measure of weight, but it lacked reliability. A reliable measure is one that yields identical results when conditions are identical;

psychologists give careful attention to the measures they use to assure high degrees of reliability.

Experimental control. In experimental studies, the researcher exercises control over the independent or causal variable and frequently can manipulate when or how much of the independent variable is present at any given time. Let's return to our hypothesis about the effects of attractiveness on memorability. We have postulated that, all other things being equal, an attractive face is going to be more memorable than an average face. We might test our hypothesis by conducting a true experiment. To test our hypothesis experimentally, we must manipulate our independent variable: attractiveness. One possible way to do this might be to take a set of faces that have been rated in advance for attractiveness by a large number of raters. We could then show our research witnesses either a set of attractive faces or a set of less attractive faces for a short period of time and later test their ability to recognize these (attractive and not so attractive) faces by showing the subjects a second set of faces – some of which they saw before and some of which are new. Let's suppose that we do observe the difference that we predicted: Faces previously rated attractive are better remembered than less attractive faces are. If we have designed our experiment properly and observed the experimental research guidelines about to be discussed, we may well be able to rule out the null hypothesis (that attractiveness and memorability are unrelated). But does this prove our research hypothesis? Unfortunately it does not, for there are other grounds on which our conclusions can be questioned.

Internal validity and rival hypotheses. Suppose that somebody comes along and challenges the "internal validity" of our study. Our study would be internally valid if our attractiveness manipulation truly had produced the rating differences. However, our critic might quarrel with our initial measure of attractiveness – perhaps she could take our original pictures and have them rated for "happiness" and demonstrate that faces rated high in happiness are the same faces rated high in attractiveness. Thus, our results might just as easily be attributed to happiness of appearance as to attractiveness. The critic's rival hypothesis is that it is really the apparent happiness of the people in our pictures that produces the observed differences in memorability.

The critic asserts that we have confounded (mixed up) these variables so that we cannot determine accurately whether happiness or attractiveness produced the results. As long as rival alternative hypotheses and possible confounds of variables can be identified it is essentially impossible to prove the validity of the theory that generated the original research hypothesis. We may be able to rule out rival alternative hypotheses effectively by demonstrating in soundly designed experiments that the predictions made in those alternative hypotheses are not supported by experimental results – but we can never be entirely certain that someone else won't come along with a new theory and generate yet another plausible rival hypothesis.

Random assignment of subjects. Yet another critic might point out that our two groups of witnesses were systematically different from one another. Perhaps we unwittingly assigned males to rate only the attractive faces and females to rate the average faces. Our ratings might be attributable to a difference between males and females. As researchers we might react by saying: Well, we can see that we should have made sure that the two groups of witnesses were as much alike as possible by matching the characteristics of raters in both groups. Perhaps we should have identified every characteristic that could be related to remembering others. We should have asked how attractive each witness is, how outgoing and personable each witness is, whether the witness is male or female, how mature the witness is, how good each individual's memory is, and so on. But as you can see, the problem with matching witnesses in the two groups is that the list of matching variables quickly grows very long, and it may become very difficult (in fact, it will soon become impossible) to find people who match on a large number of characteristics.

The alternative to matching is a random assignment of witnesses to the different experimental conditions. What happens if, as each subject enters our lab, we flip a coin and send all "heads" to be smiled at and all "tails" not to be smiled at? The answer is that by chance alone, approximately half the males, half the females, half the attractive people, half the mature subjects, half the people with good memories, indeed, half of every type of subject we can (and cannot) think of should end up receiving smiles, and half should end up not receiving smiles. By randomly assigning subjects to conditions, we have in effect guaranteed that the two groups will not be significantly different in a way that could produce a difference in our outcome variable.

External validity. So far, so good: We have done everything right and are feeling confident about our results and the support they lend to our theory. But along comes another critic who argues: Your laboratory experiment is a nice demonstration that smiling *can* affect liking, but I doubt that your results generalize to the real world. In other words, the study may be internally valid, but it is not externally valid.

The challenge to external validity can take many forms. Some may argue that the laboratory study lacked realism and that its results would not generalize to settings and situations in which subjects had more at stake than a few postsession ratings. Some may argue that the results are true only for undergraduates and that if the experiment were run with more mature adults, smiling would not affect liking. Still others might argue that the results are solely attributable to some quirky characteristic in our confederate and that most people could not affect significantly the impressions they make by smiling or not smiling at strangers.

The most effective way to respond to critiques about the external validity of studies is to repeat or replicate the study using a wide variety of situations and settings, with equally diverse confederates, a wide variety of subjects, and interrelated manipulations of the independent variable. A single experimental study is seldom regarded as conclusive evidence. Psychologists recognize that all studies and findings are strengthened by replications.

Nonexperimental research methods

The vast majority of studies discussed in this book have used experimental methods. Psychologists and other scientists generally prefer to use experimental methods because the degree of control they permit also allows them to reach more definite conclusions about causal relationships. However, there are many instances in which it is impossible for researchers to conduct true experiments because the researchers cannot manipulate independent variables. For example, many psychologists are interested in the differences in performance of eyewitnesses to crimes in which there has been violence as compared to crimes without violence. Although one can easily imagine an experiment to test the effect of violence, it is clearly unethical for researchers to perpetrate crimes and randomly assign people to be victims of violence or nonviolence. Even though it is more difficult to make unambiguous causal judgments using nonexperimental methods, such methods are nonetheless important tools for researchers. Two types of nonexperimental research used by eyewitness researchers are archival studies and surveys.

Archival studies. Archives are places where public records and documents are stored – for example, court records and police files. Researchers study archives to learn about natural patterns in behavior and events. For instance, psychologists have used police records to study the reports of crime victims.

The archival method has the advantages of being unobtrusive and not requiring interaction with the people who originally supplied the data. Because it is unobtrusive, it eliminates the possibility that people's responses will be influenced by the fact that they have been asked to give a direct response to the researcher. Other advantages are that the data already exist, may be readily available, may be highly reliable, and may provide a record spanning many years. But the archival method's disadvantages are that sometimes the appropriate data may not exist, may be hard to locate, and may take a lot of time to reduce to analyzable form. Most important, because the data are not experimental in origin and lack the controls previously discussed, it is extremely difficult, if not impossible, to make authoritative statements about the causal relationship between variables of interest (e.g., the level of stress experienced by a witness and his or her identification accuracy) from archival data.

Surveys. Perhaps the most familiar nonexperimental research method is the survey. Surveys are used to assess people's attitudes and to gather information from them about their behavior. In surveys reported in this book psychologists have used surveys to learn about public knowledge concerning factors that influence eyewitness performance and to assess eyewitness experts' agreement about the implications of eyewitness research findings. As with archival studies, the lack of controls available in experiments limits the ability of survey researchers to make causal statements about relationships among the variables they study.

In short the hallmarks of scientific research include the falsifiability/testability of research hypotheses; the testing of hypotheses using experimental research methods; experiments in which the variables or processes examined by researchers are carefully controlled by the researchers in order to assess their causal effects on outcome variables (such as identification accuracy). The results and conclusions summarized in the next section are the products of precisely the methods underscored by the Supreme Court in *Daubert*.

Peer review

The second *Daubert*-inspired question that might be posed about eyewitness research is: Has the scientific research been subjected to the peer review process? In fact, in the research studies relied upon here findings have often survived two levels of peer review. Much of the research upon which the proffered testimony is predicated is the product of research supported by funding sources such as the National Science Foundation, the National Institutes of Mental Health, the National Institute of Justice, the Research Council of Canada, and equivalent agencies in Great Britain, Australia, and Germany (the vast bulk of the research has been conducted by researchers from these countries). These national funding agencies typically subject research proposals to a review process in which anonymous evaluations are solicited from a half-dozen to as many as 20 scientific reviewers. Proposals are evaluated for soundness of research design and analysis and the contributions they are likely to make to our understanding of the processes under study. At an agency such as the National Science Foundation only one in five such proposals receives funding.

Once data collection and analyses are completed and the results are written up for publication, a second round of peer review begins. Articles are submitted to a *single* scientific journal for peer review (in contrast to the publication process in law journals where an author could, in fact, submit the same article to any of the more than 200 law reviews – which are overwhelmingly student edited – and wait for one of them to accept the paper). The editor of the journal will typically solicit three anonymous outside reviews of each submitted manuscript (and will also evaluate the manuscript herself). Relatively few articles are accepted for publication (the rejection rate in most psychology journals is around 80%). Authors of rejected manuscripts may choose to revise their manuscripts and submit them to another journal – where the manuscript will once again go through the peer review process. Although some original research first appears in edited scientific books and is not subjected to as rigorous a form of peer review, these chapters typically undergo review by the volume editors and therefore reflect the input of peers who were not directly involved in the research.

What do reviewers look for in a manuscript? An essential requirement is that a study be sufficiently well designed so that it can be relied upon to address the questions posed by the researcher. Thus, all the design and analysis features discussed in the first half of this chapter are evaluated by reviewers. Poorly designed studies (e.g., studies with significant confoundings of variables, studies with poor measurement of dependent variables, studies with poor operationalizations of independent variables, studies that provide no new insights into the questions addressed, studies that are not properly analyzed with appropriate statistical tests, and so on) do not pass muster and are not published. The standards are high and in leading journals it is not unusual for 80–90% of all submissions to be rejected.

How much research is there? When was the research conducted?

One way to gauge the extent and vintage of research on eyewitness reliability is to examine writings that review the research. Two chapters published in volumes separated by a decade provide some insights. The chapters were by Penrod, Loftus, and Winkler (1982) and by Williams,

Table 4.1. *References cited in* Adult Eyewitness Testimony *(Ross, Read, & Toglia, 1994)*

era	number of cites
pre-1950	9
1950s	11
1960s	29
1970s	106
1980s	306
1990–1992	100 (a rate of 330 for 90s)

Loftus, and Deffenbacher (1992) and they were designed to provide overviews of the theoretical and empirical context within which eyewitness reliability research has been conducted. These writings reveal that the research producing psychological insights into factors that influence eyewitness performance is of relatively recent vintage. Of the approximately 250 citations in the Penrod et al. 1982 chapter (which was written in 1981), nearly 200 had appeared in 1970 or after. Of the nearly 150 studies cited in the William et al. 1992 chapter over 80% were conducted after 1980.

A 1994 volume on *Adult Eyewitness Testimony* (Ross, Read, & Toglia) has nearly 600 references dating to the time-periods identified in Table 4.1.

The recent vintage of this research is very important, for as we have already seen, some of the significant appellate cases that created precedential impediments to eyewitness expert testimony predate the vast bulk of the research, for attempts to introduce expert psychological testimony on eyewitness memory began to flourish in the early 1970s. Evidence of these efforts can be found in appellate court decisions. In the state courts, two states, Kentucky (*Pankey v. Commonwealth*, 1972) and Massachusetts (*Commonwealth v. Jones*, 1972), upheld their trial courts' decisions to exclude such expert testimony. Trial court exclusion of such testimony was also upheld in an early and widely cited decision by the U.S. Court of Appeals for the Ninth Circuit (*United States v. Amaral*, 1973). The novelty of the research was one of the factors that influenced these decisions and raises the question: What has changed in the past 20 years?

There is little doubt that there is now a very large and growing body of research on eyewitness reliability – one of the authors maintains a bibliography on eyewitness research that now contains over 2,000 references (most of them scientific studies). This is a body of research that has expanded at an accelerating rate since 1980.

Table 4.2. *Consensus about eyewitness research findings (percentages)*

	Reliable Enough?	Would Testify	Have Testified
Suggestive lineup instructions	95	86	26
Weak confidence-accuracy relation	87	83	37
Exposure duration at crime	85	72	26
Retention interval	83	78	28
Cross-race recognition	79	71	32
Foil bias in identification test	77	79	27
Eyewitness's level of stress	71	65	38
Weapon focus	57	53	27
Event violence	36	30	14

The growth of research on factors influencing eyewitness performance is also underscored by the number of scholarly books psychologists have written in recent years (Ceci, Toglia, & Ross, 1987; Clifford & Bull, 1978; Lloyd-Bostock & Clifford, 1983; Loftus, 1979; Ross, Read, & Toglia, 1994; Shepherd, Ellis, & Davies, 1982; Wells & Loftus, 1984). Furthermore, there is also a much larger body of research (numbering in thousands of studies) on human memory generally that provides a broader and deeper empirical and theoretical context for the research that focuses specifically on eyewitness performance and the factors that influence such performance.

Is there a consensus on the content of expert testimony?

Courts have traditionally required that the content of expert testimony reflect scientific principles generally accepted in the field, though the more modern trend, reflected in the Supreme Court's 1993 decision in *Daubert* is to look less to general acceptance and more to the scientific validity of the procedures that have produced the knowledge represented in the expert testimony. Nonetheless, general acceptance remains one of the criteria a court may examine when making an admissibility decision. Of course, it can easily be argued that a reliable and valid assessment of consensus in the field requires a systematic sampling of opinion and several such studies have been undertaken.

Yarmey and Jones (1983b) were the first to attempt to address the level of consensus empirically. They provided 16 eyewitness experts with hypothetical scenarios and forced-choice response formats to assess their predicted outcomes. High levels of agreement were obtained on many topics. Kassin, Ellsworth, and Smith (1989) replicated and expanded significantly upon Yarmey and Jones's findings. They conducted a large-scale survey of eyewitness experts from the United States, Canada, and Europe. A total of 63 experts responded to the survey (a response rate of 56%). The respondents completed a 24-page questionnaire in which they evaluated the reliability of 21 eyewitness phenomena and provided personal information concerning their educational background, employment, publications, and experience as eyewitness experts. The vast majority of the respondents had Ph.D.s, and the average number of relevant publications was 6.35 (most of which were in scientific journals). Most (56%) had testified as experts on eyewitness memory at least once. In total they estimated having testified on 478 occasions: Three hundred sixty-four times for the defense in criminal cases, 29 times for the prosecution in criminal cases, 54 times for the plaintiff in civil cases, and 31 times for the defendant in civil cases.

With respect to eyewitness phenomena, the experts were asked whether they perceived each factor to be "reliable enough for psychologists to present it in courtroom testimony," whether they would testify about that factor, and whether they have testified about that factor. We review only those phenomena pertaining to eyewitness identification. Table 4.2 summarizes the experts' opinions about the most reliable phenomena pertaining to eyewitness identification. More than 70% of the experts opined that suggestive lineup instructions, the weak confidence-accuracy relation, exposure duration retention interval, cross-race recognition, foil bias, and the eyewitness's level of stress were findings sufficiently well established to testify about in court and almost as many indicated that they would testify about these factors. Each of these factors was testified about by at least 25% of the experts. Considerably less consensus was obtained for the phenomena of weapon focus and event violence.

Kassin et al. noted several limitations to their study. First, the results are time-bound and reflect the state of knowledge about the factors that influence eyewitness memory at the time the survey was conducted. For example, the consensus about weapon focus was modest. But the survey was carried out before much of the relevant research and, most important, before Steblay's (1992) analysis of 19 weapon focus studies was published. If the survey were conducted again, it is likely that consensus levels would increase on topics such as weapon focus effects (but might decline on other topics). Such movements in the levels of consensus would depend upon the results of recent research.

In sum, the existing data suggest that considerable consensus does exist regarding the influence on eyewitness memory of a variety of factors.

5   Summarizing eyewitness research findings

Of the research topics reviewed in this book, none have received more empirical attention than the factors that influence eyewitness identification. The research literature on this topic is vast. Reviewing, summarizing, and integrating a large body of empirical research is no easy undertaking. In addition to the tasks of identifying and locating relevant research, a reviewer faces the problem of extracting broad empirical and theoretical generalizations from disparate research findings. Furthermore, not all studies yield consistent results – indeed, inconsistencies in research findings seem to be the rule rather than the exception. How are these inconsistencies to be interpreted and how should they influence efforts to distill a general set of conclusions from research?

How to summarize research findings

Conventionally, reviewers have steeped themselves in research literature and attempted to arrive at their generalizations after a thorough consideration of the theories, methods, and findings found in the literature. However, in the past decade there has been an explosion in the use of so-called *meta-analytic* methods, which use quantitative techniques to develop integrative reviews of empirical research.

Quantitative approaches to research synthesis are displacing conventional forms of review because they offer a number of significant advantages to traditional qualitative reviews. For example, Beaman (1991) systematically compared related groups of traditional and meta-analytic reviews and found the latter superior in such domains as:

♦ extensiveness of citations and critiques of previous reviews,
♦ effectiveness of study retrieval,
♦ exhaustiveness of bibliographic searches,
♦ presence of summary conclusions,
♦ explanations for exclusions of studies,
♦ attention to study characteristics,
♦ testing of interactions and theoretical hypotheses, and
♦ explicitness of the criteria used in conducting the reviews.

71

Similarly, Becker (1991) examined the values of review journal editors and found that the review characteristics they most value include: breadth; clarity of purpose, arguments, presentation, and conclusions; coverage of literature; replicability; and a systematic approach.   These are all characteristics more commonly found in meta-analyses than in conventional qualitative reviews.

What is a meta-analysis?

In one variant of meta-analysis, individual research findings are treated as separate data points in a secondary data analysis. For example, one can imagine 10 experiments using the same independent variable (i.e., perpetrator disguise) in which the same experimental treatment (the perpetrator in a staged crime is disguised in some way) is tested against the same control condition (the perpetrator is not disguised). For each experiment, the investigator can compute the difference in a criterion score (an outcome variable such as the percentage of witnesses who correctly identify the perpetrator from a photoarray or the percentage of witnesses who incorrectly identify a foil) between the experimental and control conditions. In meta-analysis, these different scores serve as data points in further data analyses. In a simple example, the 10 data points (one difference score for each of the 10 experiments) can be combined to obtain an overall average that reflects the average difference in performance rates for the experimental versus the control conditions. This average difference score provides a succinct summary of the findings or "effects" generated by the 10 studies.

As we will explain, simply computing average treatment effects is not the only objective of a meta-analysis, but it is one of the characteristic features of this method. The idea of pooling results across studies is not new. The theoretical and methodological foundations of meta-analytic methods can be traced back over 50 years. However, Cohen (1962) significantly advanced the meta-analytic revolution by recognizing the value of reducing study results (the differences between control and treatment groups) to an effect-size measure such as the correlation coefficient that is standardized across studies.   As Glass underscored, with sufficient information it is possible to reduce the relationship between any independent variable and dependent variable to a measure that is common across studies – even though the operationalizations of the independent and dependent variables (the actual manner in which the independent variable is represented and the dependent variable is measured) may not be identical. Indeed, as we will show, the differences in the ways that independent variables are manipulated can, themselves, be the object of study.

One might want to use existing studies to estimate the likely size of the effect in question. Indeed, many social scientists have long recognized the advantage of examining prior research in their domain of interest in order to estimate the size of the effects they plan to study. Such estimates permit the researcher to determine the size of the samples that are required to assure – to a particular probability – that the effect will produce statistically significant differences in dependent measures. This process of "power analysis" has generated entire volumes designed to guide researchers (see, especially, Cohen, 1977). In fact, one major advantage of meta-analysis is that it systematically uses prior research findings to generate a fairly precise estimate of the effect sizes detected in a body of research and thereby provides a succinct summary of the status of scientific research in a particular domain.

Since the late 1970s hundreds of meta-analyses have been conducted and reported by social psychologists, clinical psychologists, educational psychologists, epidemiologists, and medical researchers (indeed, medical meta-analyses have permitted much stronger conclusions about a variety of phenomena that were left ambiguous when reviewed with traditional methods and the results of meta-analytic reviews of prior medical research appear regularly in the popular press). At the same time the methods of meta-analysis have grown in sophistication and acceptance.

Cumulation of scientific findings

Meta-analyses have grown in popularity because they address several traditional problems within social and other scientific communities. It has sometimes been observed that the social sciences do not exhibit the orderly patterns of empirical and theoretical development shown by more established scientific disciplines such as chemistry and physics. Although part of the problem of cumulation in the social sciences arises from the failure to undertake systematic replications of previous research findings, there are many domains in which replications and partial replications can be found in large numbers. Researchers who recognize the existence of such replications often conduct literature reviews that are meant to summarize the findings from related bodies of research, but these efforts have been hampered by the lack of a method that permits quantified integrations of research results.

Traditional reviews that seek to go beyond a verbal characterization of the reviewer's impression/integration of findings have often tried to introduce an element of quantification by providing nose counts of studies that have yielded significant and nonsignificant findings using a conventional p-level such as .05. These tallies, especially when they produce roughly equal numbers of studies with significant and nonsignificant results, have led some reviewers to conclude that the relationships being examined are of an inconclusive status.

Sophisticated reviewers recognize that simply looking at the numbers of significant and nonsignificant findings can, in fact, yield an extremely distorted picture of the relationships involved. Statistical significance is a function of both the size of treatment effects and sample size. In an extreme case one can easily imagine a half-dozen studies, all of which detect statistically significant differences, each based on a sample size of 200, and another half-dozen studies with nonsignificant findings, each based on a sample size of 20. It might be tempting to conclude from these 12 studies that there is no reliable relationship between the variables even though the magnitude of the observed effect might be the same in the two sets of studies.

Theoretical versus practical significance of findings

Another criticism that has been directed at much research in the social sciences is that researchers have given too little attention to the problem of assessing the social and theoretical importance of the effects of their independent variables. This point is perhaps most easily illustrated with a policing example. All other things being equal, the police are interested in practices or treatments that are maximally effective – those that produce the largest benefits such as reductions in crime rates. Given a choice between two practices that differ *only* in effectiveness, the police should logically choose the most effective – the one that produces the largest "effect size." Traditional research reviews in applied domains have been ill-equipped to provide summaries of findings that differentiate treatments (or, more broadly, independent variables) on the basis of their effectiveness.

Indeed, the fixation of social scientists on statistical significance levels has often obscured the fact that not all treatments/independent variables are equal in terms of the effects they produce. The same criticism can be leveled at research directed at purely theoretical issues. Theories designed to provide explanatory, causal accounts of particular phenomena are not all equal. Some theoretical accounts are more elegant than others, some encompass more findings than others, and some, just as important, account for more of the variability in critical dependent variables. That is, some theories embody relationships that capture larger effect sizes. Although the strength of relationships (sometimes referred to as explained variance) is only one of the criteria with which theories should be evaluated, it can be an important criterion – especially insofar as knowledge about the explanatory power of theories can serve as a valuable guide to policy decisions. Meta-analysis is extremely useful in assessing the relative size of effects examined in a body of research and in distinguishing the explanatory power of alternative theories.

Integrating research findings

A third criticism directed at much social science research and the process of cumulation is that social scientists have not been very enterprising in finding ways to use existing research to test and evaluate theoretical and practical issues not originally addressed in the preexisting research. As bodies of descriptive research and theories develop, researchers often wish that they could employ prior research to address new questions. Meta-analytic techniques can, in many instances, achieve this objective. It is possible, by drawing on a larger body of research, to examine relationships within the body of studies that cannot be investigated by looking at the studies individually.

In fact, many meta-analytic researchers have been interested in examining variables that may moderate the effects studied by a related body of research. Eagly and Carli (1981), for instance, established that the oft-asserted difference in male and female influenceability was a methodological artifact attributable to the fact that the vast majority of studies in this domain had been conducted by male researchers who choose influence tasks on which males were generally more knowledgeable. Once the difference in task sophistication was considered, the gender difference disappeared.

Meta-analytic methods

At least two basic forms of meta-analysis can be distinguished (Bangert-Drowns, 1986), and each has its unique strengths.

The first method, the *Glassian study-wise approach* (Glass, McGaw, & Smith, 1981) uses three steps:

1. All relevant studies are identified.
2. Outcomes in all studies are converted to a common effect-size metric (e.g., a correlation coefficient r or Cohen's d, which divides the difference between treatment groups by the control group's standard deviation, which has the result of placing outcomes from different studies in the same unit of measure). This means that every cell in a research study can contribute a separate effect-size

estimate for each dependent variable employed by the original researcher and that studies employing multiple independent variables tested at multiple levels can contribute large numbers of effect sizes to a meta-analysis.

3. Studies are grouped according to theoretical, methodological, validity, publication, and other criteria and average effect sizes within these groupings are computed.

A corollary of the third step, developed by Hedges (1982; Hedges & Olkin, 1985) and Rosenthal and Rubin (1982) emphasizes statistical tests of the homogeneity of variance in outcomes across studies. If variances are large or significant, then efforts can be made to differentiate among studies on methodological, design, operationalization, and other criteria in order to account for the variability in outcomes.

A second meta-analytic method advanced by Rosenthal (1978, 1979, 1991) emphasizes the combination of probabilities across studies. This procedure requires computation of an effect size for each study, an exact one-tailed p (test of statistical significance) for each study, and the complementary standard normal Z (another standardized effect-size measure) for each study. Average effect sizes and combined Zs (often weighted for sample size) are then computed for each independent variable. The weighted Z further permits a computation of a "fail-safe" N – the number of unreported studies with null effects that would have to be stashed away in file drawers or trash cans in order to "wipe-out" the effect reported in published and otherwise available studies.

Reporting meta-analytic results

Typically, the results of effect-size analyses are expressed in d-units (difference in means divided by the standard deviation) or in r-units (the correlation coefficient) that index the magnitude of an effect. A d-value of 0.0 would indicate no effect whereas an absolute value larger than 0.0 would indicate better recognition in one condition in comparison to another. In the following discussion of the Shapiro and Penrod findings, where a d is presented, we also present (when available) the results of Shapiro and Penrod's means analysis, which refers to the average percentage correct in the conditions being compared. Note that the means analysis did not include data from all of the studies in the effect-size analysis, as means were not always available in individual studies. Further, Shapiro and Penrod caution that studies are more likely to present the means when they differ significantly, so the mean analysis might overestimate the impact of some variables.

Table 5.1. *Rates of correct classification and values of r and d*

Percent Correctly Classified	Percent Incorrectly Classified	r	d
50	50	0	0
60	40	0.2	0.41
70	30	0.4	0.87
80	20	0.6	1.5
90	10	0.8	2.67
100	0	1	x

Table 5.1 shows the general pattern of relationships among some representative distributions of correctly and incorrectly classified cases in two groups and the d and r associated with those distributions. The meaning of the table can be illustrated with an example in which we are confronted with 100 witnesses, 50 of whom have made a correct identification and 50 of whom have made an erroneous identification.

If we know nothing about these witnesses that would permit us to differentiate accurate from inaccurate witnesses then we would have to guess whether each witness is correct or incorrect. Simple guessing would be expected to produce 50 correct guesses and 50 incorrect guess – half right and half wrong and a corresponding $r = 0.0$ (and $d = 0.0$), which indicates that we possess no useful information with which to classify the witnesses. On the other hand, if we had access to some very useful information and could use that information to correctly classify 80% of the witnesses (much better than guessing), the strength or usefulness of our information would be captured with an $r = .6$ and a $d = 1.5$.

Forming summary judgments

Meta-analytic methods permit the following sorts of summary judgments:

1. For which variables is there substantial variability in findings (e.g., conflicting findings and findings in which effect sizes are highly variable) that makes interpretation of findings difficult? With meta-analysis it is possible to assess the extent to which such variability can be accounted for

with moderating variables such as research methods, operational definitions of independent variables, differences in subjects, and so on. Where it is impossible to account for such variability, further research is clearly required. Fortunately, the results of the meta-analysis can provide guidance about avenues of further research that are likely to be more or less fruitful.

2. For which variables are there insufficient numbers of studies or studies with such low statistical power that further investigations are needed in order to pin down effect sizes and causal relationships?

3. Which variables show sufficient promise to merit further investigation? Variables that play a key role in theoretical formulations probably deserve the most research attention. However, researchers often must choose among a host of such variables. The meta-analysis can identify variables and relationships that are well documented and also identify variables that are not well documented but merit further investigation (because, for instance, the results from a limited number of studies indicate potentially strong relationships).

4. Most important, the meta-analysis permits tests of interactions or moderating effects *across* studies that have not been examined within studies. A clear-cut example of this is the testing of effect sizes as a function of research method. There are, for example, sound reasons to believe that field and laboratory studies may yield different estimates of the effect size of at least some independent variables. Hypotheses about such interactions can be tested and a number of such hypotheses are specified below. As in any conventional review, meta-analysis permits the reviewer to examine findings in light of conflicting theories and can yield much more precise judgments about the degree of support for alternative theories. The techniques permitting use of meta-analysis for such theory testing are well worked out (see Cooper & Lemke, 1991; Harris, 1991; Rosenthal, 1991).

Given the power of meta-analytic techniques, including the fact that they are built on explicit codings of existing research, that the underlying codings can easily be transported to other reviewers for re-analysis, and that meta-analyses can serve as the foundation for any of the integrative approaches that underlie traditional reviews, it can well be argued that no review of a literature that pretends to be exhaustive should be conducted using methods other than meta-analysis.

6   Factors that influence eyewitness accuracy: Witness factors

The most ambitious existing meta-analytic summary of eyewitness research is one conducted by Shapiro and Penrod (1986). Their meta-analysis focused on facial identification research and thus does not encompass all eyewitness research, but it represents a sound starting point for the review contained in this and the next chapter. Shapiro and Penrod examined the results of 128 eyewitness identification and facial recognition studies, involving 960 experimental conditions and 16,950 subjects. Virtually all of this research had been reported in peer-reviewed scientific journals. The meta-analysis was designed to summarize the knowledge that psychologists have accumulated on factors that reliably influence facial identification performance.

The analytic strategy

Two analytic techniques were employed. The first was an "effect-size" analysis, which combined the effect sizes of eyewitness factors across studies that manipulated a particular factor. This is analogous to the example in the previous chapter in which the results of the 10 studies were averaged.

The second approach employed by Shapiro and Penrod was a "study characteristics" analysis. In this analysis experiments were grouped on various factors (e.g., viewing conditions, the manner in which identification accuracy was tested, and methodological factors such as live versus photographic lineups) that might influence identification accuracy. The influence of these grouping variables on identification accuracy rates was then examined. Some of the study characteristics analyzed (e.g., exposure time and retention interval) also served as independent variables in many studies. However, the analyses of study characteristics are potentially more informative since they have more than 950 data points (based on judgments from more than 16,500 subjects) for correct identifications, whereas effect-size analyses have fewer than 30 data points (even though they are often based on between 1 and 2,000 subjects). For variables that appear in both sets of analyses, each analysis can be considered a validity check for the other.

One advantage to the study characteristics analysis over the effect-size analysis is that it uses multiple regression to examine the explanatory value of one factor while controlling for the influence of other factors. This element of statistical analysis is important because a problem of multicollinearity arose – that is, some study characteristics proved somewhat redundant with one another because they varied together across the studies. This occurred largely because laboratory researchers make use of one set of procedures whereas field researchers characteristically make use of somewhat different procedures. For example, laboratory researchers frequently made use of greater numbers of faces for subjects to remember, exposed faces to subjects for shorter periods of times, and tested memory after shorter delay periods. To clarify the analyses and results, correlated variables were combined into groups for analysis and variables that were independent of one another were analyzed independently.

The results of the study characteristics analysis are expressed in terms r and R^2 and in terms of a partialled r (or sr) or partialled R^2. The squared terms index the proportion of variance in the criterion (correct or false identifications) accounted for by a variable. The unpartialled terms indicate the strength of the relationship between the criterion and a variable considered by itself, whereas the partialled terms "control" for the influence of other variables in the analysis and indicate the strength of the "unique" relationship between a variable and the criterion. We use r rather than sr in some cases because there are no other variables being controlled for in the analysis; in such a case, r and sr are identical. The B in the study characteristics analyses indexes the percentage difference in hit or false alarm rates associated with a particular variable.

Variables in an eyewitness meta-analysis

Shapiro and Penrod's meta-analysis is the most comprehensive and sophisticated review of the eyewitness literature to date. We therefore rely heavily on it in this review. Still, some potentially important factors were not included in the meta-analysis, primarily because, at the time at which the meta-analysis was conducted (between 1983 and 1985), the research identifying these variables was not available to Shapiro and Penrod. One such factor, for example, is the effect of alcohol intoxication on eyewitness memory. The first published study did not appear in print until after the meta-analysis had been completed (Yuille & Tollestrup, 1990). Weapon focus is another example. Most of the studies were published after the meta-analysis. In the following review, if meta-analytic results are not mentioned for a given factor, it is because the factor was not included in the meta-analysis.

We categorize eyewitness factors as: stable eyewitness characteristics, unstable eyewitness characteristics, eyewitness testimony, stable target characteristics, malleable target characteristics, eyewitnessing environment, and postevent procedures. Within each category we review the available research and include tables in each section summarizing the results of the meta-analyses conducted by Shapiro and Penrod. For many variables we describe details of individual studies. The purpose of describing these studies is to illustrate the methodology used and to give the unfamiliar reader a flavor of the research. The studies chosen for illustration should not be given excess weight over other studies not used as examples.

Stable eyewitness characteristics

Stable eyewitness characteristics are features of the eyewitnesses that are generally not subject to change, such as their demographic characteristics.

1. Sex. In the Shapiro and Penrod meta-analysis, females were slightly more likely to make correct identifications ($d = .10$) but also more likely to make false identifications ($d = .08$) – see Table 6.1. Put another way, females were slightly more likely to make a positive identification but their improvement in correct identification performance appears to be offset by higher levels of false identification.

2. Race. In Platz and Hosch's field study (described above), identifications were obtained from Anglo, black, and Mexican-American convenience store clerks. Average identification accuracy for these three groups was 42.6%, 54.5%, and 38.1% correct, respectively. These percentages did not differ significantly. In Shapiro and Penrod's meta-analysis, black subjects made more correct identifications than did white subjects ($d = .17$) but these groups did not differ in their number of false identifications ($d = -.04$).

3. Intelligence. Several studies of the relation between eyewitness intelligence and identification accuracy reveal no significant association (Brown, Deffenbacher, & Sturgill, 1977; Feinman & Entwistle, 1976; Witryol & Kaess, 1957). One study did report a significant correlation between intelligence and face recognition accuracy (Howells, 1938: $r = .27$). Shapiro and Penrod reviewed research that examined the influence of eyewitnesses' verbal ability, verbal ability for pictures, and ability to describe faces and imagery on identification accuracy. Three studies examined verbal ability and found that subjects with high verbal ability made more correct identifications than subjects with low verbal ability (d = .11). Verbal ability was not associated with the number of false identifications. Two studies investigated verbal ability for pictures and found it to be unrelated to the number of correct identifications. Data on false identifications were unavailable.

4. Age. A substantial number of studies have examined developmental trends in identification accuracy. Chance and Goldstein (1984) reviewed many early studies and concluded that all except one showed that correct identifications improved with age. Chance and Goldstein (1984, p. 71) noted that "[a]t kindergarten level, percent correct falls between 35 and 40% – or slightly above chance; at 6 to 8 years, between 50 and 58%; at 9 to 11, between 60 and 70%; and at ages 12 to 14, between 70 and 80%." Parker, Haverfield, and Baker-Thomas (1986) showed a slide presentation of a simulated crime to groups of elementary school (with an average age of 8 years old) and college students. The two groups did not differ with respect to identification accuracy, but the elementary school subjects were more likely to change their lineup choices. Chance and Goldstein noted that few of the developmental studies examined false identifications. In the studies that did, false identifications generally declined with age.

Brigham, Van Verst, and Bothwell (1986) conducted a field study of children's eyewitness identification accuracy. Subjects were 40 fourth, 50 eighth, and 40 eleventh graders from a Florida school. An experimenter led groups of 10 subjects through hallways and corridors to a research trailer. Upon reaching the trailer, the experimenter asked the children to refrain from talking. This cued an assistant, posing as a thief, to rush from the trailer carrying a portable cassette tape player. The experimenter: "reacted with surprise, exclaiming, 'Hey, what are you doing in there! You're not supposed to be in there. We're using this trailer for an experiment. Give me that thing! You're not supposed to have that! I'm taking you to the office; come with me!'" The experimenter grabbed the thief by the arm and led him past the students. Subjects had about 15 to 30 seconds to see the thief's face. About 10 minutes later another assistant, dressed either as a security guard (authority figure condition) or casually (nonauthority condition) entered and announced that he had been assigned to investigate robberies at the school and that he needed to ask everyone some questions. He questioned each student individually. The interviews included a six-person photoarray that contained the thief. Identification performance was significantly more accurate among eighth graders (88% correct) and eleventh graders (93% correct) in comparison to fourth graders (68% correct). These results were not qualified by whether or not the interviewer was an authority figure.

These results are further corroborated by Shapiro and Penrod's meta-analysis. They compared identification performance from "young" versus "old" subjects. Older subjects were much more likely to make correct identifications (d = 1.10; 70% vs. 58%) and less likely to make false identifications (d = .66; 15% vs. 25%) – see Table 6.2 for a summary of these results.

Some studies show that elderly eyewitnesses (usually 60 years old or older) perform less well on identification tests as compared to younger adults (Adams-Price, 1991; Bartlett & Fulton, 1991; O'Rourke, Penrod, Cutler, & Stuve, 1989). O'Rourke et al., for example, showed videotaped enactments of a liquor store robbery to groups of college students and community members and had them attempt to identify the robber from robber-present and robber-absent videotaped lineups. The percentage of correct decisions on the identification test were 51% for the 18 to 19-year-old group; 47% for 20 to 29; 46% for 30 to 39; 42% for 40 to 49; 29% for 50 to 59; and 25% for 60 to 72 (r = -.18) Identification accuracy dropped off sharply at around age 50. O'Rourke et al. also found that, despite the age differences in identification performance, other factors affected the decisions of young and old comparably. Others (Smith & Winograd, 1978; Yarmey & Kent, 1980) found no recognition differences between adult and elderly populations (Baltes & Schaie, 1976).

5. Face recognition skills. Woodhead, Baddeley, and Simmonds (1979) conducted a study in which they first characterized subjects as "good recognizers" or "poor recognizers" on the basis of their performance on a face recognition test. On a subsequent face recognition test, good recognizers outperformed poor recognizers, suggesting that face recognition skills are somewhat stable across tests. Woodhead et al. also found that self-reported face recognition skills were uncorrelated with performance on the recognition test. This finding suggests that we should not place more confidence in identifications by eyewitnesses who claim to be good at recognizing people or devalue identifications from eyewitnesses who claim to be poor at recognizing faces. Relatedly, ability to describe faces, examined in two studies in Shapiro and Penrod's meta-analysis, had a substantial effect on correct identifications (d = .41). Eyewitnesses with high ability to describe faces, in comparison to those with low ability, made more correct identifications. In those studies, the relation between verbal ability and number of false identifications was not assessed.

6. Personality characteristics. In Shapiro and Penrod's meta-analysis, field independents (as opposed to field dependents) made significantly more correct identifications (d = .24) but did not differ with respect to false identifications. Field independents are better than field dependents at distinguishing foreground from background information and were therefore expected to be better at such recognition tasks.

Table 6.1. *Meta-analytic results from studies of stable eyewitness characteristics*

Witness characteristics	Hits					False alarms				
	N	n	D	Z	P	N	n	D	Z	P
Women/men	48		0.1	4.11	***	26		0.08	2.77	**
Blacks/whites	14		0.17	2.64	**	10		-0.04	2.05	0
High/low verbal ability			0.11	1.95	*	3		0	0	n.s.
Subject age (young vs. old)	9	603	1.1	13.34	***	5	408	0.66	13.33	***
Verbal ability for pictures	2		0	0	n.s.					
Ability to describe faces	2		0.41	2.31	*					
High/low imagery	4		0.11	0.68	n.s.					
Field independence	8		0.24	4.46	***	3		0	0	n.s.
Low/high anxiety	6		0.11	1.83	n.s.	6		0.33	3.69	***
Low/high self-consciousness	3		0.09	0.5						

The construct of self-monitoring (Snyder, 1979) was designed to differentiate individuals who guide their cognition and behavior in accordance with social expectations (high self-monitors) from individuals who guide their cognition and behavior in accordance with personal attitudes and beliefs (low self-monitors). Hosch, Leippe, Marchioni, and Cooper (1984) reasoned that self-monitoring might relate to identification accuracy in several ways. First, as compared with low self-monitors, high self-monitors should demonstrate superior memory for salient persons in a situation. Second, high self-monitors would be more susceptible to biased lineup procedures than would low self-monitors. Though there was some evidence for the second hypothesis, there was no support for the first. In a second related experiment (Hosch & Platz, 1984), self-monitoring was found to be significantly correlated with correct identifications ($r = .51$). The influence of self-monitoring on false identifications was not assessed.

Shapiro and Penrod reviewed six studies that examined whether chronically anxious eyewitnesses differ from less anxious eyewitnesses in identification accuracy. Chronic (trait) anxiety was not significantly correlated with the number of correct identifications. In contrast, eyewitnesses low in trait anxiety made more false identifications than eyewitnesses high in trait anxiety ($d = .33$).

7. Conclusions. Stable eyewitness characteristics (for which the meta-analytic results are summarized in Table 6.1) are not particularly useful predictors of identification accuracy. Sex, race, various forms of intelligence and personality characteristics appear to be weakly, if at all related to the tendency to make correct or false identifications. Age does appear to be an important predictor, with young and elderly subjects performing more poorly than other adults. Face recognition skills, as measured not by self-reports but by prior face recognition performance, also appear promising as a predictor of identification accuracy. Verbal ability also seems to be weakly correlated with face recognition skills. It might be noted that the personality and cognitive factors, in particular, have relatively little forensic value insofar as no one is testing or even proposing to test these witness characteristics in actual witnessing situations. Only witness age, which can generally be assessed through observation, holds significant forensic promise.

Malleable eyewitness characteristics

Unlike demographic characteristics and personality traits, some characteristics of eyewitnesses are subject to change, such as what the eyewitness is thinking at the time of the crime and the eyewitness's state of intoxication. We will now review the influences of these types of factors. Four outcome variables are reported (in Table 6.2) for these factors and the factors reported in subsequent sections: hits, false alarms, d', and B". A hit is a correct identification and a false alarm is an incorrect "identification." d' measures overall sensitivity (i.e., the ability to detect a signal when it is present, and to detect that there is no signal when the signal is absent) and B" indexes subjects' decision criterion (a lax criterion means that subjects are more willing to guess).

1. Expectation of future identification test. Bank tellers and convenience store clerks are often instructed, if confronted with a robber, to attend to the perpetrator's facial characteristics so that an identification could later be made. Does knowing that one will later attempt to identify a perpetrator improve subsequent identification accuracy? In Cutler, Penrod, and Martens's (1987a) experiment, subjects viewed videotaped enactments of a liquor store robbery and later attempted to identify the perpetrator from videotaped lineups. Half of the subjects were told, prior to seeing the videotape, that they will be viewing a crime and later attempting to identify the robber from a lineup. The remainder were merely told that they will be viewing a videotape and answering some questions about it. Of those who expected the identification test, 34% gave a correct decision. Of those who were unaware of the recognition test, 38% gave a correct decision, a nonsignificant difference. In Shapiro and Penrod's meta-analysis expecting an identification test had no significant effect on either correct ($d = .10$; 56% vs. 58% for expected/not expected) or false ($d = 27$; 27% for both) identifications.

2. Training in racial recognition. In the Pigott et al. (1990) field study described earlier, 77% of the bank tellers who participated indicated that they had some kind of training on eyewitnessing techniques. Does training work? Penry (1971) hypothesized that training people to analyze and categorize facial features would improve face recognition skills and so devised a training method. Woodhead, Baddeley, and Simmonds (1979) conducted three experiments to evaluate the effectiveness of Penry's training course. In the three facial recognition experiments subjects who *had not* taken the training course performed equivalently or better than subjects who *had* completed the course. In their first experiment, for example, subjects took part in a simple face recognition experiment before and after taking the training course. A group that did not take the training course was also tested. During the encoding phase, subjects were shown a series of slides of 24 unfamiliar targets. During the retrieval phase subjects were shown 48 slides (24 new and 24 old). The group that completed the training program correctly recognized 60% of the targets both before and after the training program, thus showing no improvement. The untrained group performed comparably. In Shapiro and Penrod's meta-analysis, training had a nonsignificant effect on both correct ($d = .18$; 65% vs. 61% for trained/untrained) and false ($d = -.04$; 10% for both) identifications.

3. Orienting/processing instructions and strategies. Although not all customer service workers receive training for eyewitnessing, many are instructed that they should, if confronted with a robber, pay particular attention to his facial features so that they can later recognize him. But do these instructions affect an individual's ability to make a correct identification? Not only can individuals to some degree control the object of perception and attention, but they can also exert control over the qualitative nature of attention. For example, when studying someone's facial features, one could note characteristics such as thickness of the eyebrows or the color of the eyes. Or one might engage in more elaborate judgments, such as making personality assessments of the target person based on facial features. Does the difference in processing strategies affect the accuracy of subsequent identification attempts? Various forms of instructions have been examined for their relationship with identification accuracy. These instructions are designed to generate various "orienting strategies" (Devine & Malpass, 1985). Some instructions require subjects to make inferential judgments about faces (e.g., personality judgments, such as "this looks like the face of someone prone to violence"), whereas other instructions require subjects to make superficial judgments (e.g., judgments about the distinctiveness of facial features, such as "this person has a pointed chin").

Table 6.2. *Mean hit and false alarm rates from experimental studies*

Variable	Hits			False alarms			D'			B"	
	Hi	Lo	N	Hi	Lo	N	Hi	Lo	N	Hi	Lo
Stable witness characteristics											
Subject age (young vs. old)	70	58	9	15	25	4	0.8	0.23	4	0.2	0.1
Malleable witness characteristics											
Knowledge of recognition task	56	58	2	27	27	2	0.3	0.25	3	0.1	0.1
Training in facial recognitions (yes vs. no)	65	61	8	10	10	4	0.7	0.63	4	0.4	0.5
Encoding instructions (hi/ low)	74	66	26	21	27	17	0.7	0.48	17	0.1	0.1
Face was associated with rich vs . poor elaboration	78	72	10	10	11	2	0.8	0.82	2	0.3	0.3
Stable target characteristics											
Sex of target (male vs. female)	74	72	18	14	14	9	0.7	0.71	9	0.2	0.3
Race of target (white vs. minority – black or Asian)	59	53	15	16	20	9	0.6	0.44	9	0.3	0.2
Target distinctive (hi vs. low)	70	60	14	17	29	12	0.6	0.46	11	0.2	0.1
Malleable target characteristic											
Transformation (none vs. disguise)	75	54	19	22	30	5	0.7	0.32	5	0.1	0.1
Eyewitnessing environment											
Exposure time (long vs. short)	69	57	5	34	38	3	0.4	0	3	-0	0
Same vs. cross-race ID	63	57	16	18	22	11	0.6	0.51	11	0.2	0.2
Same vs. cross-sex identification	76	72	12	21	21	3	0.4	0.37	3	0.1	0.1
Postevent factors											
Retention interval (short vs. long)	61	51	16	24	32	11	0.5	0.15	11	0.1	0.1
Context reinstated (yes vs. no)	79	52	23	25	18	18	0.8	0.39	18	-0	0.3
Other factors											
Pose at study (3/4 vs. front or profile)	66	54	10	41	39	2	0.2	0.2	2	-0	0
Mode of presentation at study time (live or videotape vs. still)	72	58	4	30	38	1	0.5	0.29	1	0	0
Mode of presentation at recognition (live/video vs. still)	50	50	11	30	26	7	0.1	0.1	7	0.1	0.1
Target present/absent lineup				25	52	12					

In Shapiro and Penrod's meta-analysis two types of orienting strategies were examined. Encoding instructions and degree of elaboration were analyzed separately, but it is useful to discuss them together because they both refer to the amount of information encoded with a face. They differ in that the encoding instructions call for substantial activity on the part of subjects (requiring them to make inferences about a face while looking at it). Elaboration, in contrast, refers to whether the face was associated with one or several descriptors versus none, and in these studies subjects take a passive role.   Both variables produced large effects on correct identifications: for encoding instructions, $d = .97$ (74% vs. 66%); for elaboration, $d = 1.0$ (78% vs. 72%). The effects on false identifications was smaller: for encoding instructions, $d = .38$ (21% vs. 27%); for elaboration, $d = -.06$ (10% vs. 11%). Although these variables have a statistically significant effect (d) on correct identifications, analysis of correct identification rates showed that the improvements in performance are small. A technical note: One reason for the large effect size and small performance difference is that some of the studies included in the meta-analysis use within-subjects designs and therefore have small error terms.

As already noted, training programs have had disappointing results on identification performance, perhaps because they have generally focused on featural analyses. Results of Shapiro and Penrod's meta-analysis cause us to be somewhat more optimistic about the prospects for training programs, provided that they focus on more effective elaboration techniques.

4. Alcohol intoxication.   Evidence from police files suggests that intoxicating substances, particularly alcohol, go hand in hand with many types of crimes (Sporer, in press; Yuille & Tollestrup, 1990).   Both perpetrators and witnesses are sometimes intoxicated at the time a crime is committed. In Sporer's archival analysis of all crimes occurring within a short time period in Marburg, Germany, data on the level of intoxication were available from 62 out of 100 witnesses. Of these, seven (11%) were believed to be substantially intoxicated and the remainder were sober. Intoxication levels are likely to be underreported in police reports (Sporer, in press; Yuille & Tollestrup, 1990). What impact does intoxication have on witness performance?

Yuille and Tollestrup (1990) exposed subjects to a live, staged theft, prior to which subjects were randomly assigned to intoxicated (blood alcohol level averaging .10) and sober conditions. Following the crime some subjects from each condition were interviewed immediately while the others were excused. All subjects were interviewed 1 week after the event and attempted an identification from a target-present or target-absent photoarray. Intoxicated witnesses recalled less information immediately after the crime, as well as in the subsequent interview. Among those shown the target-present photoarray, 91% of the intoxicated and 89% of the sober witnesses correctly identified the perpetrator, a nonsignificant difference. Among those shown the target-absent photoarray, 39% of the intoxicated witnesses and 25% of the sober witnesses made false identifications. Although this trend appears to be appreciable in magnitude, the difference was not statistically significant – possibly because the study included a small sample of subjects and was, therefore, low in statistical power.

In a rather unusual experiment, Read, Yuille, and Tollestrup (1992) had subjects play the roles of thieves in a simulated robbery in conditions of low or high arousal while either sober or intoxicated (average blood alcohol level of .11). Arousal was manipulated by varying the subjects' perceptions of how likely they were to be caught by a bystander who would not know that the theft was part of an experiment. One week later (on average), subjects attempted to identify two bystanders seen while they committed the crime. Subjects were shown either bystander-present or bystander-absent photospreads. No difference in performance was found in data from bystander-absent photospreads. In contrast, in data from bystander-present photospreads, arousal interacted significantly with level of intoxication. In the low arousal conditions, 31% of intoxicated subjects and 69% of sober subjects made correct identifications. In the high arousal condition, 56% of subjects in the sober and intoxicated conditions made correct identifications. Read et al. concluded that high levels of arousal subjects overcame the debilitating effects of alcohol intoxication. Note that Read et al. controlled for expectancies by having subjects in the sober condition believe they were drinking alcohol.

It is difficult to draw firm conclusions about the effects of intoxication on identification accuracy based on these two experiments, especially given that their results are somewhat mixed. Indeed, at some level of intoxication, perception and storage can be expected to deteriorate. Further research is needed to determine this level.

5. Conclusions. Malleable eyewitness characteristics (for which the meta-analytic results are summarized in Table 6.3), as a class of variables, produce mixed results. Expectation of a lineup test, while viewing the crime, had little effect in Shapiro and Penrod's effect-size analysis or in the study characteristic analysis. In the latter, expectation was entered in a block with five other attentional variables that together produced a pr^2 of only .02 for correct identifications (meaning that these variables together accounted for only 2% of the variance in correct identification performance) and a pr^2 .06 for false identifications. The overall results of the study characteristics analyses of hits and false alarms are shown in Tables 6.4 and 6.5. Orienting strategies were also included in the "attention" block in Shapiro and Penrod's study characteristics analysis (as degree that attention

Table 6.3. *Meta-analytic results from studies of malleable witness characteristics*

Witness characteristics	Hits					False alarms				
	N	n	D	Z	p	N	n	D	Z	p
Knowledge of recognition task	5	703	.10	.42	n.s.	5	1100	.27	-1.03	n.s.
Training in facial recognitions (yes vs. no)	8	534	.18	.54	n.s.	5	371	-.04	-.15	n.s.
Encoding instructions (high vs. low)	29	1868	.97	9.87	***	19	1733	.38	2.07	*
Face associated with rich vs. poor elaboration at exposure time	10	362	1.00	8.15	***	2	72	-.06	-.27	n.s.

was focused on targets). Thus, the effects of encoding instructions and elaboration are reliable but comparatively small in magnitude. Training appears to have little effect on identification accuracy, perhaps because it relies on less effective orienting strategies. Alcohol intoxication is a potentially important predictor, but more research is needed to examine specific levels of alcohol intoxication.

Eyewitness testimony

This section addresses the extent to which certain aspects of the eyewitness's testimony can be relied upon to evaluate the accuracy of the eyewitness's identification. Throughout an investigation, eyewitnesses are interviewed numerous times: at the scene of the crime by uniformed officers, later by detectives (sometimes several times by the same or different detectives), by attorneys in deposition and again, in court, during examination and cross-examination. These interviews provide a rich and diverse set of information that may or may not be diagnostic of identification accuracy. Researchers have focused on several classes of information provided by eyewitness testimony: quality of the description of the perpetrator given by the eyewitness at the time of the crime, consistency of the eyewitness's accounts across interviews, and confidence of the eyewitness in his or her identification accuracy. We review the diagnostic value of each.

Table 6.4. *Study characteristics analysis of hits*

Block Variables	Zero order R^2	r	Partialled R^2	sr (Full model)	B Coefficient
Attention	.33*		.02 *		
Degree attention on targets		.52		.09	4.64
Mode of presentation at study		-.53		.07	4.95
Knowledge of recognition task		.35		.07	5.44
No knowledge of task		-.23		.01	.92
Seconds of exposure per face	.07*		.003		
at study		-.22		.05	.075
Seconds (squared) of exposure	.03 *		.00		
per face at study		-.18		-.01	-.0004
Pose	.25*		.03 *		
Mixed vs. others		-.49		-.14	-11.07
Front vs. others		.43		.00	.17
Load at study	.17*		.01*		
Number of targets at study		.41		.06	.14
Number of faces at study		.35		-.02	-.03
Total exposure time at study		.19		.03	.001
Target race	.02*		.02*		
White targets		.13		.11	7.02
Black targets		-.14		-.01	-1.11
Target sex	.15*		.01*		
Males		-.38		-.02	-1.56
Mixed sex		.36		.03	2.98
Retention interval	.07*		.01*		
Minutes		-.29		-.11	-.000075
Minutes squared	.03*		.00		
		-.18		.03	.00
Load at recognition	.15*		.00		
Number of simultaneous faces		-.15		.03	.27
Mode of presentation		-.16		-.01	-1.08
Number of decoys		.22		-.01	-.009
Ratio of targets to decoys	.27			-.01	-.64
Type of study	.35*		.03*		
Eyewitness vs. face recognition		-.59		-.16	-16.15

Note: Intercept = 43.51. Total r^2 = .47, (.45 adjusted), $F (22, 671)$ = 27.18, $p < .00005$.
$p < .05$ for $r = .08$; $sr = .06$; $p < .01$ for $r = .11$; $sr = .08$; $p < .001$ for $r = .13$; $sr = .1$; $p < .0001$
for $r = .16$; $sr = .12$. For R^2 -- *$p < .001$

Table 6.5. *Study characteristics analysis of false alarms*

Block Variables	Zero order R^2	r	Partialled R^2	sr (full model)	B Coefficient
Attention	.21**		.06**		
Degree attention on targets		.32		-.06	2.48
Mode of presentation at study		.37		-.12	-7.04
Knowledge of recognition task		-.32		-.18	-9.12
No knowledge of task		.12		-.12	-6.56
Seconds exposure per face	.13**		.02**		
at study		.36		.13	.17
Seconds (squared) of	.08**		.00		
exposure per face at study		.28		-.04	-.001
Pose	.08**		.02*		
Mixed vs. others		.18		-.04	-2.37
Front vs. others		-.28		-.12	-6.95
Load at study	.06**		.03**		
Number of targets at study		-.25		.09	-.20
Number of faces at study		-.20		.07	.12
Total exposure time		-.07		-.02	-.002
Target race	.00		.01**		
White targets		.04		-.03	-1.51
Black targets		.05		.07	4.80
Target sex	.10**		.01 **		
Males		.31		.02	2.06
Mixed sex		-.30		-.02	-1.73
Retention interval	.01		.00		
Minutes		.09		.02	.00
Minutes squared	.00		.00		
		.02		-.05	.00
Load at recognition	.19**		.11**		
Number of simultaneous faces		.23		-.04	-.39
Mode of presentation		.21		.11	5.10
Number of decoys		-.36		-.21	-.16
Ratio of targets to decoys		-.19		-.13	10.15
Type of study	.30**		.02**		
Eyewitness vs. face recognition		.54		.17	13.58

Note: Intercept = 24.60. Total r^2 = .43 (.40 adjusted), F (22, 406) = 13.93, $p < .00001$.
$p < .05$ for $r = .11$; $sr = .09$; $p < .01$ for $r = .14$; $sr = .11$; $p < .001$ for $r = .17$; $sr = .14$; $p < .0001$
for $r = .20$; $sr = .18$. For R^2 -- *$p<.05$, **$p<.01$

1. Quality of description. To what extent can the quality of the eyewitness's description of the perpetrator at the time of the crime be relied upon as an indicator of the eyewitness's identification accuracy? Several studies have examined this question. In Pigott et al.'s (1990) field study (described earlier in this chapter), bank tellers' descriptions of the perpetrators were coded for accuracy (the extent to which the description matched the person who committed the mock crime), completeness (amount of detail in the description), and congruence (the extent to which the description matched the person identified from the lineup). Wells (1985) noted that congruence is perhaps more relevant to actual cases than is accuracy. In an actual case, the investigators do not know the identity of the perpetrator, so they cannot obtain a true measure of accuracy. Congruence, in contrast, can be assessed in actual cases.

In Pigott et al.'s field study, among eyewitnesses who made a positive identification from the lineup (either target-present or target-absent), the correlations between identification accuracy and description accuracy, and completeness and congruence were nonsignificant: .03, .09, and .25, respectively. The findings from this field study corroborate those of laboratory studies that showed null or weak relations between description quality and identification accuracy (Cutler, Penrod, & Martens, 1987a; Wells, 1985). Although Wells (1985) found that ability to describe a face accurately was not associated with ability to recognize a face, he did find that faces that were more accurately described were also significantly more accurately recognized. In other words, better describers were not better identifiers, but faces that were better described were more accurately identified. Unfortunately, as Deffenbacher (1991) notes, in a forensic situation we have no way of knowing which faces lend themselves to accurate description.

2. Consistency of description. As already mentioned, eyewitnesses are usually interviewed repeatedly: They provide descriptions at the scene of the crime and during depositions, and during examination and cross-examination. An analysis of an eyewitness's multiple accounts may reveal inconsistencies in recall for certain details. A common strategy among attorneys who wish to discredit an eyewitness is to highlight these inconsistencies for the jury and encourage them to conclude that the inconsistencies cast doubt on the quality of the eyewitness's entire memory for the event. For example, an attorney might encourage the jury to conclude that the identification from an eyewitness should not be trusted because the eyewitness stated, at the scene of the crime, that the perpetrator had a blue shirt but stated, in a later deposition, that he had a red shirt. Is such a conclusion defensible based on the empirical research? Are these inconsistencies diagnostic of identification accuracy?

Fisher and Cutler (in press) reported the results of four separate studies in which the association between consistency of witness statements and identification accuracy was explored. In each study, subjects witnessed a staged theft during a course lecture. Each subject was interviewed on two separate occasions. After the second interview, each eyewitness attempted to identify the perpetrator(s) from a photoarray, videotaped lineup, or live lineup. Descriptions were scored for consistency across interviews. Three of the studies used multiple perpetrators, so eight identifications were tested in all. The eight correlations ranged in magnitude from -.04 to .23 and only one was statistically significant. The average correlation was .10. In sum, consistency of testimony is a poor predictor of identification accuracy.

3. Memory for peripheral details. Is ability to recall details of the crime associated with identification accuracy? There are at least two conceptual ways to address this question. First, memory for details may be associated with quality of encoding and retrieval of the entire event. An eyewitness who barely saw anything would not be expected to recall details accurately or accurately identify the perpetrator. In contrast, a vigilant eyewitness might, under some circumstances, be capable of recalling most details and making a correct identification. The second approach recognizes that attentional capacity is limited and that eyewitnesses cannot attend to all information in a crime. For example, in a crime involving two perpetrators, an eyewitness who focuses her attention on one has less attention to encode the other's characteristics. Two studies favor the latter interpretation.

In Cutler, Penrod, and Martens's (1987a) study, subjects, after viewing a videotaped crime and before attempting identifications, were asked to recall the hand in which the robber held his weapon, the color of the victim's sweater, and the number of people who interacted with the victim before she was accosted. Memory for peripheral details was found to be correlated with the tendency to make a positive identification ($r = .22$) but inversely correlated with identification accuracy ($r = -.21$). Both of these correlations were significant. They indicate that subjects who accurately recalled peripheral details, as compared to those who were less accurate, were more likely to make a positive identification but less likely to give accurate judgments on the identification test. Wells and Leippe (1981) found similar results; in their experiment, subjects who performed better on the identification task performed more poorly on an 11-item test of memory for peripheral details, whereas subjects who performed better on the test of memory for peripheral details performed more poorly on the identification task.

4. Confidence. It is typical for police investigators to ascertain the eyewitness's confidence in her ability to make an identification during the crime scene interview ("do you think you can identify him?"). It is also typical for them to ask the eyewitness how sure she is after making a decision on an identification test ("how sure are you that this is the guy?"). Eyewitnesses might be asked the latter question several more times throughout depositions and in-court examinations. A substantial amount of research has been devoted to the association between the witness's confidence and the accuracy of the identification.

We (Cutler & Penrod, 1989) meta-analyzed nine studies examining the relation between identification accuracy and *confidence in ability to make an identification*. For example, in our studies (Cutler & Penrod, 1988; Cutler et al., 1986; Cutler, Penrod, & Martens, 1987b), subjects viewed a videotaped robbery and later attempted an identification from a lineup. After viewing the crime but before seeing the lineup, subjects indicated their confidence in their abilities to (a) correctly identify the robber if the robber is in the lineup, and (b) avoid making a false identification if the robber is absent from the lineup. Across the nine studies reviewed in the meta-analysis the correlations between confidence in ability to make a correct identification and subsequent identification accuracy ranged in magnitude from .00 to .20. In short, confidence in one's ability to make a correct identification is a poor predictor of identification accuracy. Most provocatively, these findings imply that witnesses should be asked to attempt identifications irrespective of their confidence in their ability to identify a perpetrator insofar as any resulting identifications may yield other, confirming evidence that would reinforce identifications made by low-confidence witnesses.

In many experiments witnesses are asked, after making a decision on a lineup test, to indicate their confidence in their decision. A meta-analysis of nearly 40 separate tests of the relation between *decision confidence and identification accuracy* (Bothwell, Deffenbacher, & Brigham, 1987) found the average correlation to be .25. Witnesses who are highly confident in their identifications are only somewhat more likely to be correct as compared to witnesses who display little confidence in their identifications – see Table 5.1 for one index of the practical value of a correlation of .25.

5. Conclusion. In summary, aspects of eyewitness testimony are poor indicators of identification accuracy. A large body of studies have demonstrated that accuracy, completeness, and congruence of prior descriptions of the perpetrator are weakly related to identification accuracy. Memory for peripheral details is inversely (though weakly) related to identification accuracy. Consistency of testimony (of crime details and person descriptions) is unrelated to identification accuracy. Confidence in ability to identify a perpetrator is unrelated, but confidence in having made a correct identification is modestly associated with identification accuracy.

Note, however, that confidence in having made a correct identification is suspect for other reasons. Confidence judgments are malleable. Luus's (1991) dissertation (see Wells, 1993) demonstrates how confidence can be influenced by information learned after both the crime and the identification test. It is reasonable to assume that information learned throughout the investigation, depositions, and pretrial preparation can influence an eyewitness so that the confidence expressed to the jury differs from the level of confidence expressed at the time of the identification. It is also reasonable to assume that such changes reduce the reliability of confidence as a predictor of identification accuracy. Given that confidence, when measured immediately after the identification, is a modest predictor of accuracy, reductions in reliability may render it equivocal. Overall, aspects of the eyewitness's testimony should not be used to evaluate the accuracy of the eyewitness's identification.

7   Factors that influence eyewitness accuracy: Perpetrator, event, and postevent factors

Although the eyewitness is a natural focus of attention for researchers interested in eyewitness reliability, eyewitness characteristics tell only a portion of the story about sources of eyewitness unreliability. Features of the perpetrator and of the circumstances surrounding the viewing of the perpetrator are also logical targets of investigation as are the circumstances under which identifications are made. Although identification circumstances have long interested the courts – largely because those circumstances are under the control of investigators and police, research on perpetrator and event characteristics reveals that concern with these factors is also justified.

Target characteristics

Stable target characteristics

Like stable witness characteristics, some features of the target are not subject to change. The effects of these factors are reviewed here.

1. Sex. Sex of target was examined in Shapiro and Penrod's meta-analysis. The effects were trivial in magnitude. For correct identifications, $d = .02$ (74% for males vs. 72% for females); for false identifications, $d = -.07$ (14% for both).

2. Race. In Shapiro and Penrod's meta-analysis, race of target was examined by comparing identifications of white targets versus identifications of non-white targets (blacks or Asians). White targets were somewhat more often correctly recognized ($d = .24$; 59% vs. 53%) and less often falsely recognized ($d = .18$; 16% vs. 20%). In Platz and Hosch's field study (1988, in the previous chapter described), identifications of Anglos, blacks, and Mexican-Americans were obtained. The Anglo customers were correctly identified by 48% of the clerks; the black customers were correctly identified by 38% of the clerks; and the Mexican-American customers were correctly identified by 47% of the clerks; these percentages are consistent with the meta-analysis results although the differences did not reach statistical significance.

97

Table 7.1. *Meta-analytic results from studies of stable target characteristics*

Witness characteristics	Hits					False alarms				
	N	n	*D*	*Z*	*p*	*N*	*n*	*D*	*Z*	*p*
Sex of target (male vs. female)	19	2052	.02	1.88	n.s.	12	1690	-.07	-3.40	***
Race of target (white vs. minority)	18	1894	.24	2.05	*	15	1626	.18	.23	n.s.
Target distinctiveness (hi vs. low)	22	2174	.76	12.53	***	18	1957	.78	7.89	***

3. Distinctiveness and attractiveness. Several investigations (Cohen & Carr, 1975; Davies, Shepherd, & Ellis, 1979; Fleishman, Buckley, Klosinsky, Smith, & Tuck, 1976; Going & Read, 1974; Light, Kayra-Stuart, & Hollander, 1979) have revealed that faces that are rated as highly attractive or highly unattractive are better recognized than neutrally rated faces. This suggests that facial distinctiveness rather than attractiveness is related to facial recognition. In Shapiro and Penrod's meta-analysis, target distinctiveness was a substantial predictor of identification accuracy. Distinctive targets were more often correctly recognized (d = .76; 70% vs. 60%) and less often falsely recognized (d = .78; 17% vs. 29%).

4. Summary. Of the stable target characteristics examined in the research, (and for which the meta-analytic findings are summarized in Table 7.1) only distinctiveness of appearance is found to be diagnostic of identification accuracy. In Shapiro and Penrod's study characteristic analysis of correct identifications, pr^2 was .02 for race and .01 for sex. The comparable values for false identifications were both .01. (Target distinctiveness could not be examined in the study characteristics analysis.)

Malleable target characteristics

The physical appearance of crime perpetrators sometimes changes between the crime and the identification, particularly when there has been a considerable time lapse. This section reviews the influence of those changes.

1. Changes in facial characteristics. Patterson and Baddeley (1977) examined the influence on identification accuracy of changes in hair style, facial hair, and the addition or removal of glasses. In their first experiment, large differences in recognition accuracy were obtained with simultaneous changes in hair style and facial hair. If the targets were identical at encoding and recognition, d' (a signal detection measure of sensitivity, or accuracy; zero means the inability to discriminate and a higher number means better discrimination – d' indexes differences in mean levels of performance in the same way as the d reported throughout this chapter – see especially Table 5.1) was 3.00, which indicates that the subjects could fairly easily recognize faces they had seen before. However, if the targets' hair style and facial hair changed, d' was .58. This difference was predominantly due to a dramatic drop in correct identification rates. In their second experiment, the changes in hair style and beard were manipulated independently, and both changes resulted in poorer recognition accuracy.

More recently, Read, Vokey, and Hammersley (in press) exposed subjects to high school students' photos as to-be–recognized targets, and used photos of the same targets taken 2 years later in a later recognition task. The photo pairs were categorized in terms of low, intermediate, or high similarity. Subjects were less able to recognize correctly older photos when the photo pairs were low in similarity, suggesting that natural processes of aging and facial hair transformations may reduce identification accuracy. The meta-analytic results are described below.

2. Disguises. It is common for individuals to don disguises before engaging in criminal acts. Full face masks and stockings can be quite effective in diminishing the facial feature cues that are necessary for recognition. In our research (Cutler, Penrod, & Martens, 1987a, 1987b; Cutler et al., 1986; O'Rourke et al., 1989) we have examined the effects of masking a target's hair and hairline cues on subsequent identification accuracy. In these experiments participants viewed a videotaped liquor store robbery and later attempted an identification from a videotaped lineup. In half of the robberies the robber wore a knit pullover cap that covered his hair and hairline. In the other half the robber did not wear a hat. The robber was less accurately identified when he was disguised. For example, in one of the experiments (Cutler et al., 1987a) 45% of the participants gave correct judgments on the lineup test if the robber wore no hat during the robbery, but only 27% gave a correct judgment if the robber wore the hat during the robbery. The effectiveness of covering the cues to hair and hairline are compellingly illustrated in Figure 7.1, which was constructed using a desktop computer-based facial composite production system. The six composites look very different when not disguised; however, they look very similar when the hair and hairline are covered by a hat.

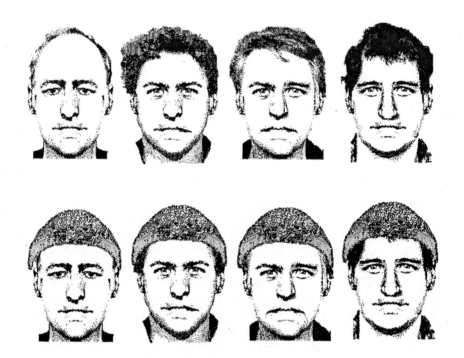

Figure 7.1.   An illustration of the effects of a simple disguise on appearance. When a hat is used to conceal hairstyles the faces in the bottom row are much more similar than those in the top row.

   In Shapiro and Penrod's meta-analysis, experiments were coded for whether or not the facial stimuli had undergone changes in facial features between the encoding and recognition phases. Facial transformations included changes in facial hair and deliberate disguises such as those used in the experiment just described. Nontransformed faces were more accurately recognized ($d = 1.05$; 75% vs. 54%) and less often falsely identified ($d = .40$; 22% vs. 30%) than transformed faces.

3.   *Summary.* Malleable target characteristics (the meta-analytic results for disguises and other changes in appearance are summarized in Table 7.2) are important predictors of identification accuracy. They are important not only because of their reliable and substantial effect on identification accuracy but also because disguises and facial transformations are common in crimes involving eyewitnesses.

Table 7.2. *Meta-analytic results from studies of malleable target characteristics*

Witness characteristic	Hits					False alarms				
	N	n	D	Z	p	N	n	D	Z	p
Transformation (none vs. disguise)	19	2682	1.05	13.46***		6	1494	.40	5.64***	

Eyewitnessing environment

This section concerns the influence of aspects of the crime environment, with "environment" broadly defined. It refers not only to the physical layout of the environment but to other situational influences as well.

1. Exposure duration. Common sense tells us that the amount of time available for viewing a perpetrator is positively associated with the witness's ability to subsequently identify him. But common sense does not tell us much about the nature of this relationship. Some investigations show a linear increase in face recognition accuracy with exposure time (Hall, 1980; Laughery, Alexander, & Lane, 1971). Others show a logarithmic relationship (Ellis, Davies, & Shepherd, 1977); that is, as exposure duration increases, face recognition accuracy improves, but the improvements become smaller as duration increases. Shapiro and Penrod's study characteristics analysis showed that the linear trend for exposure time was a stronger predictor than the quadratic trend, but both were relatively small in magnitude (see the results for the Attention block, described above).

2. The presence of a weapon. Several investigators (e.g., Loftus, 1979) have posited that the presence of a weapon during a crime attracts the attention of the witness to the weapon, leaving less attention to the perpetrator's facial and physical characteristics. This phenomenon is often referred to as "weapon focus." The notion is that when confronted with a handgun, a knife, or another weapon, there is a tendency to attend primarily to the weapon. In a compelling demonstration of the weapon focus effect, Loftus, Loftus, and Messo (1987) exposed students to a series of slides depicting a crime and monitored their eye movements with the use of video recorders. Subjects tended to focus more often and for longer periods of time on the weapon in comparison to other objects appearing in the scene.

One result of weapon focus is that because less attention is paid to the perpetrator, identifications are less likely to be correct. There have now been several other direct tests of the weapon focus hypothesis. In some of our studies, half of the videotaped robberies showed the robber outwardly brandishing a handgun, whereas the remaining half show the robber hiding the handgun in his coat pocket. In one study (Cutler, Penrod, & Martens, 1987a), 26% of the subjects who viewed the weapon-present videotapes gave correct judgments on the lineup test. In contrast, 46% of the subjects who viewed the weapon-hidden videotapes gave correct decisions, a significant difference. Similar effects for weapon focus have been reported by Cutler et al. (1986) and by Loftus et al. (1987; Experiment 2). Maass and Kohnken (1989) simulated weapon focus through the use of a syringe (compared to a pen in the "no weapon" condition) coupled with the very real threat of injection. Subjects exposed to the syringe showed significantly poorer performance on a subsequent lineup test than subjects in the no weapon condition. Steblay (1992) meta-analyzed 19 studies of weapon focus effects and found an average effect size (Cohen's [1977] difference between proportions) of .13 – a small but statistically significant effect. Some of these studies compare the performance of witnesses who view events such as robberies in which a weapon is either plainly visible or is concealed (but nonetheless present) – the effects observed in these studies are smaller than average. Larger effects are observed in studies that compare performance in conditions where a weapon is visible versus conditions in which there is no weapon.

3. *Crime seriousness.*   Crime seriousness can be operationalized in a variety of ways. It can refer to the amount of danger in a crime situation, the monetary worth of objects that are stolen or damaged, or the personal stake one has in the object of the crime. Leippe, Wells, and Ostrom (1978) staged a theft for their subjects. Crime seriousness was manipulated by the monetary worth of the stolen item. Subjects were led to believe that either a pack of cigarettes or a calculator had been stolen. In addition Leippe et al. manipulated whether or not subjects had knowledge of the value of the stolen item before the crime occurred. When witnesses believed the stolen item to be expensive, they correctly identified the thief more frequently than if the stolen item was believed to be inexpensive.

Hosch and his colleagues (Hosch & Cooper, 1982; Hosch, Leippe, Marchioni, & Cooper, 1984) examined whether being a victim, or merely a bystander-witness, influences eyewitness identifications. In these studies subjects were exposed to an elaborate staged theft. Either a laboratory calculator or the subject's own wristwatch was stolen. It is reasonable to assume that a crime is viewed as more serious by the victim of the crime than by an uninvolved witness. Were victims more likely to make correct identifications than bystander eyewitnesses? In the experiments by Hosch and his colleagues victimization had no clear-cut effect on identification accuracy. In Hosch et al. (1984) witnesses gave accurate lineup judgments more often than did victims, but not significantly so. Identification accuracy was not significantly affected by victimization in Hosch and Cooper (1982).

Crime seriousness, as operationalized by monetary worth of the item, has shown some ability to influence identification accuracy, but as operationalized by personal involvement, has shown no direct relationship with identification accuracy. Caution must be exercised in the interpretation of the findings discussed here, however. First, there are obvious ethical limitations on the type of experiments that can be performed. Second, the studies bearing on the question of crime seriousness are few, and the ones discussed here (Hosch & Cooper, 1982; Hosch et al., 1984; Leippe et al., 1978) did not employ target-absent lineups.

4. Stress, arousal, and violence. The issue of arousal and its effect on identification accuracy is controversial. On the one hand, it is of strong interest to the legal community because violence and threat of violence are present in many crimes. Such threats are likely to affect the ability to encode information and subsequently make accurate identifications. But adequate laboratory research on the effects of such stress is lacking because of obvious ethical constraints. Despite the importance of knowledge in this area, one cannot simulate violent crimes and pose a threat to the well-being of naive experimental subjects. Researchers have therefore resorted to a variety of manipulations including the use of violent versus nonviolent videotaped crimes. Increased violence in videotaped reenactments of crimes has been shown to lead to decrements in both identification accuracy and eyewitness recall (Clifford & Hollin, 1981; Clifford & Scott, 1978; Johnson & Scott, 1976; Sanders & Warnick, 1980), but this finding is not universally obtained (Cutler, Penrod, & Martens, 1987a; Sussman & Sugarman, 1972). Read, Yuille, and Tollestrup (1992; discussed earlier) examined the joint influence of arousal and alcohol intoxication. Subjects in these experiments committed a mock crime in two different arousal conditions. Their first experiment demonstrated no effect for arousal. The second experiment showed that increased arousal led to better identification of persons central to the event, but did not affect identifications of a "peripheral" target, or bystander.

Deffenbacher (1983, 1991) appealed to the "Yerkes-Dodson Law" when explaining the effects of arousal on identification. Stress or arousal demonstrates an inverted U-shaped relationship with identification accuracy. Low levels of arousal, such as when waking up, produce low attentiveness; moderate levels of arousal, such as that felt by an athlete preparing to

compete, serve to heighten perceptual and attentiveness skills; and, higher
levels, such as that felt by an individual under extreme danger or duress,
debilitates perceptual skills. Some critics (e.g., McCloskey, Egeth, &
McKenna, 1986) argue that the Yerkes-Dodson law is not relevant to the
eyewitness situation and the research is too inconclusive to advance any
conclusions regarding the effects of stress on identification accuracy.
Further complaints are raised because no objective measure exists to allow
between-study comparisons of subjects' arousal levels.

In point of fact, most of the studies reviewed by Deffenbacher (1983)
and, more recently, by Christiaanson (1992), do not examine the influence
of arousal on eyewitness identification accuracy. They examine the
influence of arousal on eyewitness reports.

5. Cross-race identification. As reviewed in item 2 above, neither the race
of the witness nor the race of the perpetrator, if considered alone, is strongly
associated with identification accuracy. But considered together, an
interesting finding emerges. Own-race recognitions are more accurate than
other-race identifications. Lindsay and Wells (1983) reviewed 11 separate
experiments that all show an interaction between race of witness and race of
target (although the patterns of main effects differ). Shapiro and Penrod
(1986) included own- versus other-race in their meta-analysis and found
that, indeed, own-race recognitions were correctly identified more often (d
= .53; 63% vs. 57%) and falsely identified less often (d = .44; 18% vs. 22%).
Bothwell, Brigham, and Malpass (1989) meta-analyzed 14 separate tests of
the own-race recognition bias (d = .71 for black subjects and d = .69 for
white subjects). Thus, the cross-race recognition effect is substantial and
comparable in magnitude across races. Anthony, Cooper, and Mullen (1992)
also meta-analyzed this literature and located a larger set of studies that
permitted 22 separate tests of the cross-racial effect. For white subjects the
d = .82 and for blacks d = .46. Based on this larger set of studies, the cross-
racial effect appears to be stronger for whites than for blacks.

In Platz and Hosch's field study discussed in the previous chapters,
white, black, and Mexican–American convenience store clerks attempted to
identify white, black, and Mexican customers. All three groups showed an
own–race bias in identification accuracy.

6. Cross-gender identification. Like race, gender of witness and gender of
target, when considered independently, have little effect on identification
accuracy. In Shapiro and Penrod's meta-analysis, there was a small but
significant tendency for subjects to identify correctly persons of their own
gender (d = .14; 76% v. 72%) more often than persons of the opposite
gender. No significant difference was observed for false identifications (d
= .02; 21% for both).

Table 7.3. *Meta-analytic results from studies of eyewitnessing environment*

Wiitness characteristics	Hits					False alarms				
	N	n	D	Z	p	N	n	D	Z	p
Exposure time at study (long vs. short)	8	990	.61	4.48 ***		8	1389	.22	.67	n.s.
Same vs. cross-race identification[a]	17	1571	.53	6.99 ***		14	1432	.44	7.4	***
Same vs. cross-race identification[b]	22	1725	.62	13.71***						
Same vs. cross-sex identification	13	1197	.14	3.18 ***		5	784	.02	.06	n.s.

[a] Shapiro and Penrod (1986); [b] Anthony, et al. (1992).

7. *Summary.* The eyewitnessing environment comprises an important class of predictors. Exposure duration, weapon presence, and cross-race recognition all have reliable effects on identification accuracy (see the summary of the meta-analytic findings in Table 7.3). It is, at this point, more difficult to specify the effects of arousal, whether operationalized as crime seriousness, violence, or in other ways. But, as Christiaanson (1992) points out, arousal may not be a unitary construct and various forms of arousal might differentially influence eyewitness memory. Clearly, arousal is a factor in dire need of additional research.

Postevent factors

This section reviews how time passage and other factors that intervene between the crime and identification influence identification accuracy.

1. *Retention interval.* Common sense tells us that memory declines over time. Can we expect eyewitness identification accuracy to decline as the time between the crime and the identification test increases? Shepherd (1983) reported the results of three experiments that included time delay as a factor. In his Experiment 2, time delays of 1 week, 1 month, 3 months, and 11 months were tested. Results showed a clear linear decline in correct

identifications across the four time delays (65%, 55%, 50%, and 10%, respectively). False identifications, though, remained largely unchanged (15%, 20%, 20%, and 15%, respectively). In his Experiment 3, time delays of 1 month and 4 months were tested, but this time delay had little influence on the percentage of correct identifications (21% vs. 27%) or false identifications (25% vs. 35%). In his Experiment 4, identification accuracy was tested for either 0, 1, or 2 targets, and after either 1 or 4 months. Correct identifications differed as a function of time delay (30% vs. 23%). Thus, Shepherd concluded that delays of less than 4 months have little influence on correct identification rate, but identification accuracy declines after 4 months. Shepherd also concluded that the false identification rate is relatively stable across time.

Though the research by Shepherd and colleagues is extensive, it is not entirely corroborated by other findings. Malpass and Devine (1981), for instance, found that a time delay influences *both* correct identifications and false identifications. Subjects in their experiment attempted identifications of a vandal (from a staged incident) within 3 days of the incident or 5 months after the incident. The 5-month delay caused an increase in false identifications (0% vs. 35%) as well as a decrease in correct identifications (83% vs. 36%).

With respect to shorter retention intervals, in Krafka and Penrod's (1985) field experiment, convenience store clerks attempted identifications of customers from photoarrays after either 2 hours or after 24 hours. The time delay resulted in a significant and large increase in false identifications from 15% to 52%, and a small decrease in percentage of correct identifications, from 43% to 39%. Davies, Ellis, and Shepherd (1978) tested recognition accuracy after a period of 48 hours or 3 weeks and found recognition performance to be superior in the shorter interval condition.

In an attempt to shed some light on these disparate results for retention interval, Shapiro and Penrod included retention interval in their meta-analysis. When studies that manipulated retention interval were grouped into long versus short time delays, longer delays led to fewer correct identifications ($d = .43$; 51% vs. 61%) and more false identifications ($d = .33$; 32% vs. 24%). Across experimental cells in all the studies examined in the meta-analysis (including those that did not directly manipulate retention interval) retention interval also proved to be an important determinant of correct identifications ($r = -.11$, $p < .05$), though there was no significant relationship with false identifications.

2. *Mugshot searches.* Eyewitnesses are sometimes asked to browse through books of mugshots to see if they recognize a crime perpetrator. Mere exposure to mugshots apparently does not influence subsequent identification accuracy (Cutler, Penrod, & Martens, 1987a; Davies,

Shepherd, & Ellis, 1979; Shepherd, Ellis, & Davies, 1982). Difficulties apparently arise if the subsequent lineup parades contain people who appeared in the mugshot arrays. Several experiments (Brown, Deffenbacher, & Sturgill, 1977; Doob & Kirschenbaum, 1973; Gorenstein & Ellsworth, 1980) have shown that persons appearing in lineup parades who also appeared in prior photoarrays or mugshots may even be identified at a rate similar to the rate at which the actual target is identified!

For example, Gorenstein and Ellsworth staged a disruption during a course lecture. After 25 minutes, half of the students who witnessed the event were asked to identify the intruder from a set of mugshots from which the intruder was absent (all subjects made a selection). The other half were dismissed prior to the mugshot phase of the experiment. Four to six days later, all subjects attempted to identify the intruder from a photoarray. Included in the photoarray were a photo of the intruder and a photo that was also included in the mugshots. Of the subjects who participated in the mugshot phase, 44% identified from the photoarray the photo that was present in the mugshot phase. This photo was not of the perpetrator. This familiar but incorrect photo was chosen twice as often as the photo of the actual intruder. In contrast, among subjects who did not participate in the mugshot phase, 39% correctly identified the intruder. Thus, in a case in which a suspect is first identified from mugshots and then from a lineup, it is not clear whether the lineup identification is due to a recognition of the crime perpetrator or to a recognition of a person seen previously in the mugshots.

In another study of mugshot effects, Brigham and Cairns (1988) had 99 undergraduates view a videotaped attack. The students were then randomly assigned to one of four mugshot conditions. Subjects in the "attractiveness control" condition rated 18 photos (not containing the perpetrator) for attractiveness but did not provide recognition judgments. Subjects in the "experimental" condition viewed the same 18 photos and decided whether the target was present in the mugshots. Within the experimental condition, half the subjects made their identification decisions known to the experimenter whereas the other half kept their decisions private. A fourth group did not see the mugshots. Two days later all subjects attempted to recognize the target from either a standard photoarray (consisting of the target, two individuals pictured in the mugshots, and two new foils) or a commitment-biased photoarray (consisting of the target, the mugshot identified by the subject, another previously seen mugshot, and two foils).

Subjects in the public (30%) and private (36%) choice of the experimental conditions performed significantly less accurately than subjects in the no-mugshot (69%) and attractiveness control (64%) conditions, and the public- and private-choice conditions did not differ significantly from each other. Making a commitment at the mugshot phase also significantly enhanced the likelihood of a positive identification at the lineup phase. Whereas 77% of subjects who made a positive identification from the mugshots also made positive identification from the photoarray test, only 50% of subjects who did not make a positive identification from the mugshots did positively identify a person from the photoarray.

Despite the influence of the prior choice, those who made a mugshot identification performed with the same degree of accuracy on the photoarray test as those who did not make a mugshot identification. The performance difference between these two groups occurred in the errors they made. Subjects who made mugshot identifications were most likely to err by making a false identification (most often of the mugshot) from the photoarray (65%). In contrast, subjects who did not make mugshot identifications were more likely to reject the photoarray (59%) incorrectly. In addition, subjects who publicly stated their mugshot choice were more likely to repeat their incorrect choice from the photoarray (78%) than were subjects whose mugshot choices remained private, although this finding was not statistically significant.

In conclusion, Brigham and Cairns found that prior exposure to mugshots indeed interferes with later identification accuracy but that the identification errors depend on the decision at the mugshot stage. Subjects tended to remain committed to their decisions. False identifications from mugshots led to false identifications from photoarrays, whereas rejections of the mugshots tended to lead to incorrect rejections of the photoarrays.

3. *Experiential context.* Changes in experiential context can have effects similar to transformations in appearance such as disguise. Consider the experience of encountering an acquaintance whom you have seen a few times in a particular context, such as the workplace, and in another context, such as at a grocery store. The change in context can make it difficult to recognize the person. At first the person might seem familiar but because the person is not in the normal context it is difficult to recognize the person or recall the person's name. Criminal identifications generally involve a change in context as well as changes in appearance such as clothing.

There are sound reasons to believe that efforts to restore the original conditions or context in which a face was previously viewed will enhance recognition performance – much as placing the acquaintance in the workplace makes it easier to recognize him or her. Attempts to reinstate original contexts have met with some success in improving identification accuracy. In Krafka and Penrod's (1985) field study, for example, half of the convenience store clerks participated in a context reinstatement procedure prior to attempting to identify the customer. Clerks were instructed to reconstruct mentally the event and the perpetrator's characteristics and were provided with objects that the customer possessed (a nonpicture identification and a signed check). The remaining half of the clerks did not participate in this context reinstatement procedure. Among clerks who attempted identifications from customer-present photoarrays, 55% of those for whom context was reinstated and 29% of those for whom context was not reinstated correctly identified the target. This difference was of marginal statistical significance.

Among clerks who attempted identifications from customer-absent photoarrays, the corresponding percentages of subjects who made false identifications were 35% and 33%, respectively – a nonsignificant difference. In Shapiro and Penrod's meta-analysis, change in context was, found to be one of the most important predictors of recognition accuracy. Reinstatement of context led to more correct identifications ($d = 1.91$; 79% vs. 52%) but also to more false identifications ($d = -.44$; 25% vs. 18%). Clearly the effect of context reinstatement was much larger on correct identifications than on false identifications. Subsequent laboratory research (Cutler, Penrod, & Martens, 1987b) indicates that the effectiveness of context reinstatement varies inversely with the quality of the viewing conditions under which the crime was witnessed. Context reinstatement is most effective in situations in which memory is poor to begin with or has undergone some degradation.

Smith and Vela (1990) conducted two experiments with significant forensic implications. The object of the studies was to test whether there is a difference in the influence of actual versus imagined context reinstatement on eyewitness identification accuracy. In Experiment 1, 212 undergraduates viewed a staged incident during a class and attempted to identify the target from a set of 10 sequentially presented photos (in which the target was present) after either 1 day, 2 days, or 1 week. Two different targets were used in order to test the generality of the results. As a manipulation of context, one-third of the subjects were either tested in the same room in which the incident occurred (same context condition) and the two-thirds in a different room. Of the subjects tested in a different room, half were instructed to reinstate mentally the environment in which the incident occurred (imagined same-context condition) and the other half were not (different context condition). The correct identification rate was significantly higher for subjects in the same context condition (66%) than it was for subjects in the different context (50%) and imagined same-context (47%) conditions. Imagined reinstatement of context did not significantly improve identification accuracy in comparison to the different context condition. This effect was not qualified by retention interval or target.

In Experiment 2, 83 students participating in a mass testing session were interrupted by a man (an assistant to the experimenter) attempting to deliver a pizza. Four days later subjects attempted to identify the target from a six-person photoarray. This time half of the subjects were shown target-present and half were shown target-absent photoarrays. In addition, subjects were tested in the same room (same context) or in a different room (different context). The photoarray procedure was as follows. Subjects viewed simultaneously presented photos (slides) for 1 minute and were asked to make a decision. Following this, all subjects were asked to reinstate mentally the context of the original incident. They were shown the photoarray again and asked to make a decision again.

In the target-present condition, 44% of subjects in the same context condition correctly identified the target at both the first and second viewing. In contrast, 27% of subjects in the different context correctly identified the target after the first viewing and only 13% did so after the second. The difference in performance between subjects in the same and different context conditions was statistically significant only after the second viewing. With respect to the target-absent conditions, differences as a function of viewing and context condition were nonsignificant. Among subjects in the same context condition, 17% made false identifications after the first viewing and 9% after the second. The corresponding percentages for subjects in the different context condition were 0% and 4%. In conclusion, Smith and Vela's research supports the notion that returning to the scene of the crime improves one's ability to make a correct identification but has less of an effect on false identifications.

4. Summary. Postevent factors are potentially important for evaluating eyewitness identification accuracy (see Table 7.4 for a summary of the meta-analytic findings). Retention interval emerged as an important predictor in Shapiro and Penrod's effect-size analysis both in studies that manipulated retention interval and in their study characteristics analysis of all studies. Context reinstatement could not be examined in the study characteristics meta-analysis, but it was a strong predictor of performance in studies that manipulated it – a result reinforced by research such as the studies conducted by Smith and Vela. And, although mugshot procedures were not examined in the Shapiro and Penrod meta-analysis, recent research clearly indicates that mugshot procedures are important in situations in which a suspect has been identified first from a mugshot and later from a lineup. Most important, it is clear that the latter identification is probably not an independent recollection of the crime perpetrator but is based in part on familiarity rooted in having identified the person from a mugshot. Recent research is shedding new light on the manner in which mugshot searches and context may influence identification performance; see especially Read (1994) and Ross, Ceci, Dunning, and Toglia (1991).

Table 7.4. *Meta-analytic results from studies of postevent factors*

Postevent factors	Hits					False alarms				
	N	n	*D*	*Z*	*p*	*N*	*n*	*D*	*Z*	*p*
Retention interval										
(short vs. long)	18	1980	.43	8.03	***					
	14	1868	.33	2.02	***					
Context reinstatement										
(yes vs. no)	23	1684	1.91	17.54	***	18	1982	-.44	-2.75	*

The generalizability of laboratory findings

Several additional findings from Shapiro and Penrod's study characteristics analysis are also noteworthy. First, in their study characteristics analysis, their predictors accounted for 47% of the variance in correct identifications and 43% of the variance in false identifications – a very strong indication that eyewitness performance is subject to a variety of systematic influences. They also tested whether "type of study" (face recognition studies conducted in laboratories versus eyewitness identification studies conducted under field conditions) was related to performance. When considered separately, study type accounted for 35% of the variance in witness performance for correct identifications (and 30% of the variance for false identifications – see Tables 6.4 and 6.5). That is, there were major differences in performance levels in the two types of studies – with performance levels much higher in laboratory studies. It is interesting, however, that the setting of the studies accounted for only 3% of the difference in laboratory versus field performance for correct identifications (and 2% for false identifications – see Tables 2.6 and 2.7) when all the other witnessing characteristics were partialed out/taken into account. This result underscores that the laboratory/field distinction is almost entirely confounded with the many variables that predict identification performance – indeed, over 90% of the differences in laboratory versus field performance can be systematically accounted for by the other variables included in Tables 6.4 and 6.5.

Stated another way, the argument that laboratory results may not generalize to performance under more realistic conditions is substantially weakened by the results of Shapiro and Penrod's meta-analysis. Instead, differences in performance in laboratory versus realistic settings are almost entirely accounted for by the systematic differences in the methods used in the two settings – laboratory studies are conducted under circumstances that produce higher rates of performance than is true of field studies. Furthermore, those systematic differences also mirror the natural variations in witnessing and identification conditions that exist in real-world eyewitness situations. Laboratory, field, and real eyewitness situations all vary along dimensions such as how attention-getting events are, how much substantial a cognitive load is imposed on witnesses at the time of viewing (e.g., the number of faces to study and the study time available) and recognition (e.g., the size and fairness of lineups), same versus cross-race identifications, the extent of transformations in the appearance of targets, and so on. Knowledge about the effects of these variables on eyewitness performance is, irrespective of the setting in which the variables have been studied, of value to anyone (police, district attorneys, judges, jurors, and psychologists) trying to evaluate the reliability of an identification made under a particular set of circumstances.

Conclusions

Existing research does not permit precise conclusions about the overall accuracy of the eyewitness identifications that are a common feature of criminal prosecutions, but the research does lead us to conclude that identification errors are not infrequent. The research is more informative about the factors that do and do not influence eyewitness identification accuracy.

Overall, stable eyewitness characteristics (with the notable exception of witness age) and eyewitness representations of confidence are perhaps the least important factors for diagnosing the accuracy of eyewitness identifications. With respect to target characteristics, malleable ones, such as disguises, are important, but stable ones, such as sex and race, are less so. Distinctiveness of appearance, a stable target characteristic, is important. Aspects of the eyewitnessing environment (e.g., exposure time and cross-racial identification) and postevent factors (e.g., retention interval and especially context reinstatement) prove to be important predictors of identification accuracy.

8 The effects of suggestive identification procedures on identification accuracy

The studies reviewed in Chapters 6 and 7 clearly demonstrate that eyewitness identifications are fallible and that witness fallibility is, in many respects, systematic: That is, certain encoding, storage, and retrieval factors reliably influence eyewitness identification accuracy. In this chapter we further explore factors associated with the retrieval stage. Our particular concern is how factors that are under the control of police investigators and prosecutors can influence the suggestiveness of eyewitness identification procedures and hence eyewitness identification performance. We begin with a discussion about bias in identification tests and then examine five forms of identification test bias.

Suggestion and fairness

Eyewitness identifications take place in a social context in which the eyewitness's performance can be influenced by her expectations and inferences, which in turn can be influenced by the verbal and nonverbal behaviors of investigators, the structure of the identification test, and the environment in which the identification test is conducted. At the outset, the fact that the investigator has taken the time to put together a photoarray, made an appointment with the eyewitness and driven across town to meet her may suggest to the eyewitness that the police think they have the perpetrator. This is likely to be so even if the police are unsure about whether the suspect is the perpetrator. For example, the police might be conducting a photoarray identification test as a "shot in the dark" or in order to eliminate a suspect. But there would be no reason for an eyewitness to know this, and she may be inclined to infer that the police are reasonably certain that they know the identity of the perpetrator. It is reasonable to expect that the eyewitness will be inclined to act on this inference and make a positive identification – whether correct or incorrect.

The tendency to make a positive identification may be further strengthened by a number of factors. One such factor is the degree to which the investigator pressures the eyewitness into participating in an identification test. An eyewitness who is told that it is very important for her to view a photoarray or lineup immediately is more likely to infer that the investigators have identified the perpetrator than is an eyewitness who is told that she could drop by the station whenever it is convenient for her to do so. Another factor might be the zealousness of the investigator. The more zealous the investigator, the more confident the eyewitness might be that the investigator knows the perpetrator's identity. A cooperative eyewitness might therefore "do her part" by making a positive identification. Although there is no research testing the hypotheses concerning the effects of effort exertion and zealousness on the part of investigators, if these factors operate as described, we would deem them suggestive procedures for the reasons we will soon describe.

In this chapter we are concerned with two interrelated characteristics of identification procedures: suggestiveness and fairness. These characteristics have sometimes been confused in the legal literature, but they can be distinguished. We define suggestive procedures as any aspects of the identification test that are under the control of police investigators and that enhance the likelihood that an eyewitness will make a positive identification – whether it is correct or not (a crude example is a procedure in which a police officer informs a witness that: "we have a firm suspect and he has already been identified by other witnesses – can you identify him from this array?"). We define unfair procedures as those aspects of the identification task (other than the quality of witness memory) that are under the control of police investigators and enhance the likelihood a witness will select a suspect from a lineup rather than a foil (a crude example is a lineup comprising one black suspect and five whites – an unfortunate real-world occurrence reported by Ellison and Buckhout, 1981).

The criminal justice system acknowledges that mistaken identifications occur and that suggestive and unfair identification procedures used by police or prosecutors enhance the likelihood of mistaken identification. Said Supreme Court Justice William Brennan, writing for the majority in *United States v. Wade* (1967), "The vagaries of eyewitness identification are well-known; the annals of criminal law are rife with instances of mistaken identification. . . . A major factor contributing to the high incidence of miscarriage of justice from mistaken identification has been the degree of suggestion inherent in the manner in which the prosecution presents the suspect to witnesses for pretrial identification. . . . Suggestion can be created intentionally or unintentionally in many subtle ways."

We examine five factors that enhance the suggestibility and unfairness of identification tests. These are lineup instruction bias, foil bias, clothing bias, presentation bias, and investigator bias.

Lineup instruction bias

Instructions given to an eyewitness prior to an identification test can vary in their degree of suggestiveness. Suggestive instructions can convey to the eyewitness the strong impression that the suspect is in fact in the photoarray or lineup, thereby increasing the likelihood that the eyewitness will make a positive – though not necessarily correct – identification. How can instructions convey this message? The following experiments examine this question empirically.

Buckhout, Figueroa, and Hoff (1975) studied the influence of suggestive instructions combined with suggestive presentations of a photoarray. During a lecture, 141 undergraduates witnessed a staged assault on the professor by another student. Seven weeks later the eyewitnesses attempted to identify the assailant from one of two photoarrays. In the "leading" array, five of the six photographs were aligned squarely but the assailant's photograph was crooked. In the "nonleading" array, all six photographs were squarely aligned. Half of the eyewitnesses in each condition were given "low-biased" instructions, which merely asked them if they recognized any of the persons in the photoarray. The remaining eyewitnesses were given "high-biased" instructions, which informed them that the assailant's photograph was, in fact, in the photoarray. Subjects who received "high-biased" instructions and viewed an unfair "leading photoarray" identified the assailant at a significantly higher rate (61.3%) than did subjects in the remaining three conditions (which averaged about 40%). In short, this experiment demonstrates that suggestive instructions combined with an unfair leading photoarray can increase witness willingness to attempt an identification.

One criticism of Buckhout et al.'s experiment is that the suggestive instructions were unrealistic. Explicit statements by the police to the effect that the perpetrator's photograph is in the photoarray are probably the exception rather than the rule and do not reflect the type of suggestiveness associated with most photoarrays. Thus, one might argue that Buckhout et al.'s experiment overestimates the impact of suggestive instructions. However, given that their "low-biased" instructions still did not explicitly inform eyewitnesses that they were free to reject the photoarray, these instructions might also underestimate the impact of suggestion. Further research using more realistic instructions presents a clearer picture of the role of suggestion in photoarrays.

Malpass and Devine (1981) reasoned that suggestive instructions would' be more detrimental when the suspect resembled, but was not, in fact, the perpetrator. To test this hypothesis, they staged an act of vandalism during a lecture attended by about 350 undergraduate students, 100 of whom were asked to identify the vandal from one of two live lineups within the next 3 days. Half of the eyewitnesses attempted to identify the vandal from a vandal-present lineup and the other half from a vandal-absent lineup. Half of the eyewitnesses in each condition were given the following "biased" instructions (p. 484): "We believe that the person . . . is present in the lineup. Look carefully at each of the five individuals in the lineup. Which of these is the person you saw . . ." The form on which these eyewitnesses were to indicate their decisions contained the numbers 1 through 5 (so that eyewitnesses could circle their choices) but no option for rejecting the lineup. The remaining eyewitnesses were given the following "unbiased" instruction: "The person . . . may be one of the five individuals in the lineup. It is also possible that he is not in the lineup. Look carefully at each of the five individuals in the lineup. If the person you saw . . . is not in the lineup, circle 0. If the person is present in the lineup, circle the number of his position."

Among eyewitnesses who viewed a vandal-present lineup, 100% of those who received biased instructions made a positive identification, 75% of whom correctly identified the vandal. In contrast, 83% of eyewitnesses who received unbiased instructions made a positive identification, all of whom were correct. Although biased instructions increased the positive identification rate among eyewitnesses who viewed a vandal-present lineup, accuracy rates did not differ. Among eyewitnesses who viewed a vandal-absent lineup, 78% of those who received biased instructions made a positive identification. Of course, all of them were incorrect. In contrast, only 33% of those who received unbiased instructions made an incorrect positive identification from the vandal-absent lineup. Thus, significantly more false identifications were obtained with biased instructions than with neutral instructions.

Although Malpass and Devine's (1981) research compellingly illustrates the dangers of suggestive instructions for innocent suspects, it suffers from the same limitation as does the Buckhout et al. (1975) experiment. The biased instructions still might be unrepresentative of the degree of suggestion that is typical of photoarray procedures.

We (Cutler, Penrod, & Martens, 1987a) attempted to address empirically the criticism of the Buckhout et al. (1975) and Malpass and Devine (1981) experiments by testing instructions that are more subtly suggestive. In this experiment, 165 undergraduates viewed a videotape of a staged liquor store robbery and attempted to identify the robber (after either 1 hour or after 7 days) from a videotaped robber-present or robber-absent lineup. Roughly half of the eyewitnesses in each lineup condition received "biased" instructions. Eyewitnesses were not told that the robber was in the lineup; rather, they were merely instructed to choose the lineup member whom they believed was the robber. The remaining eyewitnesses received "unbiased" instructions that explicitly offered them the option of rejecting the lineup. As in Malpass and Devine (1981), instructions did not significantly influence accuracy when the robber was present in the lineup. In contrast, when the robber was absent from the lineup, eyewitnesses who received biased instructions were significantly more likely to make a false identification (90%) than were eyewitnesses who received unbiased instructions (45%).

Our experiment demonstrated that suggestive lineup instructions can have a substantial impact on false identifications even when they are more subtle. We replicated the effect of subtly biased instructions in three additional experiments (Cutler, Penrod, & Martens, 1987b; Cutler, Penrod, O'Rourke, & Martens, 1986; O'Rourke, Penrod, Cutler, & Stuve, 1989). In one of those (O'Rourke et al., 1989), the effect of suggestive instructions was found to be comparable among student and community member samples. Overall, we have observed strong evidence for the influence of suggestive instructions on false identifications in data from 895 participants in crime simulation experiments.

Kohnken and Maass (1988) challenged the generalizability of the research on instruction bias. They argued that the suggestibility effect may arise because eyewitnesses in these experiments know that they are taking part in a simulation and that there are no real consequences of their judgments. The presumed cautiousness of eyewitnesses to actual crimes was hypothesized to mitigate the effect of suggestive instructions. They conducted two experiments in an effort to test this notion using students from a German university. Their experiment differed from the research we have already reviewed in two important respects: (a) some eyewitnesses did not know they were participating in a crime simulation and therefore believed the crime and the identifications to be real; and (b) during the lineup test, all eyewitnesses were given the option of making no identification by indicating "I don't know."

In their first experiment, 76 students witnessed a staged dispute between a professor and a student about a bag that a student wanted to carry out of the classroom. Eventually, the student grabbed the bag and ran out of the room, leaving the remaining students to believe that he stole it. One week later the student-witnesses attempted to identify the thief from a thief-absent lineup conducted by an officer of the Criminal Investigation Department. A considerable effort was made to convince subjects of the seriousness of the identification. Half of the subjects were informed, just before the identification test, that the crime and identification test were simulated but that, for the purposes of the research, they should behave like eyewitnesses. The other half of the subjects were not so informed and were led to believe that the crime and identification were real and important.

Within each belief condition, half of the subjects were given "biased" lineup instructions. They were told (p. 365): "There are indications that one of these persons is the perpetrator. Please, try to recognize this person."

They were also given a response sheet containing those instructions and a space to write the number of the lineup member believed to be the perpetrator. Three additional options appeared on the response sheet. One stated: "If you are absolutely sure that the culprit is not here, please mark here." Two other responses allowed subjects to indicate: "I don't know which of the persons is the perpetrator/I cannot remember the perpetrator" or "The perpetrator is not present."

The remaining subjects were given "unbiased" lineup instructions. They were told: "Please check whether you can recognize any of these persons as the one that you have observed last week." These instructions appeared in writing on the response form together with the three response alternatives (the number of the lineup member believed to be the thief, don't know/can't remember, and the thief is not present in the lineup). The statement "If you are absolutely sure that the perpetrator is not present, please mark here" was not on the response sheet.

Subjects who were not informed that the crime and lineup test were simulated and who received biased instructions were significantly more likely to use the "don't know/can't remember" option than all other groups combined (50% vs. 25.8%). False identification rates did not differ significantly. Kohnken and Maass concluded that the biased instructions may have made eyewitnesses more cautious when they believed that they were participating in an actual identification test.

In their second experiment, Kohnken and Maass replicated the Malpass and Devine (1981) experiment described earlier using 63 German students. There was one major change in experimental procedure: The instructions given to the witnesses were modified to parallel those used in the Malpass and Devine (1981) study. Unbiased instructions informed witnesses that the perpetrator may not be in the lineup and included an explicit option for indicating the perpetrator was not in the array. The biased instructions included neither the admonition that the perpetrator might not be in the lineup, nor an explicit option for "not present." As in Kohnken and Maass's first experiment, half of the subjects were informed, prior to the identification test, that the crime was simulated. The remaining half were not so informed and were led to believe that the crime and identification test were real. This time they found that instructions produced a significantly larger effect on identification performance among eyewitnesses who were informed that the crime was simulated as compared to the uniformed witnesses. Among the informed subjects, 88% who received biased instructions made a false identification, whereas 33% who received unbiased instructions made a false identification. Among subjects who believed the crime and identification test to be real, 63% who received biased instructions made a false identification, whereas 47% who received unbiased instructions made a false identification; although sizeable, this difference was not statistically significant.

Kohnken and Maass (p. 369) concluded: "Taken together, the present findings suggest that the instructional bias effect observed in previous experiments is limited to subjects who are fully aware that they are participating in an experiment. The fact that neither study provides evidence for a reliable increase of false identifications as a function of biased instructions, suggests that eyewitnesses are better than their reputation." We disagree. We question their conclusions for several reasons. A review of the biased and unbiased instructions they used in their first experiment reveals that the difference in suggestiveness is smaller than in any experiment reviewed above (indeed, the choosing rate in their uninformed, biased condition was 42% vs. 45% in their unbiased condition). Why would the choosing rates not differ in the two conditions? The primary explanation appears to be that all eyewitnesses are explicitly given the option of indicating that the thief is not in the lineup. The fact that these less suggestive instructions have nonsignificant effects on identification performance does not threaten the conclusion that more suggestive instructions do increase the likelihood of false identifications. We do not challenge their conclusion that eyewitnesses who know that they are taking part in a simulation may be less cautious. Nevertheless, this finding also does not threaten our conclusions regarding suggestive instructions. A more rigorous test of Kohnken and Maass's conclusion would require testing the influence of the "don't know/not sure" response together with more suggestive instructions.

Kohnken and Maass's second experiment does provide strong evidence that the effect of suggestive instructions is larger in staged crimes than in real crimes. Nevertheless, their results do not indicate that the effect is absent in actual crimes. Although the difference in false identifications was not significant when witnesses were not informed that they were part of an experiment (63% among eyewitnesses who received biased instructions and 47% among eyewitnesses who received neutral instructions), the lack of statistical significance may be due to weak statistical power (i.e., the likelihood of detecting a statistically significant effect of a given magnitude with a particular sample size). Based on the magnitude of the instruction effect obtained by Malpass and Devine (1981), an experiment employing 58 participants would have statistical power of .90. This means that with a sample size of 58, the investigator would have a 90% chance of detecting the effect of instructions at a conventional significance level ($p < .05$). With a sample size of 44, power drops to .80. With a sample size of 23, power drops to .50 (see Friedman, 1982). Kohnken and Maass's nonsignificant effect of biased instructions (among eyewitnesses who believed the event to be real) was calculated on data from only 31 eyewitnesses. Clearly, weak statistical power could explain their results.

Paley and Geiselman (1989) were also concerned with the realism of instructions used in earlier research (e.g., Buckhout et al., 1975; Malpass & Devine, 1981) and conducted two experiments to examine the effects of subtly biased instructions. They tested the effects of the instructions used by the Los Angeles Police Department (LAPD). These instructions inform witnesses that the perpetrator might appear different in the lineup and the perpetrator might not be in the lineup. Because they contain more statements about the perpetrator's appearance in the lineup than about the perpetrator's absence from the lineup, Paley and Geiselman thought these instructions might enhance the number of false identifications (and the number of correct identifications) as compared to more balanced or more minimal instructions. Subjects (180 undergraduates) in Experiment 1 viewed a videotaped simulation of a woman being robbed while drawing money from an automated teller machine and attempted identifications 2 days later. Just prior to attempting an identification from a robber-present or robber-absent photoarray (each containing photos of six persons), each subject read an instruction sheet containing one of the three sets of instructions. The LAPD instructions were:

In a moment I am going to show you a group of photographs. This group of photographs may or may not contain a picture of the person who committed the crime now being investigated. Keep in mind that hair styles, beards, and moustaches may be easily changed. Also, photographs may not always depict the true complexion of a person – it may be lighter or darker than shown in the photo. Pay no attention to any markings or numbers that may appear on the photos or any other differences in the type or style of the photographs. When you have looked at all the photos, indicate below whether or not you see the person who committed the crime. Do not tell other witnesses that you have or have not identified anyone.

As Paley and Geiselman noted, the third, fourth, and fifth sentences imply that the perpetrator is in the photoarray even though the second sentence implies that the perpetrator might not be present. Thus, these instructions are believed to be unbalanced. The "balanced" instructions were as follows:

In a moment I am going to show you a group of photographs. This group of photographs may or may not contain a picture of the person who committed the crime now being investigated. It is possible that the correct suspect has not been apprehended. Keep in mind that the person you saw commit the crime may or may not be present in the photospread. If you do not see the person who committed the crime, it is acceptable to indicate that you do not think the suspect is present. Keep in mind that hair styles, beards, and moustaches may be easily changed. Also, photographs may not always depict the true complexion of a person – it may be lighter or darker than shown in the photos. Pay no attention to any markings or numbers that may appear on the photos or any other differences in the type or style of photographs. When you have looked at all the photos, indicate below whether or not you see the person who committed the crime. Do not tell other witnesses that you have or have not identified anyone.

The "minimal" instructions did not mention the presence of the perpetrator in the photoarray. These instructions were:

In a moment I am going to show you a group of photographs. When you have looked at all the photos, indicate below whether or not you see the person who committed the crime. Do not tell other witnesses that you have or have not identified anyone.

At the bottom of each instruction sheet subjects could check whether the robber was "present" or "not present" and write in the number of the robber's photograph if present.

The three different sets of instructions did not significantly influence identification performance when the robber was present in the photoarray. The percentages of correct identification rates for subjects who read actual, balanced, and minimal instructions were, respectively, 40%, 43%, and 47%. The instructions did not significantly influence identification performance among subjects who attempted identifications from robber-absent photoarrays. The respective false identification rates were 37%, 33%, and 30%, respectively.

In light of the lack of an effect for the instructions examined in Experiment 1, Paley and Geiselman tested the LAPD instructions against a more suggestive set of instructions in Experiment 2. The videotaped crime already described was shown to 60 undergraduates who, 2 days later, attempted to identify the robber from six-person, robber-present or robber-absent photoarrays. Half of the subjects were given the LAPD instructions and the corresponding response format. The other half were given the following "biased" instructions that did not mention the possibility that the perpetrator was not present in the lineup (but also did not state that the perpetrator was present): "We would like you to identify the person you saw commit the crime in the videotape you watched 2 days ago. Please indicate below which number photograph is of that suspect. Please do not discuss with anyone else which suspect you have identified." The response sheet for this condition contained one space for each photograph; subjects could check the appropriate space or a space labeled "can't recall." These instructions are comparable to the ones we used in our experiments (described earlier).

Table 8.1. *Effects of biased lineup instructions on identification accuracy*

Study	Correct identifications Target present		N	False identifications Target absent	
	Biased	unbiased		Biased	unbiased
Buckhout, Figueroa, & Hoff	.61	.40	141		
Malpass & Devine	.75	.83	350	.78	.33
Cutler, Penrod, & Martens	.43	.46	165	.90	.45
Kohnken & Maass					
(Study 2-informed)			76	.88	.33
(Study 2-uninformed)			63	.63	.47
Paley & Geiselman					
(Study 1)	.40	.45	180	.37	.32
(Study 2)	.40	.53	60	.90	.40
Unweighted means	.50	.53		.74	.38

Subjects who heard the more biased instructions were significantly more likely to make a positive identification than were subjects who heard the LAPD instructions. This increased rate of positive identifications led to somewhat more correct identifications when the robber was present (53% for biased instructions; 40% for LAPD instructions) but many more false identifications when the robber was absent from the photoarray (90% for the biased instructions; 40% for the LAPD instructions). Thus, in response to Kohnken and Maass's (1988) hypothesis, biased instructions influence identification performance even when subjects are given the option of providing no response (i.e., "don't know").

In conclusion there is convincing evidence that suggestive identification instructions influence eyewitness performance. The research shows that biased instructions substantially increase the likelihood of false identifications. As shown in Table 8.1, biased instructions fundamentally affect the choosing rates in lineups in which the perpetrator is not present – of course, all choices from these lineups are false identifications.

Data from the Kassin, Ellsworth, and Smith's (1989) survey of eyewitness experts (discussed in Chapter 4) further underscores the reliability of this phenomenon. They surveyed 63 experts on eyewitness research about their conclusions concerning the reliability of 21 effects reported in the eyewitness literature. Respondents were asked for their reactions to the following statement: "Police instructions can affect an eyewitness's willingness to make an identification and/or the likelihood that he or she will identify a particular person" (p. 1091). Of the 63 respondents, 30 felt that the statement was very reliable, 22 indicated it was generally reliable, 10 felt that the research tends to favor that conclusion, one believed the results were inconclusive, and none concluded that there was no support or that the reverse was true. Further, 60 of the 63 respondents thought that the effect of instructions was reliable enough to testify about in court. In comparison to the 20 other effects, lineup' instructions was the perceived to be the second-most reliable phenomenon.

Foil bias

The term *functional size* (Lindsay & Wells, 1980; Wells, 1993) refers to the number of viable lineup members, or the number of lineup members who plausibly match the eyewitness's description of the crime perpetrator. Having other lineup members who resemble the perpetrator in physical appearance affects lineup bias by protecting the suspect from the eyewitness's tendency to make a positive identification. For example, if an eyewitness had a poor memory for the crime perpetrator but remembered some general characteristics, such as the perpetrator's long blond hair, then having other lineup members with long blond hair safeguards the suspect from identification by deduction. The quality and the number of foils in an array clearly influence the fairness of the array – as reflected in the tendency for witnesses to make identifications, particularly false identifications.

In a compelling demonstration of foil bias, Lindsay and Wells (1980) staged a theft in view of 96 undergraduates. Shortly after the theft subjects were asked to identify the thief from thief-present or thief-absent photoarrays containing six photographs. Both the thief and the innocent suspect who replaced him in the thief-absent conditions were white males in their 20s with light brown hair and moustaches. Half of the subjects viewed photoarrays in which all of the foils were white males in their 20s with brown to blond hair and moustaches (high similarity condition). The other half viewed photoarrays in which the foils were two Asian and three white males in their late 20s with full black beards and black hair (low similarity condition). Although high similarity photoarrays produced lower correct and false identification rates than low similarity lineups, the effect was significantly greater on false than it was on correct identification rates. Among subjects shown thief-present photoarrays, 71% of subjects in the low similarity and 58% of subjects in the high similarity conditions made correct identifications. Among subjects shown thief-absent photoarrays, 70% in the low similarity and 31% in the high similarity conditions made false identifications.

Although psychologists have historically advocated maximizing the similarity of appearance between the lineup members and the suspect/perpetrator, Wells (1993; Luus & Wells, 1991) disagrees. He compellingly argues that the ideal lineup, given this advice, would be one composed of clones. The suspect, in a lineup of clones, is protected from mistaken identification, but there is little chance of a correct identification because the witness cannot discriminate among lineup members. Wells proposes that lineups be high in functional size and propitious heterogeneity. Specifically, he suggests that lineup members should match the descriptions given by the witness at the time of the crime on all features mentioned but should be permitted to vary on features not mentioned in the witness's description. For example, if the witness, at the time of the crime, described the perpetrator as a white male, about 6' tall, 180 lbs, broad shoulders, blond hair, moustache and no beard, all lineup members should fit this description. But they should be permitted to vary on features not mentioned by the witness, such as hair length, eye color, and so forth. These criteria, argues Wells, should protect the suspect from the witness's tendency to make a positive identification while not making the identification task overly difficult.

Although alternative methods have been suggested for measuring the effective or functional size of a lineup – as opposed to its apparent or nominal size (e.g., Malpass & Devine, 1983; Wells, Leippe, & Ostrom, 1979), the method suggested by Wells et al. (1979) is perhaps the most straightforward. In order to test the functional size of a lineup or photoarray one assembles the description of the perpetrator provided by the witness or witnesses and presents the descriptive information, together with the lineup to be assessed, to a set of "mock witnesses" who were not present at the scene of the crime. These mock witnesses are then asked to select the person who best matches the description. If, for example, 10 out of 30 mock witnesses select the suspect/defendant, the functional size of the array is 30/10 or 3. Another way to view the functional size is to observe that in a perfectly fair array of six persons one would expect mock witnesses to select each face equally often. If there were 30 witnesses, as in our example, each of the six faces would be expected to draw five identifications, for a functional size of 30/5 = 6.

An array may have a functional size of 3 irrespective of its nominal size. If 10 of 30 mock witnesses select the suspect from an array of 6 persons, the functional size is the same as if 10 of 30 mock witnesses selected the suspect from an array of 20 persons. An array with a functional size of three does not offer an innocent suspect who resembles the actual perpetrator very much protection from a mistaken identification. An actual witness who has essentially no memory for what the perpetrator looked like (beyond the description provided at the time of the crime), but is inclined to make a choice from an array with a functional size of 3 has a one-in-three chance of picking the suspect and this selection could give rise to a criminal prosecution. To minimize such chance identifications, most commentators recommend that an array contain only one suspect and a minimum of five appropriate foils (Wells, Seelau, Rydell, & Luus, 1994).

What is the functional size of the arrays actually used by police? Brigham, Ready, and Spier (1990) reported that in an evaluation of six actual lineups brought to them by defense attorneys, the three least fair arrays had an average functional size of 1.59 – a quite dubious achievement on the part of the police officers who assembled those arrays. For more information about foil bias and assessment of the quality of lineup foils, see Lindsay (1994), Brigham and Pfeifer (1994), and Wells, Seelau, Rydell, and Luus (1994).

Clothing bias

Lindsay, Wallbridge, and Drennan (1987) note that police typically ask eyewitnesses to describe the perpetrator's appearance, including the clothing worn while committing the crime. Sometimes, they note, suspects appear in the identification test wearing the same (or similar) clothing as that worn during the crime. To what extent do the clothes worn by lineup members influence identification performance? Do eyewitnesses use clothing as a cue in the identification process? Lindsay et al. hypothesize that clothing cues can enhance the likelihood of false identifications if the suspect is wearing clothing similar to that worn by the crime perpetrator. Indeed, a person might be apprehended by police officers partly because his clothing matches the description of the perpetrator. Lindsay et al. note that the Law Reform Commission of Canada, which provides guidelines for eyewitness identification procedures, contains the following:

Rule 505 (6): "Lineup participants shall be similarly dressed. Thus, ordinarily, either all or none of the lineup participants shall wear eyeglasses or items of clothing such as hats, scarves, ties, or jackets. Subject to Rule 505 (12), the suspect shall not wear the clothes he or she is alleged to have worn at the time of the crime, unless they are not distinctive."

Rule 505 (12): "If a witness describes the suspect as wearing a distinctive set of clothing or a mask, and it would assist the witness to see the lineup participants wearing such clothing, and if the item (or something similar) can be conveniently obtained, each participant shall don the clothing in the order of his or her appearance in the lineup. If there is a sufficient number of masks or items of clothing, all participants shall don the clothing or masks simultaneously."

No such guidelines exist in the United States, and Lindsay et al. expressed concern about the extent to which the guidelines are followed – even by Canadian police departments. Thus, Lindsay et al. conducted three experiments to examine whether clothing biases in fact influence identification performance.

Subjects in the three experiments witnessed a staged theft of a relatively inexpensive object, described the appearance and attire of the perpetrator, and attempted to identify him from six-person, thief-present or thief-absent photoarrays. In all three experiments three photoarray conditions were tested: (a) the "usual" condition in which each person whose picture appeared in the photoarray dressed differently and none wore clothing similar to that of the perpetrator; (b) the "biased" condition in which only the suspect (the thief in the thief-present condition and the replacement in the thief-absent condition) wore clothing identical to that worn by the perpetrator during the crime (the foils wore clothing identical to that worn in the "usual" condition); and (c) the "dressed alike" condition in which all lineup members were dressed alike. Naturally, the suspects and foils were the same people across photoarray conditions – only their clothing changed.

In Experiment 1, 144 students participated as subjects. This experiment employed the conditions just described with the exception that two "dressed alike" conditions were tested. In one, all photoarray members wore the clothing identical to that worn by the perpetrator. In the other, all photoarray members wore identical clothing but the clothing was not similar to that worn by the perpetrator. Clothing conditions did not significantly influence identification performance among subjects shown thief-present photoarrays. The correct identification rates were: 78% among subjects in the biased condition, 67% in the usual condition, 61% in the dressed alike in criminal attire condition, and 56% in the dressed alike but not in criminal attire condition. Identification performance was significantly influenced by clothing condition when the thief was absent from the photoarrays. As expected, the false identification rate was highest (28%) in the biased lineup condition followed by the usual (11%), dressed alike but not in criminal attire (6%), and dressed alike in criminal attire (0%) conditions.

Experiment 2 used a different set of 144 undergraduates, a different thief, and different photoarray members. The conditions were the same as in Experiment 1 except that the suspects in the biased lineup conditions and all of the photoarray members in the dressed alike but not in criminal attire condition wore a sweatshirt similar but not identical to that worn by the perpetrator. As in Experiment 1, identification performance was not significantly influenced by clothing condition when the thief was in the photoarray. The correct identification rates were 78%, 83%, 83%, and 89% in the biased, usual, similar, and identical sweatshirt conditions, respectively. False identification rates were significantly influenced. As in Experiment 1, false identifications were most common in the biased condition (39%) followed by the usual (28%), similar sweatshirt (22%), and identical sweatshirt (11%) conditions.

Subjects in Experiment 3 were 104 undergraduates attending a different Canadian university from subjects in Experiments 1 and 2. These subjects viewed a videotaped enactment of the theft of a wallet and, in the same session, attempted to identify the thieves from six-person, thief-present or thief-absent photoarrays. The two thieves in the videotape dressed differently and had somewhat different physical characteristics. Photoarray conditions included the biased, usual and dressed alike (but dissimilar to the perpetrator) conditions. As in Experiments 1 and 2, identification performance was not significantly influenced by clothing conditions. The rates of correct identification were 53%, 44%, and 53% for the biased, usual, and similar attire conditions, respectively. Again, as in Experiments 1 and 2, identification performance was significantly influenced by clothing condition when the thieves were absent from the photoarrays. False identifications were most common in the biased photoarray (47%), followed by the usual (24%), and the similar attire (11%) conditions.

In summarizing their results, Lindsay et al. combined the data from the three experiments for a powerful test of the influence of clothing condition. Thus, these analyses included data from 392 subjects. Across all thief-present conditions, clothing produced a trivial and nonsignificant effect on identification performance. The overall rates of correct identification were 70%, 65%, and 69% for the biased, usual, and dressed alike conditions, respectively. However, the respective rates of false identifications in these conditions were 38%, 21%, and 10%, which did differ significantly. Clothing biased lineups substantially increased the likelihood of false identifications.

Presentation bias

Traditionally, in live and photographic lineup procedures, both the suspect and foils are presented simultaneously, and the eyewitness identifies which (if any) of the individuals is the perpetrator. Recent research questions the utility of this commonly accepted presentation procedure.

Lindsay and Wells (1985) conducted staged thefts for 243 undergraduates (individually or small groups). Five minutes after the staged theft, subjects were asked to identify the thief from a photoarray containing six persons. Half of the subjects were shown all six photographs simultaneously, as in traditional identification procedures. The other half were shown the six photographs using a novel sequential presentation procedure. These subjects were instructed that they would view a series of photographs, one at a time. As each photograph was presented, they were to indicate whether or not the photograph was of the thief. They were told that they could see each photograph only once. Although the sequentially presented photoarray, like the simultaneously presented one, contained six photographs, the experimenter held a stack of 12, deliberately misleading subjects to believe they would see all 12. The purpose behind this deception was to minimize any increased tendency to make a choice as the subject watched the experimenter exhausting the stack of photographs. In addition, half of the subjects in each presentation condition viewed thief-present photoarrays and the other half viewed thief-absent photoarrays. Among subjects shown the thief-present photoarrays, presentation style did not significantly influence identification performance: Fifty-eight percent of subjects shown simultaneous presentation and 50% of subjects shown sequential presentation correctly identified the thief. In contrast, among subjects shown thief-absent photoarrays, presentation style significantly influenced identification performance. Of those who experienced simultaneous presentation, 43% made a false identification. Among those who experienced sequential presentation, only 17% made a false identification. Sequential presentation substantially reduced false identification rate.

We (Cutler & Penrod, 1988) twice replicated the results of Lindsay and Wells's (1985) experiment. In our first experiment, each of 175 undergraduates viewed one of four versions of a videotaped liquor store robbery and 1 week later attempted identifications from videotaped lineups. Each subject tried to identify the robber from either a robber-present or robber-absent lineup, which was presented either simultaneously or sequentially. Lineups contained six persons. The sequential presentation differed from Lindsay and Wells's (1985) procedure in that subjects were informed of the actual number of the lineup members. The pattern of results was comparable to that found by Lindsay and Wells. When the robber was present in the lineup, presentation style did not significantly influence identification performance. Among these subjects, 80% of subjects who experienced sequential presentation and 76% of subjects who experienced simultaneous presentation correctly identified the robber. When the robber was absent from the lineup, presentation style significantly influenced identification performance. Subjects who experienced simultaneous presentation were twice as likely to make a false identification (39%) as were subjects who experienced sequential presentation (19%). Thus, this experiment replicated not only the effect demonstrated by Lindsay and Wells but showed that it can be obtained even if subjects in the sequential presentation condition are made aware of the number of lineup members.

In our second experiment, 150 undergraduates viewed one version of the videotaped liquor store robbery and attempted to identify the robber, 2 days later, from photoarrays containing six photographed persons. In this experiment subjects were not informed of the number of photographs to appear in the photoarray. The pattern of results replicated. Among subjects shown the robber-present photoarray, 41% of subjects who experienced sequential presentation, and 47% of subjects who experienced simultaneous presentation, correctly identified the robber – a nonsignificant difference. Among subjects shown the robber-absent photoarray, subjects who experienced simultaneous presentation were twice as likely to make a false identification (43%) as were subjects who experienced sequential presentation (21%); this difference was statistically significant.

Lindsay, Lea, and Fulford (1991) conducted three additional experiments to clarify further how various aspects of sequential presentation influence identification performance. In Experiment 1 they examined the influence of providing subjects with a second opportunity to make an identification following a sequentially presented photoarray. Subjects were 180 undergraduates. Staged thefts were conducted in view of individual or pairs of subjects. Later in the same session subjects were shown photoarrays containing eight photographed persons. Photoarrays were presented simultaneously or sequentially. Two-thirds attempted identifications from thief-absent photoarrays, one-third from thief-present photoarrays. In the sequential presentation condition, after the eighth photograph was shown, all photographs were then presented simultaneously and subjects were given the opportunity to change their decisions.

As in previous studies, presentation style did not significantly influence identification performance when the thief was present in the photoarray (57% of subjects who experienced simultaneous presentation and 47% of subjects who experienced sequential presentation made correct identifications). Presentation style significantly influenced false identification rates. Among subjects shown thief-absent photoarrays, false identifications were made by 20% of subjects who experienced simultaneous presentation and 5% of subjects who experienced sequential presentation. Allowing subjects in the sequential presentation/thief-present condition a chance to change their decisions after seeing simultaneous presentation led, to a small but nonsignificant increase in correct identifications (from 47% to 53%). Among subjects in the sequential presentation/thief-absent condition, 37% changed their decisions. The rate of false identifications significantly increased from 5% to 27%. Of those in this condition who changed their decisions, significantly more subjects changed from a correct decision to an incorrect one. Overall, allowing subjects in the sequential presentation condition a second chance using a simultaneously presented photoarray eliminated any benefits associated with sequential presentation.

The goals of Lindsay, Lea, and Fulford's (1991) second experiment were similar to the first, but this experiment also examined whether second-chance performance differed as a function of whether the second lineup was simultaneously or sequentially presented. Subjects were 32 undergraduates who viewed the same crime scenario used in Experiment 1 and attempted identifications from sequentially presented thief-absent, eight-person photoarrays. The photoarrays were foil- and clothing-biased in that only one person (the innocent suspect) resembled the thief and that same person wore a shirt similar to that worn by the thief during the crime. In addition, the identification test instructions made it clear that the thief was, in fact, in the photoarray. All subjects were given a second opportunity to view the photoarray and change their decision; for half the second photoarray was presented simultaneously, and for the other half it was presented sequentially. During the first presentation, 25% falsely identified the innocent suspect. When the second presentation was sequential, only one subject changed his or her decision. Given that the decision changed to a false identification, the percentage of false identifications changed from 25% to 28% from the first to the second sequential presentation. In contrast, when the second presentation was simultaneous, 5 out of 16 (31%) changed their decisions from a correct rejection to a false identification, and two others from a correct rejection to a foil identification. Comparing the two conditions directly, on the second opportunity, correct choices were made by 72% of subjects in the sequential, second-opportunity condition but by only 12% of subjects in the simultaneous, second-opportunity condition – a statistically significant difference. This experiment demonstrates that the second opportunity at identification is particularly problematic if a simultaneous presentation is used.

Lindsay, Lea, and Fulford's (1991) third experiment examined the influence of knowledge of the number of lineup members on identification performance in sequentially presented lineups. As we have established, sequential presentation reduces false identification rates whether or not subjects know how many people are to appear in the lineup. But the influence of this knowledge had never been tested directly while holding other factors constant. Students, in three separate psychology courses, were asked to identify (from a criminal-absent photoarray) the person who introduced the lecturer. One class (108 students) was shown a six-person photoarray, presented sequentially, and was informed, in advance, that six photographed persons were to be shown. Another class (73 students) was also shown the six-person photoarray, presented simultaneously, but was not given advance notice of the number of photographed persons to be presented. The third class (73 students) was shown the six-person photoarray using simultaneous presentation. In all classes the photoarrays were target-absent. The false identification-rates were 7% among subjects who viewed sequentially presented photoarrays and were uninformed of the number of photos to be viewed, 17% among subjects who viewed sequentially presented photoarrays but were informed of the number of photos to be viewed, and 27% among subjects who viewed simultaneously presented photoarrays. Each pair of percentages differed significantly, indicating that knowledge of the size of the photoarray reduces but does not eliminate the effectiveness of sequential presentation in comparison to simultaneous presentation.

Further insights into the effects of sequential presentations are provided by a series of studies by Lindsay, Lea, Nosworthy, Fulford, Hector, LeVan, and Seabrook (1991). Experiment 1 compared "traditional" versus "ideal" lineups. Experiments 2, 3, and 4 examined whether sequential presentation reduces the impacts of clothing, foil, and instruction bias, respectively. And Experiment 5 tested whether sequential presentation reduced the combined impact of clothing, foil, and instruction bias.

Lindsay, et al.'s first experiment (with 120 subjects) examined the difference in identification performance from conventional identification tests versus sequential presentation. In the "conventional presentation" condition, the photoarray was presented simultaneously and the presence or absence of the thief in the lineup was not mentioned. Foils generally resembled the perpetrator but were not the best available. All persons in the photoarray dressed differently, but none wore clothing comparable to that worn by the thief. The "ideal" condition used sequential presentation (with no knowledge of the number of persons in the photoarray), instructions that explicitly mentioned that the perpetrator might not be in the lineup, the foils more strongly resembled the perpetrator in appearance, and they all wore identical clothing. Half of the subjects in each presentation condition viewed thief-present photoarrays and half viewed thief-absent photoarrays. When the thief was present, the type of photoarray did not significantly influence identification performance: Sixty-seven percent of subjects shown conventional photoarrays and 77% of subjects shown ideal photoarrays made correct identifications. As expected, when the thief was absent, the type of photoarray did significantly influence performance: Three percent of subjects shown ideal photoarrays and 20% of subjects shown conventional photoarrays made false identifications.

Experiment 2 examined the combined influences of clothing bias and presentation bias on identification performance. A crime was staged in view of 180 undergraduates. Identifications were attempted in the same session. The six conditions and the identification accuracy rates are displayed in Table 8.2. In the clothing-biased conditions, only the suspect-foil (in thief-absent lineups) and perpetrator (in thief-present lineups) wore clothing similar to that worn by the thief at the time of the crime. In the clothing-unbiased conditions, no lineup members wore clothing similar to that worn

Table 8.2. *Simultaneous versus sequential lineup performance*

	Presentation	Presence of thief	Clothing condition	Correct IDs	False IDs
1	Sequential	Absent	Biased		7%
2	Sequential	Absent	Unbiased		3%
3	Simultaneous	Absent	Biased		33%
4	Simultaneous	Absent	Unbiased		20%
5	Simultaneous	Present	Biased	57%	
6	Sequential	Present	Biased	47%	

Note: Based on Lindsay, Lea, Nosworthy, Fulford, Hector, LeVan, and Seabrook (1991), Experiment 2.

by the perpetrator at the time of the crime. On average, false identifications occurred significantly more often for simultaneously presented photoarrays (27%) than for sequentially presented ones (5%). When the thief was present in the lineup and the lineup was clothing-biased, identification accuracy did not differ significantly as a function of presentation type (Conditions 5 vs. 6). And, clothing bias did not significantly influence the false identification rate among subjects shown sequentially presented photoarrays (Conditions 1 vs. 2). However, clothing bias did produce a higher rate of false identifications in simultaneous arrays (Conditions 3 vs. 4). Thus, the influence of clothing bias was minimized by sequential presentation.

Experiment 3 examined the ameliorative influence of sequential presentation on foil-biased photoarrays. Staged thefts were performed in view of 120 undergraduates. During the same session subjects attempted identifications from thief-absent photoarrays. Photoarrays were either foil-biased (containing foils who minimally resembled the perpetrator) or foil-unbiased (containing foils who strongly resembled the perpetrator) and were presented either simultaneously or sequentially. As usual, false identifications occurred significantly more often among subjects shown simultaneously presented photoarrays (47%) than among subjects shown sequentially presented photoarrays (7%). Among subjects shown sequentially presented photoarrays, the false identification rate was identical for the foil-biased and foil-unbiased conditions. Among subjects shown simultaneously presented photoarrays, false identifications occurred more frequently in the foil-biased condition (53%) than in the foil-unbiased condition (40%), but this difference was not statistically significant. It appears that sequential presentation minimizes the influence of foil bias on identification performance.

Experiment 4 examined whether type of presentation reduces the influence of biased lineup instructions. As in the previous experiments, a theft was staged in view of 120 undergraduates. In the same session subjects attempted identification from eight-person, thief-absent, simultaneously or sequentially presented photoarrays. Within each presentation condition, subjects received either unbiased or biased instructions. The biased instructions were: "The guilty party is in the lineup, all you have to do is pick him out." The unbiased instructions were: "Remember, as in a real case, the guilty party may or may not be in the lineup." Overall, false identifications occurred significantly more often among subjects shown simultaneously presented photoarrays (23%) than among subjects shown sequentially presented photoarrays (8%). False identifications were also significantly more frequent among subjects who received biased instructions (33%) than among subjects who received unbiased instructions (13%). However, the influence of instructions was nonsignificant among subjects shown sequential presentation: Thirteen percent of these subjects who received biased instructions and 3% of these subjects who received unbiased instructions made false identifications. Thus, sequential presentation significantly reduces the impact of biased instructions.

Experiments 2, 3, and 4 demonstrated that sequential presentation reduces or eliminates clothing, foil, and instruction biases when they are individually present in an identification procedure. Experiment 5 tested whether sequential presentation could overcome the combined influence of these three biases. A theft was staged in front of 63 unsuspecting students who later attempted identifications from thief-absent photoarrays. All photoarrays contained the instruction, foil, and clothing biases previously described but were presented either sequentially or simultaneously. Among subjects shown the simultaneously presented biased photoarray, 84% made a false identification. Among subjects shown the sequentially presented biased photoarray, 25% made a false identification. Sequential presentation successfully reduced the combined impact of instruction, foil, and clothing biases.

Several other aspects of sequential presentation are noteworthy. Parker and Ryan (1993) examined whether sequential presentation reduces false identifications among child witnesses. A slide sequence depicting a theft was shown to 96 children (mean age, 9 years, 2 months; range, 8 years, 1 month to 11 years, 1 month) and 96 undergraduates. Later in the session subjects attempted identifications from six-person, thief-present or thief-absent photoarrays, presented simultaneously or sequentially. In addition, half of the subjects in each condition were given a practice identification

Table 8.3. *Witness performance as a function of lineup presentation*

Study	N	Correct IDs Target present		False IDs Target absent	
		Simul	Sequen	Simul	Sequen
Lindsay & Wells	243	.58	.50	.43	.17
Cutler & Penrod					
(Study 1)	175	.80	.76	.39	.19
(Study 2)	150	.41	.47	.43	.21
Lindsay, Lea, & Fulford					
(Study 1)	180	.57	.47	.20	.05
(Study 2) Second choices	32			.88	.28
(Study 3) Overall	254			.27	.13
Lindsay, et al.					
(Study 1)	120	.67	.77	.20	.03
(Study 2) Overall	180	.47	.57	.26	.04
(Study 3)	120			.47	.07
(Study 4)	120			.23	.08
(Study 5)	63			.84	.25
Parker & Ryan	192	.40	.29	.71	.46
Unweighted means		.56	.55	.53	.16

test in which they attempted to identify the experimenter from a three-person, experimenter-absent photoarray. Correct identification rate was not significantly influenced by any of the variables (40% for simultaneous arrays vs. 29% for sequential arrays). However, among subjects who did not participate in a practice trial, significantly fewer false identifications occurred among subjects shown sequential presentations (46%) than among subjects shown simultaneous presentations (71%). Most important, this pattern of results was not significantly qualified by age, indicating that sequential presentation had a comparably beneficial effect on identifications by children and adults. The practice trial significantly reduced errors in the simultaneous presentation condition (to 58%) and so reduced the relative benefit of sequential presentation.

The following conclusions can be drawn from the experiments reviewed in this chapter. As shown in Table 8.3, presentation style minimally influences identification performance when the target is present in the lineup or photoarray. However, when the target is not in the lineup or array, sequential presentation substantially reduces false identifications relative to simultaneous presentation. Sequential presentation is more effective if subjects do not know how many people are to appear in the photoarray or lineup and if the sequential presentation is not followed by a second-chance simultaneously-presented lineup. Sequential presentation reduces the separate and joint influences of clothing, foil, and instruction biases and appears to comparably influence identification performance among adults and children. The benefits of sequential presentation are somewhat lessened by the use of a target-absent practice trial – primarily because the use of the practice trial reduces false identifications in simultaneous presentations.

Investigator bias

Wells (1993; Wells & Luus, 1990) speculated that an investigator who knows which lineup member is the suspect can inadvertently (or advertently) bias the eyewitness through nonverbal behavior such as leaning forward, smiling, nodding, and so on. Wells and Luus (1990) observed that just as a good social psychological experiment requires that the experimenter with whom the subject interacts is blind to the experimental condition to which the subject has been randomly assigned, a good lineup test requires that the investigator conducting the test is blind to the identity of the suspect. Although no published data exist confirming that knowledge of the suspect influences subjects' decisions, Wells (personal communication, October 30, 1992) has reported unpublished data confirming this hypothesis. The hypothesis is also indirectly supported by an extensive literature on demand characteristics (Rosenthal, 1976). Thus, we refer to lineups in which the investigator knows the identity of the suspect as suggestive but we do so tentatively.

Summary

In conclusion, extensive empirical research documents the role of identification procedures on identification performance. A half dozen experimental studies of instruction bias involving more than a thousand participants clearly document the profound effect that biased instructions can have on false identification rates. A dozen studies involving more than 1,800 participants have compared the impact of sequential versus simultaneous presentations on identification performance. These studies clearly demonstrate that the traditional method of simultaneous presentation carries no benefit in terms of correct identifications when perpetrators are present in an array. On the other hand the traditional simultaneous method of presentation clearly fosters substantially more mistaken identifications when the perpetrator is not present in the array. Smaller numbers of studies have examined and documented the suggestive effects of foil and clothing biases on the identification performance. As a group these studies underscore that police identification practices can be (and certainly to the extent that simultaneous identification methods are in widespread use, *are*) an influential source of suggestion in identification procedures.

Part IV

Is the attorney an effective safeguard against mistaken identification?

9   Trial counsel, the eyewitness, and the defendant

A defense attorney, when defending a client in an identification case, has two major opportunities to assist his or her client's case. The first opportunity comes during jury selection, when, at least in theory, the attorney can try to identify jurors who may be skeptical about eyewitness identifications or at least thoughtfully critical in the appraisal of an identification. The second major opportunity comes in cross-examination of eyewitnesses, when, it is generally presumed by courts and commentators, the skillful attorney can expose the weaknesses of an identification. Can and do attorneys effectively use these tools? Fortunately, there is now research that can help us address these questions.

Voir dire as a safeguard

The primary purpose of voir dire is to identify and excuse potentially biased jurors (Wrightsman, Nietzel, & Fortune, 1993), thus protecting the defendant and the prosecution from an arbitrary verdict. In trials that include eyewitness testimony, the juror's role includes evaluating the credibility of eyewitnesses and the accuracy of their testimony (*United States v. Telfaire*, 1972). Thus, the fairness of the defendant's trial is partially dependent upon the ability and willingness of the jury to scrutinize and evaluate the eyewitness testimony. Prospective jurors may vary in their predispositions to trust eyewitnesses and hence their willingness to scrutinize them. Voir dire provides the opportunity for attorneys to screen prospective jurors for these predispositions. By exercising causal and/or peremptory challenges, attorneys can presumably eliminate prospective jurors who are believed to be unable or unwilling to scrutinize eyewitness testimony. If successful, this process should increase the chances that a verdict will result from careful consideration of all the elements of the evidence.

The effectiveness of voir dire depends upon the validity of the attorneys' jury selection strategies and the limits placed on the attorneys' strategies by the court. The safeguarding function of voir dire is compromised if the defense attorney uses an invalid jury selection strategy or if legally imposed restrictions on voir dire constrain the attorney from using a valid strategy. Little (if any) research has examined the voir dire strategies that attorneys use to assess jurors' potential reactions to eyewitness testimony. Considerable research has examined attorneys' voir dire strategies in other types of cases.

Fulero and Penrod (1990) comprehensively reviewed the psychological research on jury selection. Their review of trial practice manuals revealed a collection of advice about the use of juror's gender, age, race, religion, attitudes, occupation, social status, physical appearance, and other such characteristics as predictors of jurors' verdict inclinations. They concluded that the advice was frequently inconsistent and based on stereotypes that are not supported by the empirical literature on jury selection. Fulero and Penrod also reviewed studies of attorneys' actual jury selection tactics, focusing on the characteristics that attorneys are interested in, the types of jurors typically challenged by attorneys, the effectiveness of those challenges, and their impact on jury composition. They concluded that attorneys tend to be interested in characteristics that generate a profile, including most often the categories of age, occupation, demeanor, gender, appearance, and race. Several of these dimensions are vaguely defined, for example, appearance and demeanor, and most have shown little or no predictive relation with verdict. With respect to jurors who are actually challenged by attorneys, Fulero and Penrod found that attorneys tend to eliminate jurors based on simplistic profiles of dubious validity.

Fulero and Penrod (1990) concluded that general attitudes and demographics were weak predictors of juror verdicts. However, it is also possible to examine juror attitudes in a case-specific manner and there are sound reasons to believe that case-specific attitudes are more powerful predictors of juror verdicts than are general attitudes and demographic characteristics. Examples of findings from studies of case-specific predictors include the following: (a) attitudes toward the death penalty reliably correlate with verdicts in actual (Moran & Comfort, 1986) and simulated death penalty cases (Powers & Luginbuhl, 1987); (b) attitudes toward women predict verdicts in simulated rape trials (Wier & Wrightsman, 1990); (c) attitudes toward drugs predicted verdicts in a simulated controlled substance trial (Moran, Cutler, & Loftus, 1990) and (d) attitudes toward psychiatrists and the insanity defense predicted verdicts in a simulated insanity defense case (Cutler, Moran, & Narby, 1992). A recent meta-analysis (Narby, Cutler, & Moran, 1993) demonstrated pointedly that case-specific attitudes such as these are more strongly related to verdicts than are general attitudes. In the meta-analysis of 22 studies, legal authoritarianism correlated .19 with verdict, whereas traditional authoritarianism correlated .11. These findings suggest that the most effective voir dire for eyewitness cases would focus on case-specific attitudes, that is, attitudes toward eyewitnesses.

Table 9.1. *Attitudes toward eyewitness scale (Narby & Cutler, 1994)*

1. Eyewitness testimony is an important part of most trials.

2. Eyewitnesses are reliable witnesses.

3. Eyewitness testimony provides crucial evidence in trials.

4. Eyewitnesses frequently misidentify innocent people just because they seem familiar.

5. Eyewitnesses generally give accurate testimony in trials.

6. The strongest evidence is provided by eyewitnesses.

7. Eyewitnesses can usually be believed.

8. Eyewitness testimony is more like fact than opinion.

9. Eyewitnesses generally do not give accurate descriptions.

The effectiveness of voir dire as a safeguard in eyewitness cases rests on the assumption that case-specific attitudes can be reliably measured and can then be used to identify prospective jurors who differ in their willingness to scrutinize the testimony of eyewitnesses. Most of the existing research on individual differences in reactions to eyewitness testimony primarily addresses jurors' *abilities* to evaluate eyewitness testimony. These findings are reviewed in Chapters 11– 13. A study that is more directly relevant is that of Narby and Cutler (1994), who examined attitudes toward eyewitnesses and the implications of these attitudes for the effectiveness of voir dire as a safeguard in eyewitness cases. They first tested whether attitudes toward eyewitnesses can be reliably measured and, if so, whether these attitudes predict verdicts using trial simulation methodology.

Narby and Cutler constructed an attitude inventory to assess predispositions to believe eyewitness testimony. Analyses on data from 651 students and jury-eligible community residents (from South Florida) revealed that a nine-item version of the scale (the Attitudes Toward Eyewitness Scale or ATES) was sufficiently reliable for practical use (Coefficient Alpha, a standard index of internal consistency, was .80). The nine items in the scale appear in Table 9.1.

Two studies examined the correlation between the attitudes toward eyewitnesses' scale and the tendency to convict using a simulated jury trial.

It was expected that the more faith subjects had in eyewitness testimony (i.e., the higher their scores on the attitudes scale), the more likely they would be to convict. In one study 62 undergraduates and 46 community residents ($N = 108$), all of whom were eligible to be jurors, completed the attitudes scale, viewed the simulated trial, and rendered verdicts. The correlation between the attitudes scale (ATES) and verdict was nonsignificant ($r = .14$). This finding was replicated in a second study with 30 undergraduates and 27 community residents ($r = -.15$).

Thus, although attitudes toward eyewitnesses can be measured reliably, they do not appear to predict juror predispositions in eyewitness cases. It is conceivable that asking questions about eyewitnesses prior to the trial draws an unusual amount of attention to the testimony at trial. Narby (1993; cited in Narby & Cutler, 1994) addressed this issue in a follow-up study using the same stimulus materials and methodology as in the studies just described. Half of the subjects completed the ATES prior to the trial, and the other half completed it after the trial along with other dependent measures. Verdicts and culpability judgments were compared for subjects who were queried about their attitudes toward eyewitnesses ($N = 34$) versus subjects who were not so queried ($N = 35$) prior to the trial. The groups did not differ significantly on either dependent measure, suggesting that querying jurors about their attitudes toward eyewitnesses prior to the trial does not influence the weight given to eyewitness testimony.

The most likely explanation for the lack of a significant relation between attitudes toward eyewitnesses and verdicts in the trial simulations is jurors' lack of experience with eyewitnesses. Attitude-behavior relations can be expected to vary directly with the subjects' degree of experience with the attitudinal object (Fazio & Zanna, 1981). It may be that typical prospective jurors have had little or no experience with issues pertaining to eyewitness testimony. Expecting their pretrial attitudes to correlate with their posttrial verdicts may therefore be unrealistic. Narby's (1993) follow-up study provides some support for this contention. Attitudes toward eyewitnesses correlated significantly ($r = .41$) with verdict among subjects ($N = 35$) who completed the attitude inventory after viewing the trial and rendering their verdicts. Thus, subjects who experienced the eyewitness at trial showed a significant association between their verdicts and their attitudes toward eyewitnesses.

In sum, although case-specific attitudes may be the most successful class of predictors in studies of jury selection (Fulero & Penrod, 1990), it appears that some case-specific attitudes are weak predictors of perceptions of defendant culpability. Attitudes toward eyewitnesses may be one example, perhaps because of jurors' lack of experience with eyewitnesses. These findings suggest that, at best, attitudes toward eyewitnesses may predict verdict preferences only after jurors have had some trial experience. This may happen because jurors acquire information during the trial that changes or crystallizes jurors' attitudes toward eyewitnesses. It is also possible that attitudes are in fact more predictive of verdicts than these results indicate, as there may be other, more effective ways to measure attitudes toward eyewitnesses. As is true with most case-specific predictors of verdict choice, further investigation is necessary.

What are the implications of these findings with respect to jury selection as a safeguard in eyewitness cases? If case-specific attitudes best predict juror prejudice but attitudes toward eyewitnesses do not predict juror skepticism about eyewitness testimony, then voir dire may not be an effective method for identifying prospective jurors who might, because of their critical stance with respect to eyewitnesses, reduce the number of erroneous convictions resulting from mistaken eyewitness identifications.

Of course, even if these studies had produced a tool that could be used to identify jurors more or less inclined to trust eyewitness identifications, the effectiveness of voir dire may still be limited. Constraints placed on voir dire make it difficult and perhaps impossible for attorneys to obtain information on prospective jurors' attitudes toward eyewitnesses and, more generally, information on any case-specific attitudes. Cassell (1992) describes recent Supreme Court decisions that impose limits on the use of peremptory challenges. Federal courts often employ "minimal voir dire." Judges ask the questions and limit the attorneys' involvement in the process. The questions asked by the judge are superficial, soliciting information about demographic characteristics, occupation, and so on. Responses to questions asked in minimal voir dire tend not to be predictive of juror bias (Fulero & Penrod, 1990; Moran et al., 1990).

Cross-examination as a safeguard

Cross-examination is probably the most commonly relied-upon safeguard against mistaken conviction. It is a feature of almost every trial in which an eyewitness makes an identification. It is certainly more common than the use of expert testimony, which, as explained in Chapter 3, is often not admitted for the reason that cross-examination is thought to sufficiently safeguard the defendant against mistaken identification. Cross-examination is also more common than the specialized instructions about eyewitnesses that are sometimes given to jurors at the conclusion of a trial. In this chapter we address a fundamental question about cross-examination: How effective is cross-examination in exposing the factors that influence the encoding/storage of information at the time of the crime and influence the suggestibility of identification tests? We begin by reviewing the limitations imposed by the legal system on the attorney's ability to develop information for use during cross-examination. Following this we discuss research that empirically tests cross-examination as a safeguard. This section includes surveys of attorneys' knowledge about eyewitness memory.

In order for cross-examination to be effective, the following conditions must be met:

1. Attorneys must have an opportunity to identify the factors that are likely to have influenced an eyewitness's identification performance in a particular case.
2. Attorneys must be aware of the factors that influence eyewitness identification performance.
3. Judges and juries must be aware during the trial, and consider during deliberations, the factors that influence eyewitness identification performance.

The first condition pertains to the attorney's access to information necessary for cross-examination. What opportunity does the attorney have to learn about the viewing conditions at the scene of the crime and the conditions surrounding the identification test? In order for cross-examination to be effective, the attorney must have ample opportunity to develop a strategy for questioning.

The second condition requires that the attorney be knowledgeable about the psychology of eyewitness identification. In Chapters 6 and 7 we reviewed many of the witness, target, and situational factors that influence eyewitness identification performance. For the attorney to cross-examine an eyewitness, effectively he or she must know what factors to look for. Is it common for attorneys to question the eyewitness, during cross-examination, about the conditions under which the event was witnessed and the procedures used in the identification test? Undoubtedly, it is. But more to the point, do the questions asked by the attorney in fact reflect what is known in the psychological literature about the factors that influence identification accuracy? In other words, do attorneys ask about factors that are known to influence identification accuracy (e.g., the impact of disguise, weapon focus, lineup instructions, the manner in which lineup members are presented) while ignoring factors that are known not to predict identification accuracy (e.g., face recognition skills, training in witnessing, confidence)?

The third assumption pertains to the mechanisms available to the attorney for exposing relevant eyewitnessing information for the consideration of the judge and jury. Are there obstacles that make it difficult or impossible to ask the appropriate questions and expose the information necessary for effective evaluation of eyewitness identifications? Even if we assume that the attorney knows what questions to ask, has sufficient opportunity to develop a cross-examination strategy, and encounters no obstacles in asking the questions and obtaining answers from the eyewitness, we may still ask: What do the judge and/or jury do with the information exposed during cross-examination? Do they use it to evaluate intelligently the accuracy of the eyewitness's identification? Or do they ignore it? For cross-examination to be effective, the judge and/or jury must be motivated and able to use the information. In the remainder of this chapter, we review the evidence bearing on each of these conditions.

Typically, attorneys design their cross-examinations to address two classes of information: the conditions under which the event was witnessed and the manner in which the identification test was conducted. Naturally, defense attorneys are not present at the time of the crime, so information about the conditions under which the crime was witnessed must be obtained directly from the eyewitnesses or indirectly from the police who investigated the scene of the crime. The attorney generally has access to formal police reports and may also depose (or examine in pretrial hearings) investigators and eyewitnesses prior to the trial. Finally, attorneys may visit the crime scene and note physical factors that might affect an eyewitness's perception.

Clearly, most of the information used to formulate cross-examination is obtained second-hand from investigators and eyewitnesses and from the crime scene itself. Thus, the attorney's opportunity to develop information for use in cross-examination depends, to a large degree, on the quality of witnesses' memories and extent of cooperation of the investigators and eyewitnesses. For example, the attorney may ask the eyewitness about the length of time for which she viewed the perpetrator, her distance from the perpetrator, whether or not the perpetrator was disguised or had a weapon, and so forth. Of course, just as the eyewitness's memory for the crime and perpetrator may be distorted, so, too, might her memory for the conditions surrounding the event. Unfortunately, we know of no solution to this problem except to suggest that attorneys, whenever possible, rely on objective records for this information. For example, meteorological records may speak to visibility on a given day. Instead of asking an eyewitness to estimate her distance from the perpetrator, ask her to point out the locations and make a measurement. Instead of asking the eyewitness to estimate the time during which a perpetrator is visible, ask her to indicate the time by imagining it happening and saying "start" and "stop" when the perpetrator comes into view and leaves the scene. Although this system is imperfect, it is not clear if a more reliable method for obtaining information about the viewing conditions at the time of the crime exists.

Although the attorney is not present at the time of the crime, he or she may be present at the time of the identification test. Whether the attorney is or is not present at the identification test is sometimes a matter of law: Is the defendant (or suspect) guaranteed the right to counsel at identification tests? This question was addressed in a series of four U.S. Supreme Court cases decided between 1967 and 1973. We consider these cases at some length because they specify not only the circumstances under which counsel's presence at an identification procedure is required, but they also identify some of the difficulties (hotly debated by the justices in their opinions) that a defendant and counsel may encounter in developing information that might be used as a basis for later challenges to the fairness and suggestiveness of identification procedures.

Opportunity to develop information for cross-examination: The right to counsel at identification procedures

In 1967 the Court addressed the issue of whether a defendant's right to counsel during a lineup was guaranteed by the Sixth Amendment. Two cases, *United States v. Wade* and *Gilbert v. California*, hinged, in part, on the same issue and were heard by the Court simultaneously. *Wade* and *Gilbert* are given extensive treatment here because many legal assumptions about eyewitness behavior are laid bare in the majority and minority opinions of those decisions.

On September 21, 1964, a man with a small strip of tape on each side of his face entered a bank in Eustace, Texas, pointed a gun at the cashier and vice-president, and forced them to fill a pillowcase with the bank's money. The man then fled the bank and escaped with an accomplice in a stolen car. Billy Joe Wade and two others were indicted for the bank robbery on March 23, 1965. Wade was arrested on April 2, and counsel was appointed to represent him on April 26. Fifteen days after Wade was appointed counsel, an FBI agent arranged to have the two bank employees who witnessed the robbery view a lineup containing Wade and five or six other prisoners. The lineup was conducted in a courtroom of a local county courthouse. Each lineup member wore tape (as did the robber) and each spoke a line that was allegedly spoken at the robbery. Wade was identified by both bank employees. Wade's lawyer was not notified about and was absent from the lineup procedure.

During the trial, the two eyewitnesses identified Wade in court as the bank robber. On cross-examination, the eyewitnesses testified about the prior lineup. Wade's lawyer then moved for an acquittal or to strike the in-court identifications on the grounds that Wade's Sixth Amendment right was violated in that he was denied counsel during the lineup. The Sixth Amendment guarantees that in all criminal prosecutions the accused has the right to have assistance of counsel for his defense whenever necessary to assure a meaningful defense. (Wade also argued that the lineup violated his Fifth Amendment right against self-incrimination, but the court rejected this argument.)

The Supreme Court rejected the government's argument that the lineup represents a mechanical process associated with the gathering of evidence – akin to analyzing fingerprints, blood samples, and so forth – which do not invite the presence of counsel. Eyewitness identifications, argued the Court, present specific dangers that other forensic tests do not. Wrote Justice Brennan for the majority:

We think there are differences which preclude such stages being characterized as critical stages at which the accused has the right to the presence of his counsel. Knowledge of the techniques of science and technology is sufficiently available, and the variables in techniques few enough, that the accused has the opportunity for a meaningful confrontation of the Government's case at trial through the ordinary processes of cross-examination of the Government's expert witnesses and the presentation of the evidence of his own experts. (pp. 17 – 18)

Brennan noted that identification procedures pose particular problems for defendants:

the confrontation compelled by the State between the accused and the victim or witnesses to a crime to elicit identification evidence is peculiarly riddled with innumerable dangers and variable factors which might seriously, even crucially, derogate from a fair trial. The vagaries of eyewitness identification are well-known; the annals of criminal law are rife with instances of mistaken identification. . . .. A major factor contributing to the high incidence of miscarriage of justice from mistaken identification has been the degree of suggestion inherent in the manner in which the prosecution presents the suspect to witnesses for pretrial identification. . . . Suggestion can be created intentionally or unintentionally in many subtle ways. . . . And the dangers for the suspect are particularly grave when the witness's opportunity for observation was insubstantial, and thus his susceptibility to suggestion the greatest. (p. 10)

Justice Brennan argued that one purpose of having the counsel present at lineups is to monitor the fairness of the procedure, as the defendant himself cannot be expected to do so

[W]ith secret interrogations, there is serious difficulty in depicting what transpires at lineups and other forms of identification confrontations. . . . For the same reasons, *the defense can seldom reconstruct the manner and mode of lineup identification for judge or jury at trial.* Those participating in a lineup with the accused may often be police officers;. . .in any event, the participants' names are rarely recorded or divulged at trial. . . . The impediments to an objective observation are increased when the victim is the witness. Lineups are prevalent in rape and robbery prosecutions and present a particular hazard that a victim's understandable outrage may excite vengeful or spiteful motives. . . . In any event, *neither witnesses nor lineup participants are apt to be alert for conditions prejudicial to the suspect. And if they were, it would likely be of scant benefit to the suspect since neither witnesses nor lineup participants are likely to be schooled in the detection of suggestive influences. . . . Improper influences. . .may go undetected by a suspect, guilty or not,* who experiences the emotional tension which we might expect in one being confronted with potential accusers. . . . Even when he does observe abuse, if he has a criminal record he may be reluctant to take the stand and open up the admission of prior convictions. Moreover *any protestations by the suspect of the fairness of the lineup made at trial are likely to be in vain;. . .the jury's choice is between the accused's unsupported version and that of the police officers present. . . . In short, the accused's. . .inability effectively to reconstruct at trial any unfairness that occurred at the. . .lineup may deprive him of his only opportunity meaningfully to attack the credibility of the witness' courtroom identification.* (emphasis added) (p. 11)

Justice Brennan stated firmly that cross-examination proves ineffective as a safeguard against mistaken in-court identification when the in-court identifications have been strongly influenced by previous lineup identifications held in private:

Insofar as the accused's conviction may rest on a courtroom identification in fact the fruit of a suspect pretrial identification which the accused is helpless to subject to effective scrutiny at trial, the accused is deprived of that right of cross-examination which is an essential safeguard to his right to confront the witnesses against him. . . . And even though cross-examination is a precious safeguard to a fair trial, it cannot be viewed as an absolute. . .assurance of accuracy and reliability. Thus in the present context, where so many variables and pitfalls exist, the first line of defense must be the prevention of unfairness and the lessening of the hazards of eyewitness identification at the lineup itself. The trial which might determine the accused's fate may well not be that in the courtroom but that at the pretrial confrontation, with the State aligned against the accused, the witness the sole jury, and the accused unprotected against the overreaching, intentional or unintentional, and with little or no. . . effective appeal from the judgment there rendered by the witness – "that's the man." Since it appears that there is grave potential for prejudice, intentional or not, in the pretrial lineup, which may not be capable of reconstruction at trial, and since presence of counsel itself can often avert prejudice and assure a meaningful confrontation at trial. . .there can be. . .little doubt that for Wade the postindictment lineup was a critical stage of the prosecution at which he was "as much entitled to such aid (of counsel) as at the trial itself". . . . Thus both Wade and his counsel should have been notified of the impending lineup, and counsel's presence should have been a requisite to conduct of the lineup, absent an "intelligent waiver." (emphasis added) (p. 15)

The Court did not overturn Wade's conviction; rather, it decided that when this error occurs, the government must bear the burden of proving, beyond clear and convincing evidence, that the two identifications (the pretrial lineup and the in-court identifications) had an independent source. By independent source, the Court means that the government can point to some evidence that would support the strength of the in-court identification other than the prior identification of the defendant from the illegal lineup procedure. The majority proposed the following test:

[T]his test . . . requires consideration of various factors; for example, the prior opportunity to observe the alleged criminal act, the existence of any discrepancy between any pre-lineup description and the defendant's actual description, any identification prior to lineup of another person, the identification by picture of the defendant prior to the lineup, failure to identify the defendant on a prior occasion, and the lapse of time between the alleged act and the lineup identification. It is also relevant to consider those facts which, despite the absence of counsel, are disclosed concerning the conduct of the lineup. (p. 19)

The Court lacked the information to determine whether an independent source existed for the identification of Wade and sent the case back to the trial court for a hearing on this matter.

The same constitutional error applied to Wade's companion case, *Gilbert v. California.* Gilbert was convicted in the California Superior Court of robbing the Mutual Savings and Loan Association of Alhambra and the murder of a police officer who entered the bank while the robbery was in progress. During the penalty phase of the trial the jury recommended execution. Like Wade, Gilbert was forced to participate in a lineup. The lineup was conducted in a Los Angeles auditorium 16 days after Gilbert was indicted, and his attorney was not notified of nor present during the lineup procedure. Nearly 100 persons were in the audience, each of whom was an eyewitness to one of several robberies for which Gilbert was charged. The lineup members (10 to 13 prisoners) stood on the stage behind bright lights and a screen that prevented lineup members from seeing the witnesses. The lineup procedure was unusually elaborate, requiring each lineup member, when called by number, to step forward, turn in various directions, walk, put on or take off certain articles of clothing, answer certain questions, and repeat certain phrases uttered at the scene of the crime. In response to requests from several witnesses, Gilbert and two or three other lineup members repeated the procedure. Witnesses publicly called out numbers of lineup members they could identify and were allowed to speak to each other during the procedure.

During the trial and penalty phases, the defense attorney unsuccessfully moved to exclude twelve in-court identifications by witnesses who identified

Gilbert in the pretrial lineup (just described) in which Gilbert was forced to participate without the presence of counsel. Thus, the issue in Gilbert was identical to that of Wade, and the Court issued the same decision. Gilbert's conviction was vacated, and the case was sent back to the trial court. In order for the government to introduce the in-court identifications, it had to prove, beyond clear and convincing evidence, that the in-court identifications emerged from a source independent from the illegal pretrial lineup procedure. (One witness's in-court identification was permanently excluded for other constitutional reasons.)

It is critical for our analysis to consider, as well, the dissenting opinions of the Supreme Court justices concerning whether Wade's and Gilbert's Sixth Amendment rights were violated. Justices Douglas, Clark, Black, Fortas, and Chief Justice Warren concurred with Justice Brennan's opinion that the defendants' Sixth Amendment rights had been violated. Justice White, joined by Justices Harlan and Stewart, objected for a number of reasons. They regarded (p. 24) the government's burden of establishing "by clear and convincing proof that the testimony is not the fruit of the earlier identification made in the absence of defendant's counsel" as "probably impossible." They objected to a blanket ruling that designates all lineup identifications inadmissible if made in the absence of council. Argued Justice White:

The rule applies to any lineup, to any other techniques employed to produce an identification and a fortiori to a face-to-face encounter between the witness and the suspect alone, regardless of when the identification occurs, in time or place, and whether before or after indictment or information. It matters not how well the witness knows the suspect, whether the witness is the suspect's mother, brother, or long-time associate, and no matter how long or well the witness observed the perpetrator at the scene of the crime. The kidnap victim who has. . .lived for days with his abductor is in the same category as the witness who has had only a fleeting glimpse of the criminal. Neither may identify the suspect without defendant's counsel being present. The same strictures apply regardless of the number of other witnesses who positively identify the defendant and regardless of the corroborative evidence showing that it was the defendant who had committed the crime. (p. 24)

Another basis for Justice White's dissent was the majority's assumption that police and prosecutorial misconduct in identification procedures is widespread:

The premise for the Court's rule is not the general unreliability of eyewitness identifications nor the difficulties inherent in observation, recall, and recognition. The Court assumes a narrower evil as the basis for its rule – improper police suggestion which contributes to erroneous identifications. The Court apparently believes that improper police procedures are so widespread that a broad prophylactic rule must be laid down, requiring the presence of counsel at all pretrial identifications, in. . .order to detect recurring instances of police misconduct. . . . I do not share this pervasive distrust of all official investigations. None of the materials the Court relies upon supports it. . . .. Certainly, I would bow to solid fact, but the Court quite obviously does not have before it any reliable, comprehensive survey of current police practices on which to base its new rule. Until it does, the Court should avoid excluding relevant evidence from state criminal trials. (p. 24)

Justice White also questioned whether biases associated with pretrial identification procedures in fact lead to erroneous as opposed to correct identifications and whether such biases are, in fact, discoverable without counsel present at the identification test in question:

To find the lineup a "critical" stage of the proceeding and to exclude identifications made in the absence of counsel, the Court must also assume that police "suggestion," if it occurs at all, leads to erroneous rather than accurate identifications and that reprehensible police conduct will have an unavoidable and largely undiscoverable impact on the trial. This in turn assumes that there is now no adequate source from which defense counsel can learn about the circumstances of the pretrial identification in order to place before the jury all of the considerations which should enter into an appraisal of courtroom identification. . .evidence. But these are treacherous and unsupported assumptions. . .resting as they do. . .on the notion that the defendant will not be aware, that the police and the witnesses will forget or prevaricate, that defense counsel will be unable to bring out the truth and that neither jury, judge, nor appellate court is a sufficient safeguard against unacceptable police conduct occurring at a pretrial identification procedure. I am unable to share the Court's view of the willingness of the police and the ordinary citizen witness to dissemble, either with respect to the identification of the defendant or with respect to the circumstances surrounding a pretrial identification. (p. 25)

Justice White raised three additional objections to the majority's reasoning. First, White questioned why, if the majority is concerned with the suggestibility of identification procedures, does it not ban in-court identifications where there have been no previous identifications in the presence of police and when it is known that the defendant is charged with a crime? Second, the majority argued that legislative standards could satisfactorily replace the right to counsel at identification tests, but why does the Court not draft such standards? Third, the majority's decision made inadmissible in-court identifications when other records of procedures used in prior identification tests conducted in the absence of counsel exist. Other records might be photographs, videotapes, audiorecordings, and so forth. Justice White concluded his dissent by stressing that erroneous convictions are more likely to be the product of inherent problems with eyewitness identification evidence and are less likely to be the product of police indiscretion:

I share the Court's view that the criminal trial, at the very least, should aim at truthful factfinding, including accurate eyewitness identifications. I doubt, however, on the basis of our present information, that the tragic mistakes which have occurred in criminal trials are as much the product of improper police conduct as they are the consequence of the difficulties inherent in eyewitness testimony and in resolving evidentiary conflicts by court or jury. I doubt that the Court's new rule will obviate these difficulties, or that the situation will be measurably improved by inserting defense counsel into the investigative processes of police departments everywhere. (p. 26)

Limits on the right to counsel at identification procedures

Three other cases in the late 1960s and early 1970s further defined the scope of the defendant's rights during an identification procedure. In *Stovall v. Denno* (1967), the defendant was convicted of murder after having been brought, in handcuffs and without counsel, to a hospital room so that a dying eyewitness could identify him. The Court acknowledged the suggestiveness of the showup procedure and weighed it against the exigent circumstances (the witness was in no position to attend a live lineup at the police station) and decided that the defendant's Fourteenth Amendment right to due process was not violated. Further, the Court decided that the *Wade* and *Gilbert* decisions would apply only prospectively and therefore the defendant's Fifth and Sixth Amendment rights were not violated.

The issue in *Kirby v. Illinois* (1972) was whether the exclusionary rule devised in *Wade* and *Gilbert* applied to preindictment identification tests. The majority held that the rule does not apply to identification tests conducted prior to a defendant's indictment. The majority opinion focused on the historical context surrounding the right to counsel and when that right emerges. In dissent, Justice Brennan, joined by Justices Douglas and Marshall, argued that because the dangers faced by Wade and Gilbert also applied to the defendants in *Kirby*, they, too, should have the right to counsel during lineups, even though the lineups were conducted prior to indictment.

In *United States v. Ash* (1973), two men were charged with robbing a bank in Washington, D.C. Acting on a tip from a government informant, an FBI agent presented four witnesses with a photoarray that included a picture of Ash. This identification was made prior to any indictment. All four made uncertain identifications of Ash's picture. Three years later, just before Ash's trial, the prosecutor, in determining which witnesses he planned to call, decided to show them a photoarray to determine which ones would be able to identify Ash in court. An FBI agent and the prosecutor showed a photoarray containing pictures of five persons to the four witnesses who had identified Ash from the prior photoarray. Three of the four again identified Ash, and the fourth was unable to make an identification. Ash challenged the second (postindictment) photoarray identifications as a violation of his Sixth Amendment right to counsel under *Wade*. The motion was denied, and Ash was convicted. The government argued that the defendant does not participate in a photoarray, and his lack of counsel therefore does not threaten his right to a fair trial. The government also argued that the risks associated with the photoarray were trivial:

[W]hile the opinion in Wade spoke of the danger of suggestion at lineups being present "in many subtle ways," which may not be capable of reconstruction at trial, only '[t]hree types of suggestion' have been mentioned as possible during photographic displays: (1) the type of photographs used, i.e., if the photo of the defendant is markedly different from the others; (2) the manner in which the photographs are spread out or handed to the witness; and (3) suggestive comments or gestures by law enforcement agencies . . . (Brief for Petitioner, No. 71-1255, pp. 15 – 16).

Justice Blackmun, writing for the majority, rejected the notion that a photoarray was functionally equivalent to a live lineup. Blackmun opined that the historical purpose of having counsel present is to provide the accused "aid in coping with legal problems or assistance in meeting his adversary." The absence of the defendant from a photoarray prevents the accused from being misled or overpowered by his adversary. The right to counsel granted in *Wade*, therefore, does not extend to photoarrays. Justice Stewart, who concurred with the majority, further noted that although suggestive procedures are possible with photoarrays, those improper procedures can be reconstructed at trial:

A photographic identification is quite different from a lineup, for there are substantially fewer possibilities of impermissible suggestion when photographs are used, and those unfair influences can be readily reconstructed at trial. *It is true that the defendant's photograph may be markedly different from the others displayed, but this unfairness can be demonstrated at trial from an actual comparison of the photographs used or from the witness's description of the display. Similarly, it is possible that the photographs could be arranged in a suggestive manner, or that by comment or gesture the prosecuting authorities might single out the defendant's picture. But these are the kinds of overt influence that a witness can easily recount and that would serve to impeach the identification testimony.* In short, there are few possibilities for. . .unfair suggestiveness – and those rather blatant and easily reconstructed. Accordingly, an accused would not be foreclosed from an effective cross-examination of an identification witness simply because his counsel was not present at the photographic display. For this reason, a photographic display cannot fairly be considered a "critical stage" of the prosecution. (emphasis added) (pp. 39 – 40)

Justice Brennan, joined in his dissent by Justices Douglas and Marshall, took a rather different view of the dangers posed by photographic identification procedures conducted without the presence of defense counsel. The dissenters noted with approval an English rule disfavoring the use of photographic arrays:

Indeed, recognizing the superiority of corporeal to photographic identifications, English courts have long held that once the accused is in custody, pre-lineup photographic identification is "indefensible" and grounds for quashing the conviction. *Rex v. Haslam*, 19 Crim. App. Rep. 59, 60 (1925). . .(p. 54)

The dissenters also noted a set of dangers identified by Patrick Wall in a 1965 volume that anticipated a number of the research findings reviewed in Chapter 8 – in particular, problems of foil/clothing bias, presentation bias, and instruction/investigator bias:

Moreover, as in the lineup situation, the possibilities for impermissible suggestion in the context of a photographic display are manifold. . . . Such suggestion, intentional or unintentional, may derive from three possible sources. First, the photographs themselves might tend to suggest which of the pictures is that of the suspect. For example, differences in age, pose, or other physical characteristics of the persons represented, and variations in the mounting, background, lighting, or markings of the photographs all might have the effect of singling out the accused. . . . Second, impermissible suggestion may inhere in the manner in which the photographs are displayed to the witness. The danger of misidentification is, of course, "increased if the police display to the witness. . .the pictures of several persons among which the photograph of a single such individual recurs or is in some way emphasized." [Wall, 1965, p. 71]. And, if the photographs are arranged in an asymmetrical pattern, or if they are displayed in a time sequence that tends to emphasize a particular photograph, "any identification of the photograph which stands out from the rest is no more reliable than an identification of a single photograph, exhibited alone." [P. Wall, supra, at 81]. Third, gestures or comments of the prosecutor at the time of the display may lead an otherwise uncertain witness to select the "correct" photograph. For example, the prosecutor might "indicate to the witness that [he has] other evidence that one of the persons pictured committed the crime,". . .and might even point to a particular photograph and ask whether the person pictured "looks familiar." More subtly, the prosecutor's inflection, facial expressions, physical motions, and myriad other almost imperceptible means of communication might tend, intentionally or unintentionally, to compromise the witness's objectivity. Thus, as is the case with lineups, "improper photographic identification procedures,. . .by. exerting a suggestive influence upon the witnesses, can often lead to an erroneous identification". . . . P. Wall, supra, at 89. (pp. 54 – 56)

The dissenters were also not persuaded that a photographic record of the identification procedure afforded a defendant much protection – particularly with respect to investigator and instruction biases:

It is true, of course, that the photographs used at the pretrial display might be preserved for examination at trial. But "it may also be said that a photograph can preserve the record of a lineup; yet this does not justify a lineup without counsel". . . . Indeed, in reality, preservation of the photographs affords little protection to the unrepresented accused. For, although retention of the photographs may mitigate the dangers of misidentification due to the suggestiveness of the photographs themselves, it cannot in any sense reveal to defense counsel the more subtle, and therefore more dangerous, suggestiveness that might derive from the manner in which the photographs were displayed or any accompanying comments or gestures. Moreover, the accused cannot rely upon the witnesses themselves to expose these latter sources of suggestion, for the witnesses are not "apt to be alert for conditions prejudicial to the suspect. And if they were, it would likely be of scant benefit to the suspect" since the witnesses are hardly "likely to be schooled in the detection of suggestive influences." [Wade at 230.] Finally, and unlike the lineup situation, the accused himself is not even present at the photographic identification, thereby reducing the likelihood that irregularities in the procedures will ever come to light. (pp. 57 – 58)

In summary, the six cases reviewed here broadly define the scope of the defendant's right to counsel during identification tests. Defendants have the right to counsel at any postindictment live lineup. They do not have the right to counsel at preindictment live lineups nor at photoarrays at any stage of the investigation (assuming that the defendant is physically absent from the photoarray identification procedure). These six cases are important not only because they define the defendant's rights but because they also expose a number of assumptions about eyewitness and police behavior. Some of these assumptions concern psychological factors that influence eyewitness testimony. Other assumptions pertain to normative police practices. Most of these assumptions can, in fact, be tested empirically and, as we saw in preceding chapters on the factors that influence eyewitness reliability and will see in later chapters examining courtroom decision making about eyewitness identifications, a number have been subjected to such scrutiny.

These decisions speak most directly to the attorney's opportunity and ability to develop information that will be useful during trial and especially during cross-examination. It is clear from these opinions that most justices clearly *presume* that defense attorneys know about threats to fairness and suggestivity and the primary battle has been waged over the question of when attorneys should or need to be present at identification procedures in order to make most effective use of their knowledge.

As we have noted with respect to the conditions surrounding the crime, the attorney must rely on the eyewitness's and police officer's memories (perhaps as recorded in written reports). A different set of issues emerges with respect to the opportunity to develop information about suggestive identification tests. Unlike viewing conditions at the time of the crime, the attorney, in theory, can be present to scrutinize the procedures him- or herself. Defendants do have a right to counsel, but only at postindictment, live lineups. At least in these situations attorneys have the opportunity to witness the identification procedures, to note any suggestive procedures that take place (assuming that the attorney recognizes suggestive procedures), and may have an opportunity to influence the manner in which the identification procedure is conducted.

In practice, how frequently do defense attorneys attend identification tests involving their clients? Brigham and Wolfskeil's (1983) survey of Florida prosecutors, defense attorneys, and police officers (see Chapter 10 for details) addresses this question. The Florida Rules of Criminal Procedure require that an arrested person have a "first appearance" before an officer of the Circuit Court within 24 hours of the arrest. The purpose of the first appearance is to inform arrested persons of the nature of the charge(s), provide them with a copy of the complaint, and advise them of their legal rights. All attorneys reported that an attorney is seldom present at live lineups conducted prior to the first appearance. They reported that an attorney is usually present at live lineups conducted after first appearance. Most attorneys reported that an attorney is never present during photoarrays conducted prior to first appearance and seldom present at photoarrays conducted after first appearance. These findings raise serious questions about the attorney's opportunity to develop information for cross-examination in the vast majority of identification proceedings.

When identification tests take place without the attorney present, his or her opportunity to identify suggestive identification procedures is limited. At the very least the attorney is forced to rely on the recollections of the defendant, eyewitness, and police officers to describe what occurred. Memory is fallible. Police officers may not be particularly motivated to admit to suggestive identification procedures even if the suggestion arises by accident. The extent to which eyewitnesses accurately recall various aspects of identification tests is an empirical question that has not yet been examined (though experience indicates that witnesses often recall very little about what was said prior to and during such procedures and often remember little about the composition of arrays from which they have made identifications or about the verbal communications made at the time the identification procedure was conducted). Furthermore, there are other problems with relying on the defendant's account of the identification test procedure. Having the defendant testify about the identification procedure opens the door for the prosecuting attorney to introduce prior convictions, possibly damaging to the defendant's credibility. As noted in Justice Brennan's opinion in *Wade*, even if the defendant testifies, any discrepancies in accounts regarding what transpired during the identification test are likely to reduce to the defendant's word against the police officer's and the court is likely to side with the latter.

At various points in these opinions justices note that records can be kept of identification procedures. Most of their discussions concern photographic (and in contemporary terms, we presume we could include videotape) records. Although such records do permit better defense counsel insights into some of the identification problems highlighted in Chapter 8 – particularly problems such as foil and clothing biases, and to a lesser extent, presentation biases – photographic and videotaped records typically will not reveal the full array of problems associated with instruction and investigator biases. Although it is beyond the scope of this volume to consider the ways in which the recording of identification procedures might be broadened to permit better insights into instruction and investigator biases, it might be noted that the majority in *Wade* appeared to anticipate that better record keeping by law enforcement officers might offset the need for counsel to be present even at postindictment procedures: As Justice Blackmun observed in *Ash*:

The structure of Wade, viewed in light of the careful limitation of the Court's language to "confrontations,". . .makes it clear that lack of scientific precision and inability to reconstruct an event are not the tests for requiring counsel in the first instance. These are, instead, the tests to determine whether confrontation with counsel at trial can serve as a substitute for counsel at the pretrial confrontation. If accurate reconstruction is possible, the risks inherent in any confrontation still remain, but the opportunity to cure defects at trial causes the confrontation to cease to be "critical." The opinion of the Court even indicated that changes in procedure might cause a lineup to cease to be a "critical" confrontation: "Legislative or other regulations, such as those of local police departments, which eliminate the risks of abuse and unintentional suggestion at lineup proceedings and the impediments to' meaningful confrontation at trial may also remove the basis for regarding the stage as 'critical.'" 388 U.S., at 239. (p. 24)

In sum, one of the weakest links in the argument in favor of cross-examination as an adequate safeguard against mistaken conviction is the assumption that defense attorneys have adequate opportunities to develop the information required for an effective trial strategy. The attorney must rely on the police to ask the right questions concerning viewing conditions at the scene of the crime and to note the eyewitness's answers accurately. Of course, the investigating officers must, in turn, rely on the eyewitness to report the viewing conditions accurately. Furthermore, the attorney is frequently absent from identification tests (not by choice) – particularly photoarrays and identifications conducted at early stages of investigation.

In such cases, the attorney must, once again, rely on the eyewitness, police officer, and defendant to report any suggestive elements of an identification test.

10 Attorney sensitivity to factors that influence eyewitness identification accuracy

In this chapter we address the question of whether attorneys know the right questions to ask about the conditions under which the crime was witnessed, the events that occurred between the time of the crime and the identification test, and the manner in which the identification test was conducted. With the exception of the few attorneys who have been schooled in cognitive and social psychology, there is no reason to expect attorneys to keep up with psychological literature, even that bearing on eyewitnesses. Attorneys have enough difficulty keeping up with legal literature bearing directly on their day-to-day practices. Are attorneys sensitive to the factors affecting the encoding and storage of information as well as to factors affecting the suggestivity of identification tests?

General experience and knowledge surveys

In an attempt to address the issue of attorney sensitivity, several researchers have conducted surveys of practicing attorneys to determine if their knowledge about the factors that influence eyewitness identification accuracy conforms with what is known in the psychological literature. The Brigham and Wolfskeil (1983) study noted in the last chapter is one such survey. In response to a general mailing, they obtained completed survey responses from 89 public defenders, 69 state prosecutors, and 77 private defense attorneys throughout Florida. The survey was designed to ascertain the following about the respondents': (a) general background characteristics; (b) knowledge of legal procedures concerning eyewitness evidence; (c) estimates of the frequency of mistaken eyewitness identifications; (d) knowledge of factors that influence eyewitness identification accuracy; and (e) opinions about the weight that judges and jurors give to eyewitness evidence.

Most attorneys reported being involved with eyewitnesses less than once per week, though prosecutors reported more frequent involvement than did defense attorneys. Photoarrays were more commonly encountered than lineups; they were experienced at least once a week by 59% of prosecutors and 25% of defense attorneys. Live lineups, in contrast, were encountered at least once per week by 23% of prosecutors and 9% of defense attorneys.

When asked about the accuracy of eyewitness identifications, significantly more prosecutors (84%) than defense attorneys (36%) felt that "90% or more" of identifications are probably correct. Most defense attorneys (58%) thought that between 50% and 75% of identifications are correct. When asked what kinds of errors are most common in identification tests, prosecutors and defense attorneys differed significantly once again. More prosecutors (at least 75%) than defense attorneys (56%) felt that eyewitnesses more commonly fail to identify guilty suspects than falsely identify innocent ones. In contrast, 34% of defense attorneys felt that false identifications were more common than failures to identify guilty suspects.

The survey also contained questions, most relevant to the current concerns about factors that may be perceived to influence identification accuracy. Attorneys were asked four separate questions about cross-race recognition (one question pertaining to each pair of witnesses/suspects: (white/white, black/black, black/white, and white/black). Specifically, attorneys were asked whether, for each pair, 90% of identifications of that type are likely to be accurate. Although defense attorneys believed all identifications to be less accurate than prosecutors did, the pattern of beliefs about cross-race identifications was similar for the two types of attorneys. Ninety percent of prosecutors believed that white witness/white suspect identifications were 90% or more often correct. The corresponding percentages for black/black, black/white, and white/black witness/suspect pairs were: 94%, 81%, and 75%, respectively. The corresponding percentages among defense attorneys were: 46%, 47%, 31%, and 17%. Thus, consistent with the empirical literature on eyewitness identification, both groups of attorneys believed cross-race identifications to be less accurate than same-race identifications even though their estimates of the overall accuracy rates differed markedly.

Prosecutors and defense attorneys tended to agree with each other on the influence of sex, education, and intelligence on identification accuracy. With respect to sex, 61% thought that males and females would perform comparably on identification tests. Most (60% of prosecutors and 63% of defense attorneys) thought that intelligent witnesses were more likely to be accurate. Most also thought that education was not related to identification accuracy. Attorney beliefs are consistent with the psychological literature on sex and education, but, as noted in Chapter 6, there is little empirical evidence supporting the relation between intelligence and identification accuracy endorsed by the majority of attorneys.

Attorneys were also asked, in open-ended format, what factors they believed to be related to identification accuracy. The 10 characteristics most frequently mentioned by defense attorneys (and the percentage of attorneys who mentioned the characteristics) were:

- physical characteristics of the suspect (60%);
- lighting at the scene of the crime (39%);
- exposure duration during the crime (36%);
- proximity to the suspect at the crime (34%);
- physical appearance of the suspect's body (33%);
- the witness's temperament (26%);
- the witness's opportunity to view the suspect at the scene of the crime (22%);
- the witness's education/intelligence (22%);
- whether or not the witness has a good memory (22%); and
- whether the witness was calm or nervous (20%).

The 10 most common characteristics mentioned by prosecutors were:

- physical characteristics of the suspect (68%);
- lighting at the scene of the crime (60%);
- exposure duration during the crime (52%);
- whether or not the witness has a good memory (32%);
- physical appearance of the suspect's body (32%);
- whether the witness was calm or nervous (24%);
- physical characteristics of the suspect's face (24%);
- the suspect's speech/voice (24%);
- the witness's education/intelligence (21%); and
- proximity to the suspect at the crime (21%).

Most of these factors (lighting, opportunity to view the suspect at the scene of the crime, proximity of the suspect, exposure duration) are indeed potentially important factors, as explained in Chapter 7. The physical characteristics of the suspect might refer to distinctiveness of appearance, which is also a reliable predictor of identification accuracy. Research is less clear with respect to the role of memory skills. As we noted in Chapter 6, there is some evidence that face recognition skills, as measured objectively (i.e., by having subjects participate in a face recognition test multiple times), is predictive of subsequent identification accuracy. But self-reports of face recognition accuracy appear not to be associated with identification accuracy. Intelligence, personality, and education appear to be unrelated to identification accuracy.

Based on the attorneys' responses to this open-ended question, we generally conclude that, on balance, the factors mentioned by attorneys tend to be predictive of identification accuracy. But what of factors not mentioned by the attorneys? Potentially important factors such as weapon focus, disguises, changes in facial features, cross-race recognition, retention interval, and all of the factors associated with suggestivity of identification tests described in Chapter 8 did not rank on the attorneys' "top 10" lists. It is possible that these factors present themselves with sufficient rarity that attorneys do not think of them or think they are less important than those mentioned.

It is notable that there is wide variability among defense and prosecuting attorneys concerning the top 10 factors. Across the two lists only two factors ("physical characteristics of the suspect" and "lighting at the scene of the crime") were mentioned by a majority of the respondents. Whatever the explanation for the absence of important factors from the "top 10" lists, these survey data only moderately support the notion that attorneys know what questions to ask. Perhaps if they were asked to list the 20 most important factors, more support for sensitivity would have been obtained via the open-ended question.

Attorneys also differed significantly with respect to their views on the usefulness of witness confidence: Seventy-five percent of prosecutors but 40% of defense attorneys believed that witnesses who are more confident are more likely to be accurate. It is difficult to know how to evaluate these data. On the one hand, as noted in Chapter 6, the empirical literature indicates that witnesses who are more confident are more likely to be accurate, though only moderately so. The question asked by Brigham and Wolfskeil did not permit attorneys to indicate their understanding of the *strength* of the relation between confidence and accuracy. Furthermore, the eyewitness research pertains to confidence as measured immediately after identification accuracy and in the general absence of other social influence factors. As discussed in Chapter 6, the confidence level expressed on the witness stand may be influenced by a variety of other factors that can reduce the validity of confidence as a predictor of identification accuracy. The question asked by Brigham and Wolfskeil did not specify what attorneys should assume about how confidence is assessed.

Attorneys also differed in their views of the role of arousal. Significantly fewer prosecutors (31%) than defense attorneys (81%) agreed that arousal was inversely related to identification performance. As noted in Chapter 6, the empirical research is somewhat unclear on the relation between arousal and identification accuracy.

Other survey questions pertained to perceptions of how eyewitness testimony is used in court. When asked about how much weight judges and juries accord eyewitness evidence, 89% of defense attorneys and 7% of prosecutors indicated "too much" whereas 11% of defense attorneys and

87% of prosecutors indicated "the right amount." Predictably, defense attorneys were significantly more favorable than prosecutors toward expert psychological testimony on eyewitness identification. When asked whether "a psychologist's expert opinion should be considered in court when deciding the reliability of eyewitness identification," 11% of defense attorneys replied "never", 30% replied "rarely or only in unusual cases," 32% replied "fairly often," and 27% replied "routinely." The corresponding percentages for prosecutors were, respectively: 55%, 45%, 0%, and 0%.

The results of Brigham and Wolfskeil's survey suggest that attorneys are knowledgeable about some factors that influence eyewitness identification accuracy but less so about others and that there is little consensus among attorneys about the relative importance of the various factors about which they display some knowledge. Of course, it is impossible, on the basis of this survey, to determine whether attorneys do, in fact, detect the problems they have identified here (and/or problems that do not make the "top 10" lists) when those problems present themselves in actual cases.

Rahaim and Brodsky (1982) also conducted a survey that tested attorneys' knowledge of factors that influence eyewitness identification accuracy. Respondents in their survey were 42 practicing lawyers (presumably from Alabama, where the study was conducted). Five questions concerned the influence of race of witness and target, four concerned the influence of stress/violence, and one concerned the relation between confidence and identification accuracy. One item (Item 6) concerned memory for details and is therefore not reviewed below. Nine of the questions were forced choice, each having four alternative answers. The question concerning confidence and accuracy was true/false. The items concerning race are reviewed first, followed by the items addressing stress/violence, and then followed by the confidence item. Responses are summarized in Table 10.1.

Item 1 stated:

Two women are walking to school one morning, one of them an Asian and the other white. Suddenly, two men, one black and one white, jump into their path and attempt to grab their purses. Later, the women are shown photographs of known purse snatchers in the area. Which statement describes your view of the women's ability to identify the purse snatchers?

The answer scored as correct was: "The white woman will find the black man more difficult to identify than the white man." It was chosen by 58% of the attorneys.

Item 3 stated:

Two white men are held up by a black man on their way home from work. One of the victims hates blacks and the other neither hates nor loves blacks. In your view which victim will find it easier to identify the hold-up man?

The answer scored as correct was: "Both victims will have the same ability to identify the black hold-up man." This answer was chosen by 73% of the attorneys.

Item 5 stated:

Two black men are robbed by a white man on their way to a ball game. One of the black men grew up around whites and has several white friends. The other black man has had almost no contact with whites. Which statement below best describes your view of the abilities of the men to identify the robber?

The answer scored as correct was: "They will have the same amount of difficulty recognizing the robber." This answer was selected by 16% of the attorneys. In contrast, 71% chose the following response (which was scored as incorrect): "The victim who has white friends will recognize the robber more easily."

Item 7 stated:

A white man observes an Oriental woman and a black woman hold up a grocery store. Which statement best describes your view of his ability to recognize the criminals?

The answer scored as correct was: "He will recognize the Oriental woman more easily than the black woman." This answer was selected by 13% of the attorneys, and 60% selected the following incorrect answer: "It will depend upon whether he is usually around blacks or Orientals."

Item 9 stated:

A Chinese American man is robbed by a white man and a black man. Which statement below best describes your view of his ability to identify the robbers?

The answer scored as correct was: "He will find it easier to identify the black robber." This answer was given by 47% of the attorneys.

In summary, attorneys appear generally sensitive to the difficulty of cross-race recognitions but appear less knowledgeable about the role of experience in cross-race recognition. The notion that people who have more experience with members of another race are better able to recognize members of that race is intuitively plausible but has only weak empirical support.

Table 10.1. *Attorney knowledge of eyewitness factors*

Item	factor	Percentage scored as correct
1	Cross-race recognition	58%
3	Cross-race recognition	73%
5	Cross-race recognition	16%
7	Cross-race recognition	13%
9	Cross-race recognition	47%
2	Stress/violence	73%
4	Stress/violence	60%
8	Stress/violence	47%
10	Confidence	0%

Note: from Rahaim and Brodsky (1982)

The following four items pertain to the effects of stress and violence.

Item 2 stated:

Two people have witnessed a bank robbery. For some reason one of them felt extremely afraid while the other was not afraid. They both viewed the same robbery for the same amount of time. Which statement below best describes your view of these people's ability to later recognize the robbery?

The answer scored as correct was: "The unafraid person will recognize the robber more easily." This answer was selected by 73% of the attorneys.

Item 4 stated:

Suppose that two women were robbed. One was robbed at gunpoint, the other was robbed by an unarmed person. The crimes took the same amount of time. Which statement below best describes your view of these people's ability to recognize the criminal who robbed her?

The answer scored as correct was: "The woman who was the victim of the unarmed robbery will find it easier to recognize her robber." This answer was chosen by 60% of the attorneys.

Item 8 stated:

Two women have been raped by the same man. Both women had equal opportunity to view the rapist. One woman was the victim of a violent and brutal attack while the other victim's experience was not so violent. Which statement below best describes your view of the victim's abilities to identify the rapist?

The answer scored as correct was: "The victim of the less violent rape will find it easier to identify her attacker." This answer was selected by 47% of the attorneys. In contrast, 22% chose the answer: "The victim of the more violent rape will find it easier to identify her attacker."

In summary, the majority of attorneys who participated in this study tended to believe that violence leads to less accurate identifications, which is what psychologists tend to believe also (Kassin, Ellsworth, & Smith, 1989).

Finally, with respect to witness confidence, respondents were asked whether the following statement was true or false:

If an eyewitness to a crime is very confident they have identified the criminal they are most likely to be correctly identifying the criminal.

False was scored as correct, though no attorney chose this answer. Instead, 64% chose true. It is difficult to interpret these data, as the respondents' answers may be influenced more by their beliefs about the overall identification accuracy rate than by their beliefs about confidence. Thus, as in Brigham and Wolfskeil's survey, the wording of the confidence item makes it difficult accurately to assess attorney knowledge about the relationship between confidence and accuracy.

In summary, the two studies that assess attorney sensitivity to the factors that influence eyewitness identification accuracy show that attorneys tend to be sensitive to some factors and less sensitive to others. Furthermore, these studies reveal substantial confusion about the influence of a number of factors – the only time more than 75% of the attorneys agreed about any factor, it was about the confidence-accuracy relationship and the question used by the researchers does not permit easy interpretation of what this agreement means. For most questions there is substantial disagreement among attorneys about the influence of particular factors. Unfortunately methodological and conceptual shortcomings of the existing studies impose some limitations on our conclusions. The surveys were completed prior to the publication of most major integrative reviews of the eyewitness literature (e.g., Shapiro & Penrod, 1986) and prior to publication of many recent empirical studies. Thus, it is perhaps not surprising that knowledge about the factors examined in the surveys does not fully reflect what is currently represented in the eyewitness literature.

Further research on attorney sensitivity should examine knowledge of a broader base of factors, including factors that influence the encoding and storage of information as well as factors affecting the suggestivity of identification procedures. Indeed, neither of the existing studies investigated attorney sensitivity to factors affecting suggestivity. Further research should also employ methods that will permit assessment of attorney sensitivity to eyewitnessing factors in actual cases or analogues to actual cases. It is easy to "say," for example, that cross-race identifications are inferior to same-race identifications, but it may be more difficult to "detect" a cross-racial identification problem in actual cases.

Conclusion

At the outset of the chapter we noted that in order for cross-examination to be effective, the following conditions must be met:

1. Attorneys must have an opportunity to identify the factors that are likely to have influenced an eyewitness's identification performance in a particular case.
2. Attorneys must be aware of the factors that influence eyewitness identification performance.
3. Judges and juries must be made aware during trial, and consider during deliberations, the factors that influence eyewitness identification performance.

Our focus in this chapter has been on the two precursors to effective cross-examination. In particular we have (a) noted the legal and practical impediments to attorney development of case-specific information that is a necessary predicate to effective cross-examination and (b) reviewed research on attorneys' understanding of the factors that influence eyewitness performance. The attorney knowledge research raises serious questions about the extent to which attorneys are familiar with the factors that influence eyewitness performance. Of course, attorneys who are not familiar with the threats to eyewitness reliability obviously cannot hope to undertake an effective examination of witnesses that will expose such threats.

Unfortunately, even a thorough knowledge of the factors that influence eyewitness performance is no guarantee that an attorney will be equipped to undertake effective examination of eyewitnesses and law enforcement personnel involved in crime investigations and identification procedures. Even the most forthcoming witnesses and law enforcement officers may not remember critical details about crimes and identification procedures. And, although defendants do enjoy some rights to representation at postindictment lineups, counsel is not present at other identification proceedings – especially at those involving photographic arrays.

Under this combined set of conditions – reliance on witness and police memories for crime information, limited access to identification proceedings, and less-than-complete information about the threats to eyewitness accuracy – we think it likely that cross-examination in many criminal cases is built on a shaky foundation. Even when the foundation for courtroom examination of witnesses is solid, questions can still be raised about the third condition for effective cross-examination: Will effective examination of witnesses effectively alert juries (and/or judges) to the threats to eyewitness reliability and will these decision makers give appropriate consideration to these threats during deliberations on the evidence? These are questions to which we turn in the next chapter.

Part V

Is the jury an effective safeguard against mistaken identification?

11   Lay knowledge about sources of eyewitness unreliability

An attorney may enter a motion to suppress identification evidence on the grounds that an identification is the result of procedures that are unduly suggestive and may lead to a mistaken identification (*Stovall v. Denno*, 1967). In *Neil v. Biggers* (1972), the Supreme Court observed that "[i]t is the likelihood of misidentification which violates a defendant's right to due process." The courts have consequently focused their inquiries on the reliability of identifications. Identifications derived from unnecessarily suggestive procedures are excluded unless the totality of the circumstances indicates that the identification is reliable. These inquiries involve two steps (Heller, 1993): First, the defendant must prove that the identification procedures were impermissibly suggestive. Second, the court determines whether the identification was nonetheless reliable.

In assessing reliability, the courts consider five criteria articulated in *Biggers* and endorsed by the Supreme Court in *Manson v. Brathwaite* (1977):

1. the extent of the witness's opportunity to view the perpetrator at the time of the crime;
2. the witness's degree of attention at the time of the crime;
3. the accuracy of the witness's description of the perpetrator given prior to the identification;
4. the witness's degree of certainty at the time of the identification, and
5. the length of time that has elapsed between the crime and the identification.

Note that, as reviewed in Chapters 6 and 7, (1), (2) and (5) are consistent with the research findings but (3) and (4) are not supported by the research. Moreover, other factors identified as important in Chapters 6 and 7 are not mentioned in *Biggers*. In any case, an identification is considered reliable when the *Biggers* criteria (and other evidence of the defendant's guilt) outweigh the effects of the suggestive procedures. Thus, even though the court may determine that an identification is based on impermissibly suggestive procedures, it may rule the identification admissible because there are independent bases of reliability. The prosecution bears the burden of establishing an independent basis for the identification. Motions to suppress identifications are submitted to the trial court judge for a ruling, and sometimes a hearing is granted (though hearings are not mandatory and, if held, may even be held in the presence of the jury – *Watkins v. Sowders*, 1981).

Whether or not a hearing is conducted, it is clear that proper evaluation of these motions requires that judges must be sensitive to the factors that influence eyewitness identification accuracy – both encoding and suggestivity factors. Extant case law identifies factors that the appellate courts consider possibly suggestive. These include the following from *Wade* (388 United States at 228 – 229):

1. placing a suspect in a lineup with "grossly dissimilar" foils;
2. placing the suspect in a lineup in which the witness is familiar with the foils but not the suspect;
3. placing the suspect in a lineup in which only the suspect wears distinctive clothing that was allegedly worn by the perpetrator;
4. telling the witness the perpetrator has been apprehended and presenting the suspect individually to the witness or permitting the suspect to be viewed while incarcerated;
5. police pointing out the suspect during the lineup, and
6. asking lineup participants to try on a piece of clothing that fits only the suspect.

These factors are consistent with the findings reviewed in Chapter 8 regarding the suggestiveness of identification tests. In addition, in *Wade*, the Court noted:

Application of [the Independent Source Test] requires consideration of various factors; for example, the prior opportunity to observe the alleged criminal act, the existence of any discrepancy between any pre-lineup description and the defendant's actual description, any identification prior to lineup of another person, the identification by picture of the defendant prior to the lineup, failure to identify the defendant on a prior occasion, and the lapse of time between the alleged act and the lineup identification. It is also relevant to consider those facts which, despite the absence of counsel, are disclosed concerning the conduct of the lineup. (p. 241)

Other courts have added to the list of possible independent bases factors such as an independent recollection of an encounter with the suspect, familiarity with the suspect's voice, and familiarity with the suspect prior to the crime (Heller, 1993). These additional factors provide some insight into the factors that judges believe to be important. As with attorneys, judges appear to be sensitive to some factors identified in the empirical research and less so to others, at least as evidenced in the published opinions. Selected published opinions, however, represent a very limited source of data, for they say little about the knowledge of the majority of trial judges and even less about the weights that judges typically assign to factors that affect identification accuracy. Unfortunately, there is no empirical research on judge sensitivity to either encoding or suggestion factors – the most relevant studies are the surveys of practicing attorneys reviewed in the last chapter and the large number of studies of juror sensitivity reviewed in this chapter.

As we emphasized in Chapter 10, effective cross-examination requires that juries be or be made sensitive to factors that influence eyewitness identification accuracy. One can imagine a case in which the defense attorney, through cross-examination, establishes that the perpetrator was of a different race than the eyewitness, that the perpetrator was disguised and brandished a weapon, and that the lineup test from which the suspect was identified suffered from instruction bias, foil bias and presentation bias. Of what use is this knowledge if the jury does not understand how these factors are likely to influence eyewitness identification accuracy? The attorney can argue during closing argument that these factors enhance the likelihood of false identifications, but the jury may find such arguments implausible, especially if they perceive the attorney to be biased in favor of her client and view the arguments as inconsistent with common sense.

Four sets of studies have examined juror sensitivity to factors that influence eyewitness identification and all are reviewed in the next section. The first set consists of survey studies that assess lay knowledge using multiple choice questions, as in Brigham and Wolfskeil's (1983) study of attorney sensitivity reported in the last chapter. The second set examines the abilities of lay persons to predict the outcome of eyewitness identification experiments. The third and fourth sets involve simulated jury decision–making experiments: The third looks at the influence of discredited eyewitnesses on mock-juror decisions, and the fourth examines the influence of systematic variations in eyewitness evidence on juror decisions.

Survey studies of lay knowledge of factors that influence eyewitness reliability

Four separate surveys, published in three articles, have reviewed lay (i.e., juror) knowledge about the factors that influence eyewitness identification (Deffenbacher & Loftus, 1982; McConkey & Roche, 1989; Noon & Hollin, 1987). These four studies use the same survey instrument but rather different populations. Deffenbacher and Loftus collected data from a sample of 100 undergraduates from the University of Nebraska at Omaha and a sample of 76 undergraduates from the University of Washington. McConkey and Roche studied Australian students: 171 undergraduates from Macquarie University and 60 advanced law students at the University of Sydney. Noon and Hollin's sample consisted of 76 people from England: 28 undergraduates, 24 law students, and 24 nonstudents with a variety of backgrounds. In the McConkey and Roche (1989) and Noon and Hollin (1987) studies, the data from law students were, for the most part, comparable to that of the other subjects, so we do not distinguish between these subsamples in our review.

The survey studies used a questionnaire developed by Deffenbacher and Loftus (1982), the Knowledge of Eyewitness Behavior Questionnaire (KEBQ). The KEBQ consists of 14 items. Some of the items do not concern eyewitness identification and are therefore not reviewed here. Items 2, 3, and 4 pertain to the influence of stress and violence on eyewitness recall of information rather than identification performance; Item 5 pertains to the influence of misleading questions on recall; Item 11 pertains to the accuracy of time estimation, and Item 12 refers to the influence of narrative versus close-ended questions. Two other items are not included in our review for different reasons. Item 7 pertains to the influence of optimality of viewing conditions on the confidence-accuracy relation. We ignore it here because the research addressing the answer is minimal. Item 14 is not reviewed here because we do not believe the data from this item are interpretable. This leaves six items pertaining to lay beliefs about factors that influence identification accuracy. Responses are summarized in Table 11.1.

Item 1 pertained to cross-race recognitions. The question was:

Two women are walking to school one morning, one of them an Asian and the other white. Suddenly, two men, one black and one white, jump into their path and attempt to grab their purses. Later, the women are shown photographs of known purse snatchers in the area. Which statement describes your view of the women's ability to identify the purse snatchers?

The answer scored as correct was: "The white woman will find the black man more difficult to identify than the white man." It was chosen by 57% of subjects in the Omaha sample, 54% in the Seattle sample, 75% in the UK sample, and 62% in the Australia sample. Note this is the same question that Rahaim and Brodsky used (see Chapter 10) in their study of attorneys (see Table 10.1). Attorneys from their study gave responses comparable to those of the laypeople in the studies reviewed in this section – which suggests that the attorneys possess no special knowledge about this issue.

Table 11.1. *Survey studies of lay knowledge*

		Percentage scored as correct			
Item	factor	Omaha	Seattle sample	UK sample	Australia sample
1	Cross-race recognition	57	54	75	62
6	Prior photoarray	52	60	60	60
8	Retention interval	24	30	30	36
9	Training	16	16	25	35
10	Age	46	51	65	50
13	Prior photoarray	54	71	67	66

Item 6 concerned the influence of prior photoarray identifications on subsequent lineup identifications. The question was:

A robbery is committed. Later, the clerk who was robbed at gunpoint identifies someone from a set of photographs as the person who perpetrated the crime. Still later, the clerk is asked whether the robber is present in the lineup of several somewhat similar individuals. Which of the following statements is true?

The answer scored correct was: "Guilty or not, if the person identified in the photos is present, he/she is likely to be identified from the lineup as well." This answer was chosen by 52% of the Omaha sample and 60% of the Seattle, UK, and Australia samples. The next most commonly chosen answer, which was selected by 22%, 15%, 16%, and 11% of the samples, respectively, was "If the robber is present in the lineup, having seen his/her photo previously does not add significantly to his/her chances of being identified from the lineup."

Item 8 addressed the influence of retention interval on identification accuracy. It asked:

Which of the following statements do you feel best represents the truth about an eyewitness's memory for faces seen only once?

The statement scored as correct was: "It is 6–12 months before memory accuracy drops to a level where a face seen once becomes indistinguishable from ones never before seen." This answer was chosen by 24% of the Omaha sample, 30% of the Seattle and UK samples, and 36% of the Australia sample. More commonly chosen was the statement: "Even after several months, memory is still 90%–95% accurate," which was chosen by 40%, 49%, 51%, and 39% of the samples, respectively.

Item 9 referred to the influence of training on identification accuracy. It stated:

Concerning the effects of the amount of training or experience a person has had in making eyewitness identifications, which of the following statements seems most reasonable to you?

The statement scored as correct was: "It appears to be quite difficult to train people to become better at recognizing faces seen previously." This answer was selected by 16% of the Omaha and Seattle samples, 25% of the UK sample, and 35% of the Australia sample. The more commonly chosen statement was: "Police officers in general are better than civilians at recall details of another person encountered for only a few seconds." This statement was chosen by 53%, 48%, 58%, and 45% of the samples, respectively.

Item 10 addressed the influence of age on identification accuracy. It asked:

Sometimes during a criminal trial the age of the eyewitness is assumed to be a factor in the accuracy of the identification. Which statement do you think describes the actual relationship between age and identification accuracy?

The statement scored as correct was: "Ability to recognize previously seen faces increases steadily to early adulthood and then declines after age 60." This answer was indicated by 46% of the Omaha sample, 51% of the Seattle sample, 65% of the UK sample, and 50% of the Australia sample. Another answer commonly chosen (24%, 23%, 12%, and 18%, respectively) was: "Ability to recognize faces increases up until the early school years and then remains constant through old age." A third commonly chosen answer (27%, 19%, 22%, and 30%, respectively) was: "Face recognition ability remains relatively constant in accuracy after 3–4 years of age."

Finally, Item 13 pertained to the influence of a photoarray procedure that precedes an identification test. It asked:
Suppose a house were burglarized and the resident got a glimpse of the burglar through the window. At a later lineup the resident attempts to make an identification.

Assume there is a 10% chance that the resident will be mistaken. Now in addition to the above facts, assume that the resident was first shown photographs by the police, but recognized none of the people in the photos. Assume further that the person the resident later picked in the lineup was shown in one of the photos that had earlier been viewed. The chance of an incorrect identification in this latter situation would then:

The answer scored as correct was: "increase above 10%." This answer was reported by 54% of the Omaha sample, 71% of the Seattle sample, 67% of the UK sample, and 66% of the Australia sample.

It is interesting that these diverse groups of subjects showed remarkably consistent results. The American, English, and Australians appear to be somewhat sensitive to the influence of cross-race recognition and the influence of prior photoarray identifications on identification accuracy. They appear less sensitive to the negligible effects of training on identification accuracy and to the effects of age and retention interval.

In conclusion, survey studies converge on the conclusion that prospective jurors are sensitive to some factors but less so to others and generally display high degrees of variability in their responses. However, we wish to underscore that several methodological issues associated with this form of research prompts us to temper our conclusions. First, these survey studies examine only a limited number of variables. As we mentioned earlier, this is understandable, as a considerable portion of eyewitness research was conducted after the KEBQ was developed. Second, the KEBQ attempts to sample lay knowledge for a broader set of issues pertaining to eyewitness testimony (both identification and recall); we, in contrast, have reviewed only those items concerning eyewitness identification. Perhaps the KEBQ can be revised in light of more recent research on the factors that influence identification accuracy (particularly suggestive aspects of identification tests). The other limitations of the survey method will become clear as we review alternative approaches to the study of juror sensitivity to eyewitnessing factors.

Prediction studies of juror knowledge of factors that influence eyewitness reliability

In prediction studies, subjects are provided with descriptions of the methodology used in eyewitness identification experiments and are asked to predict the results (because the experiments had already been conducted, there is a sense in which these are actually postdiction studies, but we will retain the more familiar term and refer to them as prediction studies). If subjects in these studies are sensitive to the factors that influence identification accuracy, they should be reasonably accurate at predicting study outcomes.

Kassin (1979) provided students with summaries of the experimental conditions employed in the previously described experiment by Leippe, Wells, and Ostrom (1978). That experiment (reviewed in Chapter 7) examined the influence of crime seriousness on identification accuracy. Subjects witnessed a staged theft and were led to believe, either before or after the theft, that the theft was high or low in seriousness (i.e., the item stolen was more or less valuable). Among eyewitnesses who knew the value of the stolen item prior to the theft, 19% in the low seriousness and 56% in the high seriousness conditions correctly identified the thief. Kassin's subjects predicted that the two cell means would be 66% and 65%, respectively. Among eyewitnesses who learned of the stolen item's value after the theft, 35% in the low seriousness condition and 12.5% in the high seriousness condition made correct identifications. Kassin's students' predictions, in contrast, were 53% and 60%, respectively. Thus, Kassin's subjects were not sensitive to the influence of crime-seriousness on identification accuracy nor to overall levels of identification accuracy.

Wells (1984) reported several prediction studies. In one, students read the procedure section of the Leippe, Wells, and Ostrom (1978) study and were given one of two target cases to predict. In one case, the eyewitness was "completely certain" of his identification; in the other, the eyewitness was "somewhat uncertain" of his identification. Leippe et al. had found that confidence was unrelated to actual identification accuracy. In contrast, Wells's students predicted a .83 probability of a correct identification for the "completely certain" witness and a .28 probability of a correct identification for a "somewhat uncertain" witness. In short, not only did Wells's students believe confidence was related to accuracy, but they believed that it was very strongly related to accuracy.

In a second study, Wells had 80 students read a description of Malpass and Devine's (1981) study of instruction bias (described in Chapter 8). Each subject read about one of the four conditions (target-present/unbiased instructions, target-present/biased instructions, target-absent/unbiased instructions, target-absent/biased instructions) and predicted the percentage of subjects who would make correct identifications. In the vandal-present conditions, the predictions were fairly close. In Malpass and Devine's experiment, 75% of subjects who received biased instructions and 83% of subjects who received unbiased instructions made correct identifications. The corresponding predictions from Wells's students were 79% and 74%, respectively. Identification data from the vandal-absent conditions were 78% false identifications with biased instructions and 33% false identifications with unbiased instructions. Wells's students' predictions, in contrast, were 16% and 18%, respectively. This study thus provides evidence that prospective jurors are not sensitive to the influence of one factor that clearly contributes to the suggestiveness of identification procedures: instruction bias.

Brigham and Bothwell conducted their prediction study with a random sample of 90 community members from Leon County, Florida, all of whom were registered to vote and were therefore eligible jurors. Respondents participated by completing and returning questionnaires mailed to them by the experimenters. The questionnaire contained a description of the methods used in two experiments. One experiment was Leippe et al.'s (1978) study of crime seriousness – in which subjects received a description of the high seriousness, informed afterwards condition. The second was Brigham et al.'s (1982) field study of cross-race recognition. Brigham and Bothwell found that respondents reliably overestimated the accuracy of eyewitness identifications. In Leippe et al.'s study, 12.5% of identifications were correct. Survey respondents estimated that, on average, 70.6% would give correct identifications. Indeed, 91% of the survey respondents predicted that more than 12.5% of identifications would be correct. In Brigham et al.'s (1982) field study, 32% of white clerks correctly identified black clerks, but survey respondents estimated that 51% had done so. In this condition, 70% of the respondents gave estimates that were greater than the actual finding. Likewise, 31% of the black clerks correctly identified white customers in the field study. In contrast, survey respondents estimated that 70% had done so. In this condition, 90% gave estimates that were higher than the actual findings.

Brigham and Bothwell also had subjects estimate the overall accuracy of eyewitness identifications. They found that 63% of the respondents believed that more than 50% of identifications were correct, 28% thought that about 50% were correct, and only 9% felt that fewer than 50% were correct. Most respondents (55%) felt that an emotionally aroused eyewitness would be less likely to make an accurate identification, whereas 31% believed the opposite to be true. Most (56%) thought that confidence was positively associated with identification accuracy but many (42%) thought that the relation between confidence and accuracy was not so reliable. Most (58%) felt that jurors give too much credence to identification evidence but 37% felt that jurors place appropriate emphasis on identification evidence. Some of these effects were moderated by the respondent's level of education.

Conclusion

Brigham and Bothwell's results reinforce the findings of Kassin and Wells and indicate that prospective jurors overestimate the accuracy of eyewitness identifications. This conclusion seems inconsistent with our contention that we have little basis for estimating the overall accuracy rates of eyewitnesses (Chapter 1). If we cannot estimate the accuracy of eyewitness testimony in actual crimes, how can we conclude that prospective jurors overestimate accuracy? The prediction studies can do this because they have estimates of accuracy rates in specific situations – the conditions of the experiment. These estimates can be expected to be reliable, as they are based on substantial sample sizes. Of course, one major criticism of the prediction method of studying juror sensitivity is that descriptions of study methodology may not capture the essential elements of the actual experiment; if the descriptions do not, there is little reason to expect subjects to estimate accurately eyewitness performance. On the other hand, jurors confront a very similar problem: Even if we assume that jurors are perfectly sensitive to all the factors that influence eyewitness performance, they depend on the trial attorneys to develop all the information that is relevant to their assessment of the reliability of the identification in question. Ultimately, we want to know how well jurors perform when such information is available. The studies reviewed in the next chapter address this question.

12 The ability of jurors to differentiate between accurate and inaccurate eyewitnesses

The studies most relevant to the question of juror sensitivity are those that attempt to simulate the jury's actual task of evaluating eyewitness identifications. We have identified three distinct approaches to studying juror sensitivity. The first examines prospective jurors' abilities to discriminate between accurate and inaccurate eyewitnesses. The second studies the influence of credible and discredited eyewitnesses on mock-juror decisions. The third examines mock-juror sensitivity to the factors that influence identification accuracy. Throughout these studies the judgments of hundreds of prospective jurors (and some experienced jurors) are investigated in response to a wide variety of simulated cases.

Mock-jury studies of juror decision making in eyewitness cases

Wells, Lindsay, and Ferguson (1979) staged a crime in view of 127 undergraduates who then attempted identifications from six-person photoarrays. Of these witnesses, 24 who made accurate identifications and 18 who made inaccurate identifications participated in a simulated cross-examination that consisted of 25 questions pertaining to the event and identification. For half of the eyewitnesses, questions asked during cross-examination were leading and for half they were nonleading. One of the questions asked during cross-examination pertained to the eyewitness's confidence in his/her identification accuracy. The identification testimony of these witnesses was evaluated by 201 undergraduates who served as mock jurors. The mock jurors were asked whether they believed the identifications were correct. Wells et al. found a significant interaction between accuracy of the eyewitness and type of questions posed during cross-examination.

The results indicate that leading questions – typically used in cross-examination – may have a salutary effect on juror assessments of eyewitness performance. When the questions addressed to the witnesses were nonleading, inaccurate eyewitnesses were actually believed by more jurors (86%) than were accurate eyewitnesses (76%). In contrast, when the questions were leading, accurate eyewitnesses were believed by more jurors (84%) than were inaccurate eyewitnesses (73%).

Of course, simply because a juror believes an eyewitness does not make the eyewitness identification correct. How good were the mock jurors at differentiating accurate and inaccurate eyewitnesses? Significant main effects on *juror* accuracy were found for both accuracy of eyewitness identification and the type of question put to the eyewitness, but the interaction was nonsignificant. Among jurors exposed to nonleading cross-examination, 76% correctly classified accurate eyewitnesses but only 14% correctly classified inaccurate eyewitnesses. Among jurors exposed to leading cross-examination, 84% correctly classified accurate eyewitnesses and 27% correctly classified inaccurate eyewitnesses.

In short, performance was generally not very good: The 84% correct classification rate for accurate eyewitnesses is perhaps not so worrisome – if the numbers reflected what happens in real cases it would translate into one in six guilty defendants being acquitted. The numbers for inaccurate eyewitnesses are far more disturbing for they imply that nearly three out of four mistaken identifications would be believed. Of course, no one would argue that these numbers exactly parallel those of real cases, because there are other "filtering" mechanisms that help to assure that not all identifications result in courtroom appearances by witnesses and the people they identify. For example, many erroneous identifications will not result in prosecutions because the police know that the incorrectly identified foil could not have committed the crime, and others will be excluded when exculpatory evidence is developed. Other identifications are not followed up because the witness is not sufficiently confident in their identification. Of course, it is entirely plausible that the inaccurate eyewitnesses who reach courtrooms after such filtering processes are not fundamentally different from those studied by Wells et al. and real jurors are no more proficient than those in the study.

Wells et al. also found that the confidence of the eyewitness in his or her identification accuracy correlated significantly ($r = .53$) with whether or not the juror believed the eyewitness but nonsignificantly ($r = .05$) with the actual accuracy of the juror's decision. In other words, jurors were more likely to believe confident eyewitnesses but confident eyewitnesses were no more likely to be accurate than less confident eyewitnesses. This result (and the general research on the confidence-accuracy research reported in Chapter 6) unfortunately suggests that "filtering" out witnesses low in confidence is not likely to aid jurors in differentiating accurate from inaccurate eyewitnesses.

A second relevant study by Wells and Leippe (1981) involved a theft staged in view of 107 undergraduates. These eyewitnesses answered 11 questions pertaining to peripheral details of the crime, attempted to identify the thief from a photoarray, and rated their confidence in their identification decisions. A sample of 48 eyewitnesses who made positive identifications were then cross-examined. The cross-examinations, which were videotaped, consisted of 21 questions, 11 of which pertained to the same peripheral details about which eyewitnesses were queried after the crime. The confidence of the eyewitness in the accuracy of his or her identification was also assessed during cross-examination. Each of 48 eyewitnesses was also subjected to one of two types of cross-examination. In the control condition, eyewitnesses responded to each question with no follow-up questions from the examining attorney. In the peripheral detail condition, each time an eyewitness responded incorrectly to one of the 11 peripheral detail questions, the attorney followed up, demonstrating that the eyewitness's answer was incorrect according to police records.

The videotaped cross-examinations were then evaluated by 96 undergraduates playing the role of jurors. Each mock-juror indicated his or her belief in the accuracy of the eyewitness's identification. Cross-examination condition interacted significantly with accuracy of the eyewitness identification in predicting jurors' beliefs. Accurate eyewitnesses were believed by 75% of the jurors who viewed the control cross-examination but by only 38% of the jurors who viewed the peripheral detail cross-examination. In contrast, inaccurate eyewitnesses were believed by 71% of the jurors who viewed the control cross-examination and 58% of jurors who viewed the peripheral detail cross-examination. In short, cross-examination that focused on errors in recall about peripheral details dramatically reduced jurors' belief of witnesses, and unfortunately the effect was stronger for accurate eyewitnesses than it was for inaccurate eyewitnesses.

Among jurors who viewed the peripheral detail cross-examination, accuracy of eyewitness recall of the details was significantly and negatively correlated ($r = -.56$) with juror belief in the eyewitness identification. In other words, the more peripheral details recalled incorrectly, the less likely it was that the identification was believed by the jurors. This correlation was nonsignificant among jurors in the control cross-examination condition ($r = -.03$). In summary, to a substantial degree mock-jurors evaluated identification testimony on the basis of witness memory for peripheral details. Examination that underscored errors in memory for peripheral details significantly weakened the credibility of accurate witnesses but did not reveal the inaccurate witnesses. This unfortunate set of results is further compounded by the fact that, in Wells and Leippe's study, eyewitness memory for peripheral details was inversely (though weakly) associated with identification accuracy, as explained in Chapter 7.

Lindsay, Wells, and Rumpel (1981) further examined jurors' abilities to discriminate accurate from inaccurate eyewitnesses. Thefts were staged before 108 undergraduates, each assigned to one of three viewing conditions designed to produce low, moderate, and high levels of identification accuracy. The viewing conditions were manipulated by combining the influences of exposure duration, disguise, and personal interaction with the eyewitness (i.e., better identification performance was expected with longer exposures, no disguise, and interaction; see Chapters 6 and 7). Eyewitnesses later attempted to identify the thief from six-person photoarrays. A sample of eyewitnesses who made positive identifications was then cross-examined, and the cross-examinations were videotaped. The viewing condition manipulation was successful. Of the eyewitnesses who made a positive identification, 33% in the low accuracy, 50% in the moderate accuracy, and 74% in the high accuracy conditions were correct. These percentages differed significantly from one another. The videotaped cross-examinations of eight accurate and eight inaccurate eyewitnesses from each viewing condition were then shown to 96 undergraduates. Each juror viewed cross-examinations of four separate eyewitnesses and judged whether the witnesses had made correct identifications.

In this study the cross-examination consisted of 15 questions pertaining to viewing conditions, witness confidence, and other factors. Eyewitness confidence and the viewing conditions produced significant main effects and a significant interaction effect on juror beliefs. We first consider viewing condition effects. Overall, 62% of the low accuracy condition witnesses were believed, 66% of the moderate accuracy condition witnesses were believed, and 77% of the high accuracy condition witnesses were believed. Thus, jurors unfortunately gave witness identifications more credence than was merited by the performance of the witnesses in the different witnessing conditions (as noted earlier, the respective accuracy rates were 33%, 50%, and 74%). Furthermore, the jurors gave the witnesses more credence than was merited by the levels of accuracy of the cross-examined witnesses the jurors actually viewed – because half the eyewitnesses selected in each witnessing condition had actually made correct identifications, perfect performance by jurors would have produced 50% belief rates for each of the three conditions.

These problems are compounded by yet another consideration: Although the jurors were somewhat sensitive to witnessing conditions, they were not more accurate in their overall assessments of witnesses across witnessing conditions – in fact, they merely made different kinds of errors across conditions. The overall levels of juror accuracy in identifying accurate witnesses from the low, moderate, and high conditions were 51%,

50%, and 53%. Because jurors considered witnesses more believable as witnessing conditions improved, jurors appear to have successfully picked out larger percentages of *correct* witnesses across the three conditions (63%, 66%, and 80%). But, this "improvement" in performance is illusory and could result from guessing, given (as already noted) that jurors believed 62%, 66%, and 77% of the witnesses in the low, medium, and high conditions. In fact, the "improvements" in identifying correct eyewitnesses were fully offset by reduced levels of accuracy in picking out witnesses who made incorrect identifications (39%, 34%, and 25%, respectively).

As we have noted, witness confidence affected juror beliefs – 77% of confident witnesses were believed, versus 59% of low confidence witnesses. Witness confidence and witnessing condition also interacted. Among eyewitnesses with high confidence, viewing condition had a trivial influence on juror beliefs: Seventy-six percent of eyewitnesses in the low accuracy condition, 76% in the moderate accuracy condition, and 78% in the high accuracy condition were believed. In contrast, among eyewitnesses with low confidence, viewing condition had an impact on juror beliefs. The corresponding percentages of eyewitnesses believed were: 47%, 54%, and 76%, respectively. Thus, jurors ignored witnessing conditions when the witness was very confident, but gave the witnessing conditions greater consideration when the witness was not highly confident. Unfortunately, Lindsay et al. found only a (typically) weak relationship between witness confidence and witness accuracy (see Chapter 6); thus the jurors were relying on less than fully diagnostic information when using confidence to gauge witness accuracy.

Lindsay, Wells, and O'Connor (1989) conducted an experiment to test whether the findings from the above research would generalize to a more realistic trial situation. A simulated crime similar to their earlier research was staged before small groups of undergraduates who then tried to identify the perpetrator from six-person target-present or target-absent photoarrays. In all 54% of subjects shown target-present photoarrays made correct identifications and 25% of subjects shown target-absent photoarrays made false identifications. All eyewitnesses were then asked if they would participate as witnesses in a mock trial and most of them agreed to do so.

One to five weeks after the simulated crime, the eyewitnesses individually went to a courtroom in Kingston, Ontario, where they were greeted by an experimenter and a prosecutor (played by a practicing attorney). The prosecuting attorney spent 15 to 25 minutes discussing the case background and the anticipated examination with each eyewitness. Then each eyewitness was subjected to examination by the prosecutor, cross-examination by the defense attorney, and redirect examination by the prosecutor. All prosecutors obtained in-court identifications of the suspect. These proceedings were videotaped. Sixteen "trials" were created involving eight eyewitnesses who made correct and eight who made false identifications. Attorneys varied in their level of experience: Half were experienced lawyers (average 12 years since passing the bar exam) and half were advanced law students with some legal aid experience.

The sixteen simulated trials were shown to 178 undergraduates, each of whom viewed one taped trial. Mock-jurors rendered verdicts and answered other questions about the trials. The conviction rate did not differ significantly as a function of accuracy of the eyewitness (jurors could not differentiate accurate from inaccurate eyewitnesses): Guilty verdicts were rendered by 68% of subjects exposed to eyewitnesses who made correct identifications and 70% of subjects exposed to eyewitnesses who made false identifications. The degree of attorneys' experience did not significantly influence verdict nor did experience interact with eyewitness accuracy in the prediction of verdict. Overall, these findings suggest that the realism of the examination/cross-examination and the experience of the persons conducting these examinations do not qualify the results of Wells and Lindsay's earlier studies.

These studies of mock-jurors' abilities to discriminate between accurate and inaccurate eyewitnesses converge on a truly dismal conclusion about jurors' abilities. Jurors overestimate the accuracy of identifications (there are more convictions than there are accurate identifications); jurors fail to distinguish accurate from inaccurate eyewitnesses; jurors tend to undervalue viewing conditions that are known to predict identification accuracy and instead base their decisions in part on eyewitness memory for peripheral details and witness confidence – both of which tend to be poor predictors of identification accuracy (see Chapters 6 and 7).

Post-identification events and the malleability of witness confidence.

Unfortunately, juror reliance on witness confidence as a guide to witness accuracy may be doubly problematic. The reliability of confidence as a predictor of accuracy is further threatened because confidence proves to be fairly malleable and susceptible to influence by post-identification events. For example, in an early demonstration of confidence malleability, Hastie, Landsman, and Loftus (1978) found that witnesses who were questioned repeatedly grew more confident about the accuracy of details in their reports (although see Turtle & Yuille, 1994, for opposing findings). Wells, Ferguson, and Lindsay (1981) more compellingly demonstrated the malleability of confidence. After making identifications, some mock-witnesses were briefed about the types of questions they might encounter in an upcoming cross-examination and were instructed to prepare themselves for the examination. Others were not briefed. The briefing highlighted the fact that the defense attorney was likely to be antagonistic, discredit the witness's testimony, catch inconsistencies and press the witness on details. The final question in the cross-examination assessed witness confidence. Mock-jurors evaluated the cross-examined witnesses (20 of whom selected the perpetrator and 18 of whom selected an innocent foil).

Overall, accurate and inaccurate witnesses were equally confident. However, when cross-examined, briefed witnesses were significantly more confident about their identifications than were unbriefed witnesses and briefed witnesses were believed more often by the jurors ($p=.06$ for the latter effect). Of course, the accuracy of the identifications made by briefed witnesses were not and could not change as a result of briefings--they took place after the identifications had been made. Disturbingly, the briefing effect occurred among inaccurate eyewitnesses. The mean levels of confidence on a 7-point scale (and percentage of jurors believing the witness) for accurate witnesses were 5.25 (40%) and 5.33 (45%) for non-briefed and briefed witnesses respectively, whereas the means for the inaccurate witnesses were 3.83 (44%) and 6.08 (73%) respectively. The perceived confidence of witnesses was highly correlated with juror belief of the witnesses ($r=.58$) and with witnesses' self-ratings of confidence ($r=.53$). The elevated levels of confidence among incorrect witnesses appears to have resulted in more incorrect than correct witnesses being believed by jurors, although this effect was only marginally significant ($p=.08$).

The general failure to observe inflated confidence and belief levels among accurate witnesses may simply reflect a "ceiling effect". Accurate witnesses' levels of confidence were high to begin with – around 5.3 on a 7-point scale – and there was little room for them to increase. Similar briefing effects were obtained for other dependent measures including verdicts and ratings of witness confidence. Finally, although jurors thought that more than a third of the witnesses had been coached, there was no relation between those beliefs and actual briefing and jurors' suspicions also were unrelated to jurors' beliefs about witness accuracy. Wells et al. observed:

Inflating eyewitness confidence requires nothing on the order of high-powered persuasion techniques. A simple instruction to rehearse the witnesses' account, sample questions that might be asked by a cross-examiner, and warnings that the cross-examiner will look for inconsistencies in the testimony are sufficient to inflate the witnesses' confidence in his or her memory. The effect is apparently more than just enhancing the confidence of the witness as perceived by subject-jurors. The witnesses seem to convince themselves of their accuracy" (p. 694).

In light of these findings and jurors' (and judges' and attorneys') general reliance on witness confidence one would have to expect that a primary effect of such briefings would be to increase conviction rates for defendants identified by briefed witnesses. A secondary effect of differential inflation of inaccurate eyewitness (as opposed to accurate eyewitness) confidence levels would be to reduce any correlation between witness confidence and witness accuracy--the briefing has the effect of introducing non-diagnostic noise into the computation of that relation. Thus, briefings appear to reduce the (already limited) diagnosticity of witness confidence with respect to witness accuracy.

Even if briefings somehow managed to leave the confidence-accuracy correlation intact, the elevation in confidence levels among inaccurate eyewitnesses may still make it more difficult for jurors to make effective use of confidence as a guide to differentiating accurate from inaccurate witnesses. If, for example, jurors use a certain level of confidence (e.g. a perceived level of 90% confidence that the identification is correct) as a decision criterion and acquit in all instances where perceived confidence is below 90% and convict when it is 90% or greater, any differential elevation of confidence among inaccurate witnesses will necessarily increase the rate of erroneous convictions. Even if confidence was elevated to an equal extent among accurate and inaccurate eyewitnesses, the net effect would be to increase the rates of conviction from both accurate and inaccurate identifications.

More recent research by Luus and Wells (1994) further underscores the malleability of confidence. Through the use of a crime simulation followed by biased lineup instructions, Luus and Wells produced a sample of paired witnesses who made false identifications. Each witness was led to believe that he or she was second of the pair to make an identification. Each witness then received one of nine different forms of information about the identifications made by their co-witness. An assistant to the experimenter, posing as a campus police officer, then solicited the witness' confidence levels (on 10-point scales) in the accuracy of their identifications. Mean levels of witness confidence for each information condition are shown in Table12.1.

These ratings clearly reflect substantial malleability in confidence, with the highest confidence levels obtained from witnesses who believed their co-witness had identified the same individual. Confidence levels were quite high even among witnesses who were told that the co-witness had first

Table 12.1. *Mean Eyewitness Confidence in Their Identification as a Function of Co-witness Information*

Co-witness Identification	Confidence of witness	Perceived accuracy of witness
Same identification as witness	8.77a	5.00a
Same identification but withdrawn	8.53a	5.40a
Same/changed to different person	8.33a	5.07a
An implausible alternative	7.87a	4.85a
No infornation (control)	6.90b	4.16b
Different person identified/withdrawn	6.13b	3.55c
Different person identified	4.67c	3.05c
Different person/changed to same	4.60c	2.69c
Co-witness said "not there"	3.57c	2.68c

Note. Means with different subscripts differ at $p<.05$

identified the same individual but then withdrew the identification or switched to another individual. Witnesses given feedback indicating that the confederate had identified an implausible alternative from the photoarray were significantly more confident than witnesses who received no feedback. Witnesses who were told that the co-witness had identified a different person but withdrew the identification were somewhat (though not significantly) less confident than witnesses who received no feedback. The lowest confidence levels were found among witnesses who were told that the co-witness had indicated that the perpetrator was not in the array and mong witnesses who were initially told the co-witness identified someone else.

Besides demonstrating surprising levels of malleability, this study showed that initial characterizations of the co-witness's action had effects on witness confidence that were quite resistant to change. "Corrections" given to the witness within two minutes of an original 'erroneous' communication had little impact on witness confidence. This outcome raises the question of whether changes in witness confidence that arise from early (and, especially, erroneous) communications can ever be corrected with later information. Another notable finding is that the differences in confidence levels were not small; they spanned most of the 10-point scale!

As shown in Table 12.1, the pattern of ratings of witness accuracy collected from mock jurors who evaluated the witness statements (Luus &

Wells, 1994, Study 2) closely parallels the pattern of witness confidence levels (a result that is consistent with research reviewed earlier). The manipulations had similar effects on other juror ratings of the witnesses' statements, including quality of view, believability, and detail of description. Luus and Wells concluded:

We have dire concerns about eyewitness confidence malleability in terms of what it might mean in actual criminal cases. Because the confidence that an eyewitness expresses in his or her identification has been sanctioned as a reliable cue to accuracy in judicial rulings (e.g., Neil v. Biggers, 1972) and because people intuitively use confidence to judge the likelihood of identification accuracy, we argue that there is an incentive for police and attorneys to manipulate their witness's confidence" (pp. 720-721).

Luus and Wells express particular concern about intentional communications from police and prosecutors calculated to bolster witness confidence. It is perhaps just as likely, if not more likely, that witnesses will be the recipients of information provided to them by other witnesses (who may have made their own identifications) and even the news media. These communications could have the unintended effects of increasing witness confidence, reducing the diagnosticity of any confidence statements made to the jury by the eyewitness, and elevating conviction rates.

It is plausible that information learned throughout the investigation of a crime, through depositions and pretrial preparation, can influence an eyewitness so that the confidence expressed to the jury differs from the level of confidence expressed at the time of the identification. It is likely that such changes reduce the reliability of confidence as a predictor of identification accuracy. Given that confidence, when measured immediately after the identification, is a modest predictor of accuracy, reductions in reliability may render it utterly useless as an indicator of the accuracy of a witness's identification. Of course, it is difficult to imagine how to limit fact-finders to relying only on witnesses' immediate post-identification expressions of confidence. Eyewitnesses will almost inevitably be called upon to relate the details of the events they witnessed and will usually be asked how confident they are about the accuracy of their identifications. Furthermore, given that confidence is communicated by more than verbal expressions of confidence (Leippe, Manion, & Romanczyk, 1992), it is entirely plausible that juror inferences about witness confidence will be affected by the impact of post-event information on witness confidence even if witnesses were not permitted to state, anew, their level of confidence at trial. Although indices of confidence other than self-reports (e.g., decision time) show some promise as predictors of accuracy, it is unlikely that they would be made available to jurors.

Mock–jury experiments involving "discredited" eyewitnesses

Another method of assessing juror sensitivity to factors that influence eyewitness performance makes use of a discredited eyewitness. For example, Loftus (1974) provided 150 subjects with a description of a grocery store robbery in which the victim of the robbery was murdered. The subjects were asked to play the roles of jurors and render verdicts against the defendant charged with robbery and murder. Three different case summaries were presented. In one version just the incriminating evidence was presented. The second version included the incriminating evidence plus the testimony of the store clerk who positively identified the defendant as the perpetrator. The third version contained the same information as the second except that the defense attorney proved that the eyewitness had very poor vision, was not wearing his glasses at the time of the crime, and therefore could not have seen the criminal from where he stood. The conviction rates in the three conditions were, respectively, 18%, 72%, and 68%.

The presence of the eyewitness significantly enhanced the likelihood that the defendant was convicted. Furthermore, the eyewitness was just as effective even when discrediting information was presented by the defense attorney. In an attempted replication by Cavoukian (1980, cited in Weinberg & Baron, 1982), using Loftus's stimulus materials, the conviction rates were lower in general (35% for the eyewitness only and 30% for the "discredited" eyewitness), but the effects of discrediting information were just as small.

Two experiments by Weinberg and Baron (1982) further examined the influence of discredited eyewitnesses. In their first experiment, Weinberg and Baron used Loftus's stimulus materials but added several new conditions to examine potential qualifying effects. The six conditions and the results are summarized in Table 12.2. Condition (d) was included in order to test whether the lack of a discrediting effect in Loftus's study was due to the order in which evidence was presented. Condition (e) was included in order to test whether source credibility increases or reduces the influence of discrediting information. Condition (f) was included in order to test the joint influences of order of testimony and source credibility. Subjects were 217 undergraduates who read the case summaries and rendered verdicts for the defendant.

Having an eyewitness testify (Condition b) significantly enhanced conviction rate over circumstantial evidence (Condition a). Unlike Loftus (1974) and Cavoukian (1980), the discrediting information (Condition c) significantly reduced the conviction rate. The source of the discrediting information did not significantly influence the verdict, that is, Conditions (c) and (d) were not significantly different from Conditions (e) and (f).

Table 12.2. *Weinberg and Baron (1982)*

Condition	Percentage of convictions
(a) Circumstantial evidence only	32%
(b) Circumstantial + eyewitness identification	57%
(c) Circumstantial evidence + eyewitness identification + discrediting information	23%
(d) Same as (c) except that the defense's case preceded the prosecution's	39%
(e) Same as (c) except that the discrediting information was provided by a disinterested source – the eyewitness's optometrist	24%
(f) Same as (e) except the defense's case preceded the prosecution's	31%

When the defense's case was presented first, jurors were more likely to convict (Conditions c and e vs. d and f).

Weinberg and Baron's second experiment included Conditions (a) and (b) from their first but added a third condition (c) in which, despite the discrediting evidence, an eyewitness reaffirmed his positive identification of the perpetrator. The case summaries were read by 156 undergraduates who later rendered verdicts for the defendant. The conviction rates were 53%, 31%, and 29% in Conditions (a) through (c), respectively. These findings again indicate that the discrediting information significantly reduced conviction rate, and the effect was comparable whether or not the reaffirmation was provided.

Saunders, Vidmar, and Hewitt (1983) tested whether judicial instructions qualify the discrediting effect. They used Loftus's (1974) stimulus materials but for half of the subjects they added judicial instructions stressing that it was "dangerous to convict solely on the basis of the uncorroborated evidence of the identification witness, as this type of evidence is potentially unreliable." The trial summaries were read by undergraduates. Irrespective of whether the mock jurors did or did not receive judicial instructions, the discrediting information significantly reduced the conviction rate. However, the discrediting effect was somewhat larger when judges' instructions were presented (48% vs. 24%) than when they were absent (45% vs. 35%).

McCloskey, Egeth, Webb, Washburn, and McKenna (1981; cited in Kennedy & Haygood, 1992) tested the notion that Loftus's (1974) failure to find a discrediting effect was due to a lack of realism in the trial materials. They therefore created more realistic trial summaries that included opening statements, cross-examination, and judge's instructions. Their trial summaries were read by undergraduates. The conviction rates were 13%, 42%, and 17% in the no-eyewitness, eyewitness, and discredited eyewitness conditions, respectively.

Kennedy and Haygood (1992) also tested the realism hypothesis. They constructed lengthy trial summaries modeled after those used by McCloskey et al. The defendant was accused of robbing a liquor store and murdering the store clerk. Each summary included a description of the crime, opening statements, direct and cross-examination of witnesses, and closing arguments. Half of the trials contained judges' instructions concerning the elements of the crime and the standard of proof (beyond a reasonable doubt). The remaining trials contained no judges' instructions. The trial summaries were read by 147 students who rendered verdicts for the defendant.

The judges' instructions produced neither a significant main effect nor an interaction with condition. Although a higher percentage of convictions was obtained in the nondiscredited eyewitness condition (42%) as opposed to the no-eyewitness condition (27%), this difference was not statistically significant. The conviction rate in the discredited eyewitness condition (19%) was significantly lower than it was in the nondiscredited eyewitness condition.

Kennedy and Haygood's second experiment used the same conditions as their first but the stimulus materials were shortened by removing the opening statements, closing arguments, and judges' instructions. Their goal was to replicate Loftus's (1974) effect by making the stimulus materials less realistic.

The subjects in this study were 183 undergraduates who read the case summaries and rendered verdicts. The percentages of convictions were 30%, 52%, and 23% for the no-eyewitness, nondiscredited eyewitness, and discredited eyewitness conditions, respectively. Here, the nondiscredited eyewitness significantly enhanced conviction rate (in comparison to the no-eyewitness condition), and the discredited eyewitness significantly reduced conviction rate (in comparison to the nondiscredited eyewitness condition).

Kennedy and Haygood noted that in Loftus's (1974) experiment, in which the discredited eyewitness was believed to the same extent as the nondiscredited eyewitness, the discredited eyewitness reaffirmed his testimony after being discredited. In contrast, Weinberg and Baron found that the discredited witness was less credible than the nondiscredited witness, regardless of whether he reaffirmed his testimony. Kennedy and Haygood's third experiment attempted to reconcile this disparate set of findings using Loftus's (1974) stimulus materials. The four conditions tested were: no eyewitness, nondiscredited eyewitness, discredited eyewitness without reaffirmation, and discredited eyewitness with reaffirmation. Subjects were 145 undergraduates who read the trial summaries and rendered verdicts for the defendant. The percentages of convictions in the four conditions were, respectively: 28%, 72%, 44%, and 27%. The introduction of the eyewitness (Condition 2) significantly enhanced conviction rate but introduction of the discrediting information significantly reduced conviction rate, whether or not the eyewitness reaffirmed his testimony. The reaffirmation did not significantly influence verdicts; indeed, the pattern of differences for reaffirmation was opposite to what was expected.

These studies of credible and discredited witnesses converge on the conclusion that credible eyewitnesses significantly enhance the likelihood of conviction (as compared to no eyewitness). Somewhat less consistent are the results for discrediting information, but as shown in Table 12.3 the general pattern clearly indicates that discrediting information reduces juror reliance on eyewitness testimony. There is little evidence to suggest that jurors completely ignore discrediting information.

As always, the conclusions reached in a body of research must be considered in light of the methodological and conceptual limitations of the studies. Two points are noteworthy. First, it is difficult to know how large an effect discrediting information should have. Based on the information presented in the publications, it is difficult to know whether it was made clear that the eyewitness simply could not possibly make a correct identification. If so, then any reliance on the eyewitness testimony is evidence of insensitivity (to the discrediting information) on the part of the mock-jurors. If this was not the message conveyed to the jurors, then we would need additional evidence of the likely impact of the factors identified in the discrediting information, such as information about the factors described in Chapters 6 and 7. A second limitation is the lack of realism of the stimulus materials. These studies have uniformly relied on written trial summaries, often quite brief summaries. Kennedy and Haygood manipulated complexity of trial materials and found that mock-jurors demonstrated greater sensitivity to more realistic trial materials. But even their "realistic" materials were limited to relatively brief written trial summaries. Whether

Table 12.3. *Results of discredited witness studies*

Study	N	No eyewitness	Eyewitness	Discredited eyewitness
Loftus	150	.18	.72	.68
Cavoukian*#		.35	.30	
Weinberg & Baron				
(Study 1)	217	.32	.57	.29
(Study 2)	156	.53	.31	.29
Saunders et al.*#			.47	.30
McCloskey et al.#		.13	.42	.17
Kennedy & Haygood				
(Study 1)	147	.27	.42	.19
(Study 2)	183	.30	.52	.23
(Study 3)	145	.28	.72	.36
Unweighted Means*		.29	.53	.32

*Excluded from computation of means due to lack of data for "No-eyewitness" condition, # means from Kennedy & Haygood

these patterns of results will generalize to more realistic case materials is an empirical question.

Conclusions

In sum, there are a variety of reasons to be concerned about jury decisionmaking in eyewitness identification cases:

1. Jurors appear to overbelieve eyewitnesses.
2. Jurors apparently have difficulty reliably differentiating accurate from inaccurate eyewitnesses.
3. Jurors are not adequately sensitive to aspects of witnessing and identification conditions that are arguably better predictors of witness accuracy than is witness confidence.
4. A major source of juror unreliability is their reliance on witness confidence--which:

a. Is a dubious indicator of eyewitness accuracy even when measured at the time an identification is made and under relatively 'pristine' laboratory conditions, and

b. Appears to be highly malleable and influenced by post-identification factors such as repeated questioning, briefings in anticipation of cross-examination, and feedback about the behavior of other witnesses. These factors do not increase witness accuracy, are therefore likely to further reduce any relation between witness confidence and accuracy, and are therefore likely to further reduce the ability of jurors to differentiate accurate from inaccurate eyewitnesses..

13 Jury sensitivity to factors that influence eyewitness reliability

In an earlier section we reviewed a number of studies in which mock-jurors were presented with examinations of witnesses, some of whom were known to have made an accurate identification and some of whom had made inaccurate identifications. The primary question addressed in these studies was: Could jurors differentiate accurate from inaccurate eyewitnesses? The studies showed that jurors could not make this differentiation. Furthermore, the jurors believed more witnesses than they should have and they relied on inappropriate information in forming their assessments of eyewitness reliability. It is the latter issue that we wish to pursue to greater length in this section and in doing so we consider a number of studies in which the eyewitness evidence presented to mock-jurors has been systematically manipulated. In contrast to the earlier studies, the focus of these experiments is on determining juror sensitivity to a range of factors that are known, on the basis of empirical research, to influence or not influence eyewitness performance. In these experiments it is sensitivity to these factors and not ability to differentiate accurate from inaccurate witnesses that matters.

Lindsay, Lim, Marando, and Cully (1986) conducted four experiments to examine what factors influence the jurors' evaluations of eyewitnesses. Experiment 1 concerned the influence of the consistency of identification testimony across eyewitnesses. The subjects were 288 undergraduates who read a brief trial transcript involving a defendant charged with purse snatching. Lindsay et al. manipulated the physical evidence (strong vs. weak evidence against the accused), the number of eyewitnesses for the prosecution (0, 1, or 2) and the number of eyewitnesses for the defense (0, 1, or 2). The physical evidence was varied by having the victim's purse either found or not found in the defendant's possession. After reading the transcript (800 to 1,500 words) jurors rendered verdicts. The physical evidence did not significantly influence verdicts: Twenty-five percent of the subjects in the weak and 33% of the subjects in the strong evidence conditions convicted. However, the number of eyewitnesses for each side produced significant effects. The overall conviction rates were 41% for 0, 28% for 1, and 21% for 2 defense eyewitnesses, and 10% for 0, 34% for 1, and 45% for 2 prosecution eyewitness conditions. Convictions were most likely when the prosecution's witnesses were unopposed (50%), less likely with conflicting testimony (34%), and least likely with unopposed defense witness testimony (2%). Lindsay et al. concluded that the number of eyewitnesses was less important than whether or not there is conflicting eyewitness identifications.

Lindsay et al.'s second experiment focused on the effectiveness of defense witness testimony. A videotaped enactment of an assault trial was shown to 75 undergraduates. In all versions the victim testified that the defendant assaulted him during an attempted robbery. Five conditions were tested:

(a) no additional evidence;
(b) a second prosecution eyewitness who positively identified the defendant;
(c) a defense eyewitness who testified that the defendant was not the perpetrator;
(d) a defense witness who provided an alibi for the defendant; and
(e) a defense witness who provided the same alibi but was a relative of the defendant.

Although more convictions were obtained with two unopposed prosecution eyewitnesses (b = 80%) than one (a = 60%), this difference did not attain statistical significance. When a defense eyewitness testified that the defendant was not the perpetrator (c) or provided an alibi for the defendant (d), fewer jurors (27% in each condition) convicted. The 27% is significantly lower than the combined no defense witness (b) and the single unopposed prosecution witness (a) conditions. In comparison to the no-defense witness conditions, the alibi provided by the relative (e) did not significantly reduce the conviction rate (57% guilty). This experiment demonstrates that jurors do evaluate eyewitness identifications in light of other evidence presented in the case.

Lindsay et al.'s third experiment (study four in their published article) examined the impact of viewing conditions at the scene of the crime on jurors' perceptions. Audiotaped versions of a simulated burglary trial were played for 60 undergraduates. The defendant was identified by an eyewitness in an apartment near the scene of the burglary. In half of the trials the crime was described as occurring "at 9 AM on a sunny day." For the other half the crime occurred "at 1 AM, 60 feet from the nearest source of light (a streetlight)." Within each time-of-day condition, in one-third of the trials the viewing time was 5 seconds, in one-third it was 30 minutes, and in the remaining third, the eyewitness not only watched for 30 minutes but interacted with the burglar during that time. In all trials the eyewitness stated a high degree of confidence in his identification. Jurors rendered verdicts after hearing the audiotaped trial.

Exposure duration/quality produced a nonsignificant main effect on verdicts and did not significantly interact with time of day. The conviction rates were 45%, 40%, and 55% in the 5 seconds, 30 minutes, and 30 minutes + interaction conditions, respectively. Although jurors in the night condition convicted less often than jurors in the day condition (57% vs. 37%), this difference was not statistically significant. As in Experiment 3, perceived differences in viewing condition were significantly associated with conviction rate, even though the actual differences as reflected in the trial testimony were not. Jurors who convicted, in comparison to those who acquitted, rated the lighting conditions significantly more favorably (6.64 vs. 5.06 on a 9-point scale) and the interaction conditions superior (5.39 vs. 4.50). Again, these findings may be attributable to subjects' attempts to justify their decisions after the fact. These results indicate a lack of juror sensitivity to witnessing conditions that influence identification accuracy.

Note that these findings are not entirely consistent with the results from the Lindsay, Wells, and Rumpel (1981) study reviewed earlier. In that study mock-jurors' judgments of eyewitness accuracy were influenced by variations in witnessing conditions. It would appear that the witnessing conditions were more powerfully manipulated in the Lindsay, Wells, and Rumpel study (which also included a perpetrator disguise in the poor witnessing condition). It is, of course, worth emphasizing that jurors' sensitivity to witnessing conditions in the Lindsay, Wells, and Rumpel study did not reduce the overall number of erroneous judgments made by the jurors – it merely changed the nature of their guesses.

The fourth Lindsay et al. experiment (study three in their article) examined the joint impact of inconsistent eyewitness testimony and defendant attractiveness on mock-juror decisions. When attempting to discredit an eyewitness, it is a common strategy for an attorney to highlight inconsistencies in the eyewitness's recall testimony during cross-examination and encourage the jurors to infer, based on those inconsistencies, that the eyewitness's memory is faulty (Bailey & Rothblatt, 1985). Consistent with this recommendation, Prager, Moran, and Sanchez (1992) found that public defenders rated identification of inconsistencies in witness statements as one of the more important tasks in trial preparation. As one example of this perspective, judges' instructions in the state of Florida explicitly advise jurors to draw inferences about accuracy based on the consistency of eyewitness statements (Florida Standard Jury Instructions in Criminal Cases, 1987). In a related vein, earlier we saw that cross-examination that focused on errors in witness recall about peripheral details (Wells & Leippe, 1981) did significantly reduce juror belief of the cross-examined eyewitness (compared to eyewitnesses who were not cross-examined). Unfortunately, in that study, witnesses with poorer memory for peripheral details were actually slightly more likely to have made a correct identification.

To test whether jurors do discount eyewitness evidence when the eyewitness is inconsistent, Lindsay et al. presented an audiotaped simulated trial to 60 undergraduates. Slides of the defendant and the eyewitness were presented during the audiotaped testimony. In the consistent eyewitness condition, there were no inconsistencies in the eyewitness's testimony. In the inconsistent eyewitness condition, the eyewitness testified that she (a) originally stated the criminal was blond, (b) did not think that the defendant could be described as blond, (c) did not know if the defendant altered her hair color between the time of the crime and the lineup procedure, (d) recalled that the defendant's hair was dark when identified from the lineup, but (e) still felt certain she had made an accurate identification. Attractiveness was manipulated by showing slides of an attractive or an unattractive defendant. The defendant was the same in each condition but her makeup, hairstyle, and attire differed. Jurors rendered verdicts after hearing the audiotaped trial.

The consistency manipulation did not significantly influence jurors' verdicts. Indeed, somewhat fewer guilty verdicts were obtained when the eyewitness was consistent (43%) rather than inconsistent (50%). Despite the lack of a difference in verdict pattern, Lindsay et al. found that jurors who voted guilty perceived the eyewitness as being significantly more consistent (average rating of 7.86 on a 10-point scale) than did jurors who voted not guilty (5.90). As Lindsay et al. point out, this finding might be due to jurors' justifying their verdicts after the fact. The defendant was convicted by significantly fewer jurors when she was attractive (33%) than when she was unattractive (60%).

Berman, Narby, and Cutler (1994) have also studied the impact of witness consistency on juror evaluations of eyewitness testimony. Their study differs from Lindsay et al.'s (1986) consistency experiment in several respects. First, Lindsay et al. manipulated consistency on only one descriptive dimension and found no effect. Berman et al. devised a more powerful manipulation by increasing the number of descriptive dimensions on which the witness gives inconsistent testimony. Second, the dimension on which the witness gives inconsistent testimony was manipulated: central versus peripheral information. Witnesses are often questioned repeatedly and by different sources (at the scene of the crime by a uniformed officer, in follow-up interviews with detectives, in depositions with attorneys, and finally on the witness stand). Opportunities therefore exist for witnesses to contradict themselves on a variety of dimensions that are more or less relevant to the central issues in the case. Berman et al. therefore examined whether the centrality of the information about which the witness gives inconsistent testimony has a differential impact on juror reactions to the witness and testimony. They hypothesized that jurors exposed to inconsistent (as compared to consistent) eyewitness testimony would perceive the eyewitness as less credible, the defendant as less culpable, and would therefore be less likely to recommend a guilty verdict. They further hypothesized that inconsistent statements concerning central details would have a greater influence on mock-jurors' reactions than would inconsistent statements concerning peripheral details.

Subjects were 100 college students. They viewed a simulated examination and cross-examination of an eyewitness to a bank robbery (approximately 25 minutes in length). Inconsistencies were brought out during cross-examination. The design was a 2 (Central Details: consistent vs. inconsistent) x 2 (Peripheral Details: consistent vs. inconsistent) factorial; this required four versions of the videotaped examination and cross-examination. Whereas Lindsay et al. manipulated inconsistency on only one descriptive dimension, Berman et al. manipulated inconsistency on two descriptive dimensions. Each subject viewed one version of the videotape and completed a questionnaire assessing verdict, perceptions of the eyewitness, and perceptions of the defendant.

Conviction rates by condition were:

32% for peripheral-consistent/central-consistent,
12% for peripheral-consistent/central-inconsistent,
20% for peripheral-inconsistent/central-consistent and
8% for peripheral-inconsistent/central-inconsistent.

The main effect was significant for Central Details, X^2 $(1, N = 100) = 4.60, p < .05$, but nonsignificant for Peripheral Details, X^2 $(1, N = 100) = 1.15, p > .05$. The interaction was also nonsignificant, X^2 $(1, N = 100) = 0.29, p > .05$. The mock-jurors also evaluated the eyewitness and the defendant. Inconsistent details of both types led to significantly less positive evaluations of the eyewitness and more positive evaluations of the defendant, and on these dimensions Central and Peripheral Details had comparable effects.

The results of this experiment support the hypothesis that jurors exposed to inconsistent (as compared to consistent) eyewitness testimony perceive the eyewitness as less credible, the defendant as less culpable and, at least when the inconsistencies concern central details, are less likely to convict. In contrast, Lindsay et al. (1986) found no effect for consistency on jurors' verdicts. The difference between the Berman et al. results and the Lindsay et al. results may be attributable to the fact that the Berman et al. study manipulated inconsistency on more central details than did Lindsay et al. – the more powerful the manipulation, the greater the effect. Other explanations for the disparate results between Berman et al.'s and Lindsay et al.'s experiments are discussed in Berman et al.

Note that even though exposing inconsistencies in witness testimony may be an effective strategy for cross-examination, it is not clear whether this strategy improves the quality of jurors' decisions. The eyewitness studies reviewed in Chapter 6 indicate that description accuracy, congruence, and consistency are *not* related to identification accuracy and jurors probably should not use such inconsistencies as a basis for evaluating eyewitness reliability.

Bell and Loftus (1989) conducted two experiments that examine another aspect of eyewitness testimony: the influence of the level of detail in eyewitness testimony on juror reactions to eyewitnesses. Subjects in their first experiment were 302 students who read narratives describing a criminal trial. Within these summaries the degree of the detail provided by the prosecution witness (high vs. low), the degree of detail provided by the defense witness (high vs. low) and the degree of relationship between the detail and the perpetrator (high vs. low) were manipulated. Relatedness was manipulated by having the statements either concern the actions of the perpetrator or another party. Level of detail was manipulated by having witness statements contain either the gist of what happened (e.g., "she saw a boy purchase a few store items") or specific details about the event (e.g., "she saw a boy purchase a box of Milk Duds and a can of Diet Pepsi"). After reading the summaries, each subject indicated his or her verdict.

In general, detail of testimony did influence subjects' verdicts. With respect to the prosecution eyewitness's testimony, 33% of the mock–jurors convicted when the testimonial detail was high and 21% convicted when the testimonial detail was low; this difference was statistically significant. With respect to the defense eyewitness's testimony, 23% convicted when the testimonial detail was high and 31% convicted when it was low; this difference was marginally significant. Relatedness did not significantly influence verdicts, either as a main effect or in combination with level of detail. These findings indicate that the level of detail contained in testimony influences jurors' reactions to eyewitness testimony whether the testimony is relevant to the defendant or is not relevant – which further suggests that jurors use the presence of details to make a fairly global judgment about the reliability of the witness. This interpretation is consistent with Bell and Loftus's finding that the level of testimonial detail was positively and significantly associated with ratings of both the prosecution and defense eyewitnesses credibility, quality of memory for details, quality of memory for the perpetrator's face, and degree of attention to the perpetrator's characteristics and actions during the crime.

Bell and Loftus's second experiment used a similar methodology but several different factors were manipulated. The trial summary was changed to reflect a question–answer rather than narrative format. The prosecution eyewitness always gave low-detail testimony and the defense eyewitness always gave testimony related to the perpetrator. Bell and Loftus manipulated the degree of detail in the defense eyewitness's testimony (high vs. low, as in Experiment 1) and verification of the prosecution eyewitness's testimony. In the no-verification condition, the prosecution eyewitness was not asked about her memory for details provided by the defense eyewitness. In the verification condition, the witness was asked but replied that she could not remember the details. Subjects were 122 undergraduates who read the case summaries and rendered verdicts.

The main effect of level of detail of the defense eyewitness's testimony was significant. Subjects were less likely to convict when the defense eyewitness gave highly detailed testimony (6% in the verification condition; 31% in the no-verification condition) than when the testimony was less detailed (47% and 25%, respectively). This main effect was qualified by a significant interaction with verification. As the above means demonstrate, level of detail had a much larger effect in the verification condition than in the no-verification condition. This pattern helps to clarify the weak effect for detail of the defense eyewitness testimony in Experiment 1 (in which there was no verification) and supports Bell and Loftus's contention that jurors sometimes rely on superficial cues to evaluate the testimony of eyewitnesses. Additional research on the influence of testimonial detail is presented in Bell and Loftus (1988). Given that eyewitness research (see Chapter 6) shows that memory for physical characteristics and peripheral details does not predict eyewitness identification accuracy, these data provide further evidence that jurors are insensitive to some of the factors that influence eyewitness identification accuracy and inappropriately sensitive to factors that are not diagnostic of eyewitness accuracy.

One limitation that characterizes all of the juror sensitivity research described so far is the nearly exclusive reliance on undergraduates as experimental subjects. Researchers have questioned the generalizability of studies involving college students (Konecni & Ebbesen, 1979; Weiten & Diamond, 1979). Can we expect these results to generalize to the judgments of sworn jurors or even more realistic samples of prospective jurors? On the one hand, most college students are prospective jurors. They hold drivers' licenses and voter registration cards and are therefore eligible jurors in most states. It is even conceivable that results of studies using college students substantially overestimate the sensitivity of jurors, as they are better educated than many of their fellow eligible jurors and many have had at least one psychology course in which memory processes are undoubtedly discussed. Ultimately, the comparability of student subject and juror judgments is an empirical question, one that is addressed in the following section.

We (Cutler, Penrod, & Stuve, 1988; Cutler, Penrod, & Dexter, 1990) conducted a mock-jury experiment to examine the factors that jurors use to evaluate eyewitness identification evidence. A simulated trial was shown to 321 University of Wisconsin undergraduates and 129 former jurors from Dane County, Wisconsin. The trial concerned a defendant accused of the armed robbery of a liquor store. A positive identification of the defendant by the robbery victim was the primary source of trial evidence. Testifying as the first trial witness, the clerk of the liquor store and victim of the robbery described the witnessing conditions and the conditions under which she identified the defendant as the robber. Next, the police officer in charge of the investigation described the conditions under which the identification was made. Third, a character witness – a friend of the defendant – provided him with a relatively weak alibi. The defendant was the last witness. He denied all allegations against him yet offered little concrete evidence to support his case. Examination (direct and cross) of the two prosecution witnesses served as a vehicle for disclosure of the approximately 20 witness and identification factors that were discussed in the trial. In his closing arguments, the defense attorney reiterated many of the factors disclosed during cross-examination. Ten of these variables were systematically manipulated in the trial presentations (all two-levels) whereas the remainder were held constant. We refer the interested reader to Cutler, Penrod, and Stuve (1988) for a more detailed description of the videotaped trial. The two primary dependent measures were verdict (not guilty vs. guilty) and the subject's estimate of the probability that the identification was correct. Both dependent variables were equivalently influenced by the eyewitness factors, so only the verdict results are summarized in Table 13.1.

The witness testified that, during the robbery, the robber wore either (a) a knit cap fully covering his hair or (b) no hat. Disguise of robber, which normally affects identification accuracy (see Chapter 7), produced a nonsignificant main effect on jurors' judgments.

The witness testified that throughout the robbery a handgun was either (a) outwardly brandished and pointed at her or (b) hidden in the robber's jacket. This manipulation attempted to simulate the presence or absence of a "weapon focus" effect, which tends to reduce identification accuracy (see Chapter 7). The main effect weapon focus on juror judgments was nonsignificant.

According to the witness, the robber either (a) threatened to kill her, manhandled her, fired his handgun into the floor, and pushed her to the floor before leaving or (b) calmly and quietly demanded the money and then left. Generally, violence is thought to reduce identification accuracy (see Chapter 7). Violence produced no significant main effect on jurors' judgments.

Table 13.1. *Conviction rates from Cutler, Penrod, and Dexter (1990)*

Factor/Level	Percentage of convictions
Disguise	
(a) High	63
(b) Low	63
Weapon focus	
(a) High	64
(b) Low	63
Violence	
(a) High	63
(b) Low	63
Retention interval	
(a) Fourteen days	63
(b) Two days	63
Instruction bias	
(a) High	62
(b) Low	64
Foil bias	
(a) High	63
(b) Low	64
Witness confidence	
(a) 100%	67
(b) 80%	60
Juror type	
(a) Eligible & experienced	60
(b) Undergraduate	64

The witness testified that the identification was made either (a) 14 days after the robbery or (b) 2 days after the robbery. Retention interval, which influences identification accuracy (see Chapter 7), did not affect jurors' judgments.

In half of the trials the police officer who conducted the lineup testified that the witness was instructed to (a) "choose the suspect from the lineup who you believe is the robber." In these trials the witness was not explicitly offered the option of rejecting the lineup – an instruction that commonly leads to false identifications (see Chapter 8). In the other half of the trials the officer testified that the witness was instructed to (b) "choose the suspect from the lineup who you believe is the robber or indicate that the robber was not in the lineup." The main effect for lineup instructions was nonsignificant.

In half of the videotapes the witness testified that (a) very few of the lineup members looked like the robber. Added to this, the officer testified that foil selections included anyone who was available at the time. In the other trial the witness testified that (b) there were several lineup members who resembled the robber in physical appearance. To complement this testimony, the police officer added that, in constructing the lineup, he had provided another officer (not involved with the case) with the witness's original description of the robber and asked him to select foils who matched that description. Foil bias, which is known to influence identification accuracy (see Chapter 8), had a nonsignificant influence on mock-jurors' verdicts.

The witness testified that she was either (a) 100% or (b) 80% confident that she had correctly identified the robber. Recall that summaries of the eyewitness identification literature (see Chapters 6 and 7) reveal that eyewitness confidence and identification accuracy are only weakly related. Witness confidence produced the only statistically significant main effect of appreciable magnitude. The size of this effect should be considered in light of the relatively small difference in witness confidence between the low and high confidence conditions (80% vs. 100%).

The main effect for (a) eligible and experienced versus (b) undergraduate jurors was trivial and nonsignificant.

It is worth noting that the Witness Confidence by Subject Type interaction did not approach statistical significance. Thus, undergraduate and eligible and experienced jurors all gave comparable (disproportionate) weight to witness confidence.

A significant Weapon Presence by Subject Type interaction showed that weapon presence had a stronger impact on the judgments of eligible and experienced jurors than on the judgments of undergraduate jurors. Among undergraduate jurors weapon presence produced a trivial main effect on jurors' judgments, but eligible and experienced jurors were significantly more likely to convict if the weapon was present (M = .66) than if the weapon was hidden (M = .54). This finding shows that neither group is appropriately sensitive to the weapon focus effect.

There is a possibility that the failure to observe differences on most of these variables could arise if jurors did not remember the trial evidence or were confused about it. However, as shown in Table 13.2, detailed analyses of juror memory for the evidence (see Cutler, Penrod, & Stuve, 1988) indicates that the subjects paid attention to the testimony and recalled it with high accuracy rates. Hence, lack of attention and poor memory cannot explain the null effects of eyewitness evidence on mock-jurors' decisions

In sum, our research provides strong evidence that jurors are insensitive to some of the more important factors that influence identification accuracy. Testimony about disguise, weapon focus, violence, retention interval, instruction bias, and foil bias, which tend to influence identification accuracy (see Chapters 6, 7, and 8), had trivial effects on mock-jurors' evaluations of identification evidence. A modest difference in the confidence of the eyewitness – a factor that generally is only weakly related to identification accuracy (see Chapter 6) – produced a larger (and the only significant) main effect than any of the witness factors considered separately. In addition, this research indicates that the judgment processes of eligible and experienced jurors are comparable to those of college student subjects and supports the generalizability of the research we have described.

Conclusions

Opportunities for the attorney to gather eyewitness-related information for trial preparation are limited by practical constraints (the attorney is not present when the crime occurs) as well as by procedural constraints imposed by the criminal justice system (the right to counsel at identification tests applies only to live lineups conducted after indictment). The research on attorney sensitivity to the factors that influence eyewitness identification accuracy raises concerns about attorneys' abilities to employ important information even when the opportunity exists. Little is known about judges' abilities to evaluate identification accuracy. Inferences based on published opinions (e.g., *Neil v. Biggers*, 1972; see also Chapter 17) raise questions about the factors that judges' believe to be important.

More comprehensive research has been conducted on jury knowledge about the factors that affect identification accuracy and their decision processes in eyewitness cases. Taken together, the survey studies, the prediction studies, and the mock–juror experiments converge on the conclusion that jurors are generally insensitive to factors that influence eyewitness identification accuracy, often rely on factors (such as recall of

Table 13.2. *Recall of trial evidence from Cutler, Penrod, and Stuve (1988)*

Factor/Level	Recall
Disguise	
(a) High	.94[a]
(b) Low	.65
Weapon focus	
(a) High	.72[a]
(b) Low	.86
Violence	
(a) High	7.42[b]
(b) Low	3.78
Retention interval	
(a) Fourteen days	.97[a]
(b) Two days	.97
Instruction bias	
(a) High	5.93[c]
(b) Low	2.46
Foil bias	
(a) High	5.41[d]
(b) Low	6.21
Witness confidence	
(a) 100%	.97[a]
(b) 80%	.99
Exposure to mugshots	
(a) Mugshots shown	.97[a]
(b) Mugshots not shown	.95
Lineup size	
(a) Six-suspect	.85[a]
(b) Twelve-suspect	.93
Voice samples	
Not presented	.93[a]
Presented	.97

a, proportion of subjects who correctly recalled testimony; *b*, rated on nine-point scale where 9 = very threatened, *c*, 9 = unfair lineup; *d*, 9 = high similarity among foils peripheral details) that are not diagnostic of witness accuracy, and rely heavily on one factor, eyewitness confidence, that possesses only modest value as an indicator of witness accuracy.   The implications of this conclusion are profound.   Even if attorneys were given the opportunity to gather the information necessary for effective cross-examination and even if they knew what questions to ask in eliciting eyewitness identification information at trial, the effectiveness of cross-examination as a safeguard is still questionable in light of the lack of juror sensitivity to factors that are known to be diagnostic of eyewitness reliability.

Part VI

Is the eyewitness expert an effective safeguard against mistaken identification?

14 Expert testimony and its possible impacts on the jury

We have now provided evidence that expert psychological testimony is becoming increasingly common as a safeguard (Chapter 3); evidence that cross-examination, the most commonly used safeguard, appears ineffective (Chapters 9 and 10); and evidence that jurors are largely insensitive to factors known to influence eyewitness performance but are sensitive to factors with little or no diagnostic value. It light of these facts, it behooves us to assess the effectiveness of expert testimony. Research addressing expert testimony as a safeguard follows a general description of the likely content of such testimony.

The form of eyewitness expert testimony

What would a psychologist, who possesses expert knowledge about eyewitnesses, say on the witness stand? In general, an expert might – if given sufficient latitude by the judge – briefly lecture the jury on the psychology of memory processes, much as an instructor would lecture to an introductory psychology class. The expert might explain the encoding, storage, and retrieval stages of memory and the factors that influence each (see Chapters 6 and 7). Encoding factors are those relating to the crime, the perpetrator, the crime environment, and the eyewitness. Storage factors are phenomena that occur between the crime and the identification test, and retrieval factors are those associated with the identification test itself. The expert would probably limit his or her discussion to factors that are relevant to the specific crime. For example, if the witness is white and the perpetrator black, the expert would discuss the effect of cross-race recognition processes. If the witness and perpetrator are of the same race, the expert would not mention cross-race recognition processes. In identifying the factors that are likely to have influenced identification accuracy, the expert will draw upon up-to-date reviews of the eyewitness

213

research such as those presented in Chapters 6 and 7. Indeed, these chapters could be used (at least for a limited period of time) to formulate expert testimony, to check the validity of expert testimony, or to develop a strategy for cross-examination of an expert psychologist. Experts generally do not give opinions about the reliability of specific eyewitnesses (although they might be more likely to do so in other countries such as Germany – see Maass, Brigham & West, 1985).

Within the psychological community there is some debate about the appropriateness of expert testimony on eyewitness memory and on the content of such testimony. Some of this debate reflects commentators' interpretation of experts' legal and ethical responsibilities (e.g., Loftus, 1986). Other aspects of this debate, which are more the focus of the current chapter, concern the reliability of the research that forms the foundation for the expert testimony and the effects of expert testimony on jury decision processes. As we explained in Chapter 3, courts have traditionally required that the content of expert testimony reflect scientific principles generally accepted in the field, though the more modern trend, reflected in the Supreme Court's 1993 decision in *Daubert* (see Chapter 3), is to look less at general acceptance and more to the scientific validity of the procedures that have produced the knowledge represented in the expert testimony. However, if we begin by considering eyewitness expert testimony in light of the traditional "general acceptance" standard, it is obvious from the discussions in Chapters 6 and 7 that there is more agreement about some principles than others. Disagreements over the appropriateness of the content of some instances of expert testimony have surfaced in various forums.

In a special issue of the research journal *Law and Human Behavior* (1986*b*), Elizabeth Loftus, a psychologist who has, perhaps, testified as an expert on eyewitness memory more frequently than any other psychologist, gave examples of testimony she had given on numerous occasions. Hastie, in a commentary on her article, noted: "Some excerpts from Loftus's and Buckhout's [another psychologist who has testified frequently on eyewitness memory] transcripts go beyond the limits of interpretation and generalization from laboratory to everyday world that are personally acceptable to me." Hastie indicated that when he testified, he tended to focus primarily on police identification procedures. Others, such as Pachella (1986) and Konecni and Ebbesen (1986) argued against most, if not all, expert testimony on eyewitness memory. Noted Pachella about the content of typical expert testimony: "To go before a jury . . . and to present irrelevant and inaccurate generalities as if they were the critical information that a jury needs in order to determine the veridicality of a particular witness, constitutes a serious misrepresentation of the status of experimental psychology." Konecni and Ebbesen (1986) echoed this theme: "The practice of only giving such testimony is premature, given the present state of psychological knowledge, or, more specifically, given the methods by which such knowledge was obtained." Elliott (1993) expressed similar concerns. McCloskey, Egeth, and McKenna (1986) summarized the debated issues as follows: "(1) How well supported should a statement be? and (2) how much support do the available data provide for the sorts of statements experimental psychologists commonly make in expert testimony?"

Given the debate among the more outspoken experts and their critics, it comes as no surprise that trial courts have come down on both sides of the issue, with some concluding that a consensus exists (e.g., *United States v. Smith*, 1984) and others concluding that there is no consensus (e.g., *United States v. Fosher*, 1979). But to what extent does the public debate represent the views of the less vocal majority? A more reliable and valid assessment of consensus in the field requires a systematic sampling of opinion rather than a reliance on outspoken advocates on both sides. In Chapter 4 we reviewed research on eyewitness experts including that of Yarmey and Jones (1983), who found high levels of agreement on many topics among the 16 experts they surveyed. Kassin, Ellsworth, and Smith (1989, 1994) replicated and expanded Yarmey and Jones's findings in a survey of eyewitness experts from the United States, Canada, and Europe. The 63 experts completed a 24-page questionnaire in which they evaluated the reliability of 21 eyewitness phenomena and provided personal background information. Most experts (56%) had testified at least once, with a total of 478 appearances. As was shown in Table 4.1 considerable consensus was obtained for most of the phenomena examined. And, because of the continued growth in eyewitness research, it is likely that even higher levels of consensus would be found if the survey were replicated today.

What effect is this form of expert testimony likely to have on jury decisions? As we discussed in Chapter 3, expert testimony has been rejected for a variety of reasons. In that chapter we identified three basic issues raised by the courts:

1. What is the state of scientific findings regarding eyewitness performance? Are the findings reliable/do they rest on an adequate scientific foundation?
2. Do the traditional trial safeguards – cross-examination and cautionary instructions to jurors – afford adequate protection to defendants identified and prosecuted on the basis of eyewitness evidence?

3. Can eyewitness expert evidence assist jurors in their assessment of eyewitness evidence?

We have treated the first two questions at length in the preceding chapters. At this point we want to consider the third point and examine a number of assumptions about the effects of expert testimony on jury decision processes that can be identified in the legal and psychological literatures. For example, some judges believe that expert testimony will confuse the jury. Others believe that it will prejudice the jury. We have tried to classify the possible effects of expert testimony and consider these effects in the following discussion. We underscore that judicial impressions about the possible effects of expert testimony are essentially speculative and lack an empirical foundation – nonetheless, the issues raised in these speculations can, in fact, be addressed empirically. Recognition of the empirical questions has prompted some researchers, ourselves included, to bring data to bear on the question of what effects expert testimony has on jury decision making.

The expert's influence on the jury: Plausible effects

Plausible effects of expert testimony can generally be classified into three categories: juror confusion, juror sensitivity, and juror skepticism.

Juror confusion

If the expert testimony confuses jurors, they might disregard it, in which case expert testimony would have no influence on their decision processes. Alternatively, confused jurors might misapply the expert testimony. In this case, expert testimony might cause jurors to draw inappropriate conclusions about eyewitnesses. The possibility of expert testimony confusing jurors is supported by findings that show jurors have difficulty understanding and applying a variety of legal concepts at virtually every stage of the trial process (Penrod & Cutler, 1987).

Juror sensitivity: Knowledge and integration

If expert testimony does in fact influence juror decision making, what effect should it have? Clearly a desirable effect is to improve juror sensitivity to the factors that influence eyewitness memory (McCloskey et al., 1986; Wells, 1986). We use sensitivity to refer to both knowledge of how a given factor influences eyewitness memory and the ability to render decisions in accordance with that knowledge. Thus, sensitivity contains two components: knowledge and integration. Knowledge refers to awareness of the manner in which a factor influences eyewitness memory, including the direction and magnitude of the effect for a given factor. Integration, in this context, refers to the ability to render decisions that reflect knowledge. For example, a judge of beer might specify in advance that brews shall be rated on the dimensions of bouquet, palate, finish, fidelity to style, appearance, and body. Though specified a priori, there is no guarantee that the judge's ratings will actually reflect this weighing scheme. A perusal of a collection of data might indicate that palate and fidelity to style were given substantially less weight than finish, which was given less weight than body and appearance. If this were so, then the judge would show poor integration skills. If, on the other hand, a collection of judgments indicated that the judge in fact used the rating dimensions in accordance with the a priori rating scheme, then the judge would show good integration skills.

How are knowledge and integration pertinent to the issue of juror sensitivity? It might be the case that jurors are unaware of the manner in which some factors influence eyewitness memory. For example, the survey studies described in Chapter 11 revealed that jurors are insensitive to the equivocal effects of training on eyewitness identification accuracy (Chapter 6) – a majority of laypersons appear to believe that police officers are better eyewitnesses than laypersons even though the evidence indicates there are no significant differences in identification performance. On the other hand there is some evidence in these surveys that laypersons are somewhat sensitive to the influence of cross-race recognition.

Of course, even if jurors are aware of the relative effects of a given factor on eyewitness memory, the magnitude of that effect might be attenuated in the juror's integration of the evidence. In other words, the jurors' judgments might not reflect their a priori beliefs. Decision-making research in a variety of psychological domains (e.g., Goldberg, 1968) shows that integration is quite difficult to achieve, even by trained experts. One psychological factor that might be partially responsible for poor integration is the anchoring and adjustment heuristic (Tversky & Kahneman, 1974). It is conceivable that jurors have some a priori belief level in eyewitness identification evidence and fail, in light of the evidence, adequately to adjust their levels of belief from that point of central tendency. This could account for attenuation of evidence effects on jurors' judgments.

The mock-jury studies discussed in the previous chapter showed that jurors are insensitive to many forms of eyewitness evidence, but it is not clear whether this insensitivity is due to lack of knowledge, poor integration skills, or some combination of the two. One plausible effect of expert testimony is that it could improve both knowledge and integration of eyewitness evidence.

Juror skepticism

Though it is agreed that improved juror sensitivity is a desirable effect of expert testimony (McCloskey et al., 1986; Wells, 1986), there is considerable disagreement as to whether jurors should be made more skeptical of the accuracy of eyewitness identifications. There is ample evidence that eyewitness identifications are often inaccurate. As we discussed in Chapter 1, realistic field experiments (e.g., Brigham et al., 1982; Krafka & Penrod, 1985) show that, at least in a narrowly defined set of circumstances, witnesses give correct judgments on identification tests approximately 50% of the time. The prediction studies and the studies of mock-jurors' abilities to discriminate between accurate and inaccurate eyewitnesses (Chapter 12) provide some evidence that jurors "overbelieve" eyewitnesses, but the issue remains in debate (e.g., McCloskey & Egeth, 1983; McCloskey et al., 1986). And, although it is not evidence that there is a general overbelief in eyewitnesses, the fact that large numbers of convictions based on erroneous identifications have been identified by researchers such as Borchard (1932) and Huff (1987) (see also Kolata, 1994) demonstrates that jurors in too many cases give inappropriate credence to eyewitness identifications.

Research on the effects of expert psychological testimony

It is possible to examine independently skepticism and sensitization effects, and it is possible to detect juror confusion as well. Unfortunately, as we shall see in our review of early research on expert witness effects, the procedures designed to test the effects of expert testimony confounded skepticism and sensitization effects and made it difficult to determine exactly how jurors were affected by expert testimony. Tests of sensitizing effects require that subjects be presented some combination of expert versus no-expert testimony *and* good versus poor witnessing or identification conditions. In Chapters 11–13 we observed that jurors are largely insensitive to variations in trial evidence that ought to permit them to at least partially differentiate between good and poor eyewitnessing conditions and therefore, between accurate and inaccurate eyewitnesses. The critical question is whether expert testimony enhances jurors' abilities to make those differentiations. A perhaps less critical issue is whether expert testimony simply makes jurors more skeptical of eyewitness evidence but does not produce enhanced differentiation of good versus poor witnessing conditions.

In one trial simulation experiment Wells, Lindsay, and Tousignant (1980) showed half of their 192 mock-jurors a videotape of a psychologist's testimony regarding matters of eyewitness identification. The other half were not exposed to expert testimony. The expert's testimony, which lasted approximately 5.5 minutes, centered on levels of accuracy of eyewitnesses and on the weak relation between confidence and identification accuracy. In addition, the expert indicated that jurors should attend to the situational factors involved in the crime and not to the confidence of the witness. A videotape of the cross-examination of the eyewitness was viewed *after* the videotape of the expert testimony for those subjects who heard expert testimony (a reversal of the usual trial order). In total, videotapes of 108 independent witnesses were used. On the basis of group performance on an identification test in an earlier staged incident experiment (Lindsay, Wells, & Rumpel, 1981), witnesses were classified into one of three groups differing with respect to identification accuracy rates: poor (33% correct), moderate (50% correct), and good (74% correct). As noted in our earlier discussion of these procedures (Chapter 12), the differential accuracy rates were induced through manipulations of the witness viewing conditions (disguises worn by the robber and exposure quality).

Each juror watched videotaped cross-examinations of four independent eyewitnesses to a staged crime (all drawn from the same condition). The videotaped cross-examination of each witness consisted of 15 questions about what the perpetrator was wearing and the witness's opportunity to view the perpetrator. The primary dependent measure was whether or not the juror believed the eyewitness. Wells et al. found a significant main effect for expert testimony such that jurors who heard expert testimony were less likely to believe the eyewitnesses (41%) than jurors who heard no expert testimony (62%). There was also a significant main effect for witness condition indicating that jurors were somewhat sensitive to the witnessing conditions. Though there was a trend toward improved sensitivity with expert testimony (i.e., a tendency for jurors in the expert witness condition to show enhanced sensitivity to poor, moderate, and good witness conditions), the interaction term was not statistically significant. Thus, Wells et al.'s experiment demonstrated, primarily, a skepticism effect.

Loftus (1980), in her first expert witness experiment, examined the judgments of 240 subjects who participated in a mock-jury study. Jurors read a transcript of a trial involving the commission of a crime. The violence associated with the crime and the presence of expert psychological testimony were independently manipulated. The expert discussed several factors that were relevant to the case and known to influence identification accuracy: own-race bias, stress, weapon focus, and alcohol intoxication. Expert testimony, on average, significantly reduced conviction rates. The conviction rates were 58% among subjects who were not exposed to expert testimony and 39% among subjects who were exposed. Subjects who read the violent version (56%) were significantly more likely to convict as compared to subjects who read the nonviolent version (41%). The trend toward increased convictions associated with the violent crime was weakened by the expert testimony (evidence of greater juror sensitivity), though the interaction term was not tested for statistical significance. Among subjects exposed to expert testimony, 43% who read the violent version and 35% who read the nonviolent version convicted. The corresponding conviction rates for subjects who were not exposed to expert testimony were, respectively, 68% and 47%. These findings suggest that expert testimony leads to some sensitization (with respect to the effects of violence on eyewitness memory) and to some skepticism. Loftus's second experiment revealed that juries who were exposed to expert testimony spent significantly more time deliberating about the eyewitness evidence (10.6 min. on average) than did juries who were not exposed to expert testimony (6.8 min. on average).

Hosch, Beck, and McIntyre (1980) exposed 24 subjects (comprising four juries of six members each) to a videotaped trial in which expert testimony was either present or absent. Although the presence of expert testimony did not significantly influence ratings of the reliability of the eyewitness identification, juries who heard the expert testimony rated the identification as significantly less important (with respect to reaching a verdict) than did juries who did not hear expert testimony. Analysis of deliberations revealed that expert testimony significantly increased the amount of time that jurors spent discussing the eyewitness evidence. Among juries who heard expert testimony, 28% of deliberation time was devoted to discussion of the eyewitness testimony. Among juries who did not hear expert testimony, 10% of deliberation time was devoted to discussing eyewitness testimony.

Maass, Brigham, and West (1985) examined the impact of several different forms of expert testimony on jurors' perceptions of the defendant's culpability. Subjects read one of two court cases. The results from the two cases were comparable, so we will discuss the results of only one case. Expert testimony was either person-based or sample-based testimony and causal explanations were either present or absent. Person-based testimony refers to expert testimony that relies primarily on interviews with the witness whereas sample-based testimony refers to testimony that relies primarily on research findings. In the causal testimony conditions the expert offered a probability that the identification was correct and, in addition, offered a number of causal explanations for the probability (e.g., time delays, arousal, cross-racial identification). In the noncausal testimony conditions the expert offered the probability but gave no causal explanations. Ratings of defendant culpability (on a 1 to 7 scale) constituted one of the primary dependent variables. Postdeliberation data are summarized in Figure 14.1. Overall, expert testimony led to more lenient judgments. Among mock-jurors who heard person-based expert testimony, causal testimony reduced culpability ratings to a significantly greater extent than did noncausal testimony. The presence or absence of causal testimony did not significantly affect decisions among mock-jurors who heard sample-based expert testimony. Just as important, as Figure 14.1 shows, the effects of expert testimony were significantly larger in postdeliberation than in predeliberation data. The subjects who heard expert testimony deliberated for a longer period of time than did subjects in the baseline conditions. In addition causal testimony led to longer deliberation times than did noncausal testimony.

Fox and Walters (1986) exposed 128 undergraduates to videotaped segments of eyewitness testimony and expert testimony as separate segments of a trial. The witness had either high or low confidence. Three conditions of expert testimony were crossed with the eyewitness conditions: no expert testimony, general expert testimony, and specific expert testimony. General expert testimony included identification accuracy rates obtained in previous experiments, general memory processes (acquisition, retention, and retrieval), and types of memory (sensory, short-term, and long-term). Specific testimony, on the other hand, consisted of similar testimony, but instead of general memory processes the expert psychologist discussed the effects of 12 specific factors that are known to influence eyewitness memory (e.g., physical factors, exposure time, retention interval, stress, weapon focus, the fairness of lineup procedures). In addition, in all expert testimony

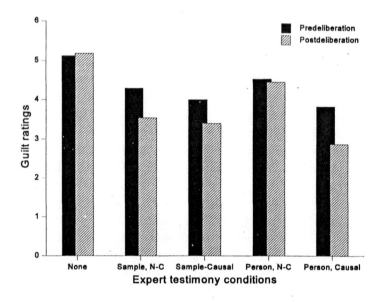

Figure 14.1. The influence of expert testimony and deliberations on juror judgments

conditions the expert psychologist discussed the weak relation between confidence and accuracy.

Among the dependent variables examined was belief in the accuracy of the identification. This belief was significantly influenced by the confidence of the eyewitness and the presence of expert testimony. The percentages of subjects who believed the eyewitness in the high and low confidence conditions were 70% and 55% among subjects who heard no expert testimony, 50% and 18% among subjects who heard general expert testimony, and 30% and 5% among subjects who heard specific expert testimony. Thus, expert testimony produced skepticism but also appeared to have a negative impact on sensitivity – insofar as jurors in the expert testimony conditions apparently gave *more* weight to witness confidence than jurors in the no-expert condition did. Although the authors did not test the interaction between confidence and expert testimony for statistical significance, our estimate from their reported data indicates that the difference in sensitivity to witness confidence was marginally significant (p = .07). And, although verdicts were not obtained, subjects rated the culpability of the defendant on a 10-point scale. General (M = 4.81) and specific (M = 4.23) expert testimony led to significantly lower culpability ratings in comparison to the no-expert testimony condition (M = 6.07).

The experiments just described reveal some consistent findings with respect to expert testimony. Most evident is that reduced belief and fewer convictions are obtained if expert testimony is presented (Fox & Walters, 1986; Hosch et al., 1980; Loftus, 1980; Maass et al., 1985; Wells et al., 1980). It is not clear whether this reduced belief is due to improved sensitivity to factors that might have impaired the witnesses' ability to make a correct identification, to increased skepticism, or to both. The experiments by Fox and Walters (1986), Hosch et al. (1980), and Maass et al. (1985) did not independently vary the presence of expert testimony *and* witnessing and identification factors that have important influences on eyewitness memory – without variations in witnessing conditions, we cannot determine whether expert testimony enhances jurors' abilities to discriminate among those conditions. Therefore, skepticism and sensitivity are confounded. Fox and Walters did vary the presence of expert testimony and eyewitness confidence simultaneously, but there was no substantial improvement in juror sensitivity to the weak relationship between confidence and identification accuracy.

The only experiments that simultaneously and independently varied witnessing factors that influence identification accuracy and the presence of expert testimony were those by Loftus (1980) and Wells et al. (1980), and both show trends toward improved sensitivity.

Data from the jury deliberation content analyses of Hosch et al., Loftus, and Maass et al. revealed that expert testimony increased the time that jurors spent deliberating about eyewitness evidence. But what can be made of deliberation time measures? Perhaps more time spent deliberating means that the jurors were attempting to reach an understanding of how a given factor might have influenced the witness's memory. If so, then expert testimony, which presumably clarifies these issues, should arguably lead to less deliberation time. On the other hand, perhaps extended deliberation time means that jurors were giving more thoughtful attention to the eyewitness evidence. Without more detailed content analyses it is difficult to characterize the effects of expert testimony on jury deliberations.

Another potential limitation of most previous studies (Fox & Walters, 1986; Loftus, 1980; Maass et al., 1985) is that they exclusively used undergraduates as subjects. Exceptions to this work include Hosch et al. (1980), who used undergraduates in one phase of the study and community members enrolled in a continuing education program in another phase of the study. In addition, Wells et al. (1980) employed jury-eligible subjects but gave no information about their demographic characteristics. As we already mentioned, some researchers have questioned how generalizable studies involving college students as subjects are to more heterogeneous populations of eligible jurors – these studies reveal no evidence of problems in generalizing across groups.

Overall, the research available through 1985 supported the conclusions of Wells (1986) and McCloskey et al. (1986) that: "At this point . . . we must acknowledge fully that there has not been a persuasive demonstration in the published literature that expert testimony on eyewitness matters improves the judgments of jurors" (Wells, 1986, p. 86).

15 Improving juror knowledge, integration, and decision making

In order to redress some of the deficiencies of the studies reviewed in Chapter 14 we (Cutler, Dexter, & Penrod, 1989; Cutler, Penrod, & Dexter, 1989) designed experiments to examine two of the three hypotheses (sensitization and skepticism) concerning the effects of expert testimony on jurors' judgments. Witnessing and identification conditions (WIC), witness confidence, and the presence of expert testimony were varied orthogonally, thus permitting independent tests of sensitivity and skepticism. Finally, we used as subjects eligible and/or experienced jurors as well as undergraduates to test whether they are comparably influenced by expert testimony.

The videotaped trial was the same as the one used in the studies described in Chapter 14 (Cutler, Penrod, & Dexter, 1990; Cutler, Penrod, & Stuve, 1988). Expert testimony was edited in to this videotaped trial. The expert testimony was organized into the following components: First the expert's qualifications were presented, and the psychologist was accepted by the judge as an expert on eyewitness testimony. Next, the expert described to the jury the case-relevant documents that he studied prior to the trial. Finally, the expert gave testimony to the jury on (a) the reconstructive nature of memory and (b) factors that affect memory at the perception, encoding, storage, and retrieval stages. In response to the defense attorney's questions, the expert discussed how the factors associated with the crime and with the identification procedures might have impaired the witness's memory for the perpetrator. The expert also discussed the effects of stress and violence, the presence of a weapon, the passage of time, suggestive lineup procedures, and the relationship between confidence and identification accuracy. The expert described the effects of disguises only in trials in which the witness testified that the robber was disguised during the robbery.

During the prosecution's rigorous cross-examination of the expert, the expert acknowledged the following points: (a) when the psychologist had previously testified it was always on the behalf of the defense; (b) the research about which the expert testified relied heavily on the use of college undergraduates as subjects and crime simulations rather than actual crimes;

225

(c) some psychologists express doubts about the reliability of the research findings and about the extent to which the research findings generalize to actual crime situations; (d) stress and violence can sometimes improve memory; (e) individuals vary with respect to their reactions to stress and violence; (f) there is no way to know how much stress a witness experienced at the time of a crime or its effect on a specific witness's memory; (g) some studies show a strong positive relation between eyewitness confidence and identification accuracy; (h) even in studies that found a low confidence-accuracy correlation, some witnesses make correct identifications and are highly confident; (i) in experiments there are usually no meaningful consequences associated with false or correct identifications; (j) the expert was being paid approximately $60.00 per hour for his appearance.

Three factors, each having two levels, were manipulated in the videotaped trial: witnessing and identification conditions, witness confidence, and expert testimony. A separate videotaped trial was constructed for each cell in the design. Several factors were combined to form a powerful manipulation of witnessing and identification conditions (WIC). In the "poor WIC" condition the eyewitness and police officer testified that the robber was disguised (i.e., wore a hat that covered his hair and hairline); the robber outwardly brandished a handgun (presumably invoking a weapon focus effect); the retention interval between the crime and the identification was 14 days, and the officer in charge of the lineup did not explicitly offer the witness the option of rejecting the lineup (instruction bias). In the "good WIC" conditions the witness and police officer testified that the robber was not disguised, that the handgun was hidden throughout the robbery, that the retention interval was 2 days, and that the lineup instructions were not suggestive. The witness testified to one of two conditions, either that she was 80% or 100% confident that she had correctly identified the robber. Disguise, weapon focus, retention interval, and instruction bias are known to influence identification accuracy (see Chapters 6 and 7). Confidence is weakly related to identification accuracy (see Chapter 6). In conditions containing expert testimony, the expert gave the testimony already described. In conditions containing no expert testimony, the prosecuting and defense attorneys nonetheless reiterated the witnessing and test conditions surrounding the identification in order to maximize their effects on jurors' decisions in the no-expert control group. After viewing one version of the trial, mock-jurors rendered verdicts and rated the credibility of the eyewitness and the strength of the prosecution's and defense's cases. Ratings were recorded on 7-point scales.

Subjects included 96 eligible and experienced jurors who were called for jury duty in Dane County, Wisconsin. All subjects were recruited by telephone within 1 year of having served (or having been called to serve) on a jury. Data from these 96 subjects were combined with data from a sample of 538 undergraduates. This large sample size ($N = 634$) allows us to test the effects of expert testimony with maximum power and permits us to test whether expert testimony differentially affects eligible jurors' and undergraduate jurors' decisions. All participants provided evaluations of the eyewitness, the defense and prosecution cases, estimates of the probability the eyewitness made a correct identification, and verdicts.

Juror skepticism and sensitivity

The WIC manipulation produced significant main effects on several dependent variables -- note that in addition to reporting mean differences we also report d, the standardized difference between the means (see Chapter 5 and Table 5.1 for details) because the d's permit ready comparison of the relative effect sizes produced by the experimental manipulations. For WIC the d for ratings of the strength of the prosecution's case was .31, for ratings of the strength of the defense's case $d = -.31$ (the coefficient is negative because the defense case was, logically, rated weaker in the good WIC condition) and for verdict $d = .28$. Jurors who viewed trials with good WIC (as compared to poor WIC) perceived the prosecution's case as stronger (6.34 vs. 5.72), the defense's case as weaker (4.68 vs. 5.27) and were more likely to convict (52% vs. 38%). Witness confidence also produced main effects on witness credibility ratings ($d = .34$), ratings of the strength of the prosecution's case ($d = .20$), and verdict ($d = .17$). Jurors who viewed a more confident witness (as compared to a less confident witness) perceived the witness as being more credible (6.25 vs. 5.51), perceived the prosecution's case as stronger (6.24 vs. 5.84), and were more likely to convict (50% vs. 41%). It should be noted that these results combine judgments of jurors who did and who did not hear expert testimony. As we will demonstrate, jurors who did not hear expert testimony were much less sensitive to the factors that influence eyewitness memory than were jurors who heard expert testimony.

Expert testimony produced trivial main effects on ratings of the eyewitness's credibility, strength of the prosecution's case, and verdict. However, jurors who heard expert testimony rated the defense's case to be significantly stronger than did jurors who heard no expert testimony ($d = .27$; 5.25 vs. 4.72). In short, there were generally no skepticism effects.

Expert testimony did produce sensitizing effects on witness credibility ratings and on prosecution and defense case strength ratings. Among jurors who heard expert testimony, witness confidence produced a weaker effect on eyewitness credibility ratings ($d = .17$) and on defense case strength

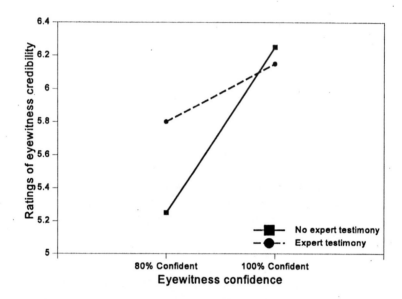

Figure 15.1. The influence of expert testimony on juror's use of eyewitness confidence

ratings ($d = .02$) than for jurors who heard no expert testimony ($d = .50$ and
.26, respectively). The results for eyewitness credibility ratings are plotted
in Figure 15.1 (the pattern is the same for defense case strength ratings). As
Figure 15.1 shows, jurors exposed to expert testimony were less likely to use
witness confidence in evaluating the credibility of the eyewitness than were
jurors who were not exposed to expert testimony. Likewise, among jurors
who heard expert testimony, WIC had a greater impact on both prosecution
($d = .49$) and defense ($d = -.56$) case strength ratings than it did on jurors
who heard no expert testimony ($d = .11$ and -.16, respectively). Effects on
verdicts were marginally significant – largely because the study with the
student mock-jurors included some variations of expert testimony that did
not increase sensitivity – the form of testimony most commonly given in
court did produce a strong sensitizing effect ($d = .94$).

The results for the sensitizing effect of expert testimony on prosecution
case strength ratings are plotted in Figure 15.2 (the pattern is the same for
defense case strength ratings). Jurors exposed to expert testimony used WIC
to a greater extent in evaluating the strength of the prosecution's and
defense's cases than did jurors who were not exposed. Thus, these findings

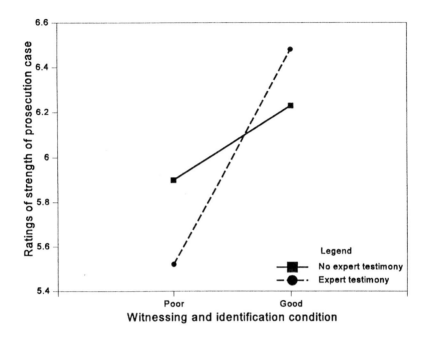

Figure 15.2. The sensitizing effect of expert testimony on juror decisions

show that expert testimony sensitizes jurors to the importance of WIC andthe relative lack of importance of witness confidence.

The fact that the witnessing and identification condition (WIC) manipulation produced very small main effects on juror decision making when no expert testimony was presented further supports the contention that jurors are not sensitive to factors complicating eyewitness evidence. The WIC manipulation consisted of the combined factors of disguise, weapon focus, retention interval, and suggestive lineup instructions, each of which, as previously noted, has an influence on the accuracy of identification (see Chapters 6 and 7). In contrast, confidence is a weak predictor of identification accuracy (see Chapter 6) but in this study, as in previous research (see Chapters 12 – 14), confidence was an important determinant of jurors' judgments, especially if jurors heard no expert testimony. As in our earlier studies (Cutler, Penrod, & Stuve, 1988; Cutler, Dexter, & Penrod, 1990; see Chapter 14), it is important to consider the influence of witness confidence on jurors' decisions in light of the fact that the difference in witness's confidence between the "high" (100%) and "low" (80%) conditions was modest and witnesses were actually highly confident in both conditions.

Jurors versus students: Are they affected differently by trial evidence or expert testimony?

Although eligible jurors gave significantly higher credibility ratings to the eyewitness than did undergraduates (d = .58; 6.91 vs. 5.70), the two groups did not differ significantly on any of the remaining dependent measures: the strength of the defense and prosecution cases and the probability the eyewitness made a correct identification, or verdict.

Witness confidence was a stronger predictor of defense case strength ratings among eligible jurors (d = .56; 5.42 vs. 4.55) than among undergraduate jurors (d = .06; 5.05 vs. 4.87). Jurors and students were comparably influenced by witness confidence on the remaining dependent variables, suggesting that the two groups were comparably sensitive to the confidence manipulation.

The interaction between expert testimony and juror type was significant in only one instance. The presence of expert testimony raised defense case strength ratings to a greater extent among eligible jurors (d = .89; 5.33 vs. 3.70) than among undergraduate jurors (d = .23; 5.22 vs. 4.78). Thus, on most measures the two groups were not differentially skeptical, nor were they differentially sensitive to the manipulations in trial evidence or expert testimony.

Assessing juror knowledge and integration

The decision-making results from these studies of expert witness effects, together with the studies of juror sensitivity reviewed in Chapters 11 – 13, underscore the fact that in the absence of expert testimony, (a) jurors' decisions are largely insensitive to factors that are known to influence eyewitness reliability; (b) jurors appear to rely too heavily on eyewitness confidence when evaluating eyewitness accuracy, and (c) jurors overestimate levels of eyewitness accuracy. The survey studies of lay knowledge of eyewitness reliability factors indicate that a significant source of juror insensitivity is simple lack of knowledge and confusion about the influence of a number of eyewitnessing factors on eyewitness reliability. However, lack of knowledge and confusion may not be the only sources of poor sensitivity. It is also possible that jurors are not making systematic use of the knowledge they do possess – or, as we posed the problem at the outset of this chapter, jurors may be poor at integrating their knowledge into their decisions.

How can we test whether jurors are poor at information integration? One of the studies discussed earlier (Cutler, Penrod, & Dexter, 1989) also explored in detail the problems of knowledge and integration. In addition to the decision-making measures already discussed, that study employed additional dependent measures of interest. *Memory* measures were employed to see what the mock-jurors remembered about the witnessing conditions in their trials (both the eyewitnessing factors that were manipulated in the WIC manipulation and other eyewitnessing factors that were mentioned but held constant), and what they remembered about the expert testimony (for those who viewed expert testimony). *Knowledge* about the effects of witnessing factors (in particular, the witnessing conditions that were manipulated in the study) was also assessed. For eyewitnessing factors that were manipulated in the WIC manipulation the jurors rated the extent to which those factors were likely to contribute to a correct identification in both the specific case they were deciding and in eyewitness cases in general. The *knowledge* measures can be used to test whether (in the absence of expert testimony) the factors (if any) that the jurors believed to influence eyewitness accuracy actually influenced their decision making. Of course we already know from our discussion of the sensitivity results that only eyewitness confidence had an effect on juror judgments. This means that if jurors believed that any eyewitnessing factors (other than confidence) affected eyewitness performance, the jurors were not making use of that knowledge.

In addition to testing knowledge and the match between knowledge and decisions made without the benefit of expert testimony, the research design also permitted us to test how expert testimony improved juror sensitivity to eyewitnessing conditions. We already know that expert testimony produced sensitizing effects. Sensitization could come about in two ways. First, expert testimony could impart new knowledge to jurors who could then employ that new knowledge in their assessments of eyewitness reliability. Second, eyewitness expert testimony could also "activate" knowledge that jurors already possess but fail to employ when making their reliability assessments. In other words, the measures of juror memory and knowledge were designed to ascertain the point in the inferential chain where jurors go awry in evaluating eyewitness evidence. Is it that jurors do not remember the evidence, that jurors do not think the evidence is important, or that jurors fail to integrate effectively important information in their inferences or judgments? The answer to this question might vary as a function of the factors being examined.

Table 15.1. *Memory for eyewitness evidence*

Evidence	Proportion correct
Witness confidence in ability to make an identification	59.7
Duration of exposure to robber in seconds	87.0
Mugshot search procedures	88.7
Number of persons in the lineup	93.5
Lineup persons viewed in front pose	97.2
Lineup persons viewed in 3/4 profile	93.1
Lineup persons viewed in full profile	91.4
Voice samples used in lineup	93.1
Disguises worn by robber	
No Disguise	96.8
Disguise	96.4
Time for which weapon was visible in seconds	
Low weapon visibility	67.7
High weapon visibility	63.9
Retention interval	
2 days	87.2
14 Days	91.8
Witness confidence in the accuracy of the identification	
80% Confident	81.0
100% Confident	74.1

Evidence	Rating
Violence of robbery [a]	6.51
Fairness of lineup [b]	
Neutral instructions	7.63
Suggestive instructions	3.53

a = rated on a 1 (not at all violent) to 9 (very violent) scale; *b* = rated on a 1 (very unfair) to 9 (very fair) scale, $t(536) = 22.99$, $p < .0001$, $r = .705$.

Table 15.2. *Memory for expert testimony*

Evidence	Proportion correct
Stages of memory	
One stage	81.0
Two stages	74.3
Three stages	54.3
Four stages	53.8
Discussion of witness and identification factors	
Disguises	77.6
Violence	94.3
Weapon presence	95.7
Retention interval	96.7
Mugshot searches	54.7
Lineup size	62.4
Lineup instructions	71.9
Witness confidence	81.9

Memory for trial evidence and expert testimony

As shown in Table 15.1, the mock-jurors demonstrated superior memory for the evidence surrounding the crime and the identification. This finding indicates that memory cannot be blamed for any lack of effects for WIC on jurors' judgments. In light of the high recall rates it is also probably the case that expert testimony does little to improve memory, as there is little room for improvement.

As shown in Table 15.2, overall memory for the expert testimony was also very good, although over half the subjects incorrectly reported that the expert discussed mugshot searches, and the effects of the size of the lineup. This latter finding suggests there was an appreciable response bias toward reporting that the expert discussed a given factor, although accuracy rates were much higher for factors actually discussed by the expert.

Juror knowledge about the influence of eyewitness factors

WIC, witness confidence, and the various forms of expert testimony were examined for their influences on juror knowledge, inference, and decisions. Analyses explored how expert testimony influenced juror knowledge as compared to the control group. In discussing the results of this study we again make extensive use of *d*, the standardized measure of effect sizes. A *d* of zero would indicate that two means are identical, whereas a *d* of .3 (or -.3) would indicate a difference in means that, in the context of this study, is worthy of note (see Table 5.1).

Juror *knowledge* in this study refers to the juror's view of how an eyewitness factor influences identification accuracy. Jurors were asked to rate on a 9-point scale whether particular witnessing conditions in their case were likely to lead to false or correct identifications. Consider, for instance, the ratings for the role of disguise and recall that jurors in the good witnessing condition learned that the perpetrator wore no disguise whereas jurors in the poor witnessing condition learned that perpetrator was wearing a hat that concealed his hairline . If jurors in both the good and poor WIC conditions rated the impact of disguise as 5 on a 9-point scale anchored at one end by "1 = produces false identifications" and at the other end by "9 = produces correct identifications," this would indicate that jurors failed to recognize a differential impact of the disguise evidence on identification accuracy. Furthermore, if juror knowledge was improved by expert testimony we would expect to see ratings of disguise impact to spread apart in the good and poor WIC conditions. Similar spreading might also be observed in the ratings of the effects of weapon visibility, retention interval, or lineup fairness and we might expect a narrowing of differences in the ratings of the impact of witness confidence if jurors who hear expert testimony believe they should rely less on witness confidence than jurors who do not hear expert testimony.

In fact, as shown in the top portion of Table 15.3, among jurors who did not hear expert testimony the WIC manipulation had a large effect on ratings of the role of *disguise* ($d = 2.26$), which indicates that jurors were well aware that disguises affect identification accuracy and jurors in the poor WIC condition were strongly inclined to believe that the disguise they heard about would impair the performance of the eyewitness, whereas jurors in the good WIC did not believe there was a problem with witness disguise (and, in fact, in their version of the trial the perpetrator was not disguised). Given the large difference in ratings of the disguise effect between jurors in the good versus poor WIC it is not surprising that expert testimony did not improve juror knowledge about the effects of disguise – among jurors who heard the expert testimony the difference in the evaluation of the effect of disguise was $d = 2.36$.

In the absence of expert testimony WIC had a trivial and nonsignificant main effect on *weapon visibility* ratings ($d = -.03$), indicating that jurors were unaware of the effects of weapon focus on identification accuracy. But, WIC had a significantly larger effect on weapon visibility ratings among jurors who heard expert testimony ($d = .41$). This finding indicates that expert testimony improved juror knowledge for the effects of weapon focus. Even without expert testimony WIC had a large effect on the ratings for the effect of *retention interval* ($d = .74$), indicating that subjects were aware that person recognition accuracy declines over time. WIC also produced a large main effect on ratings of the importance of *lineup instructions* ($d = 1.79$), indicating that jurors considered lineup instructions to be important in assessing identification accuracy. Expert testimony did not improve juror knowledge of these factors.

Witness confidence had an appreciable main effect on knowledge ratings for witness confidence among jurors who did not hear expert testimony ($d = .84$), indicating that jurors believed confidence is a good predictor of identification accuracy. Confidence was viewed as being less relevant among jurors who heard expert testimony ($d = .52$).

These analyses show that jurors believed that disguise, retention interval, and lineup instructions all have appreciable effects on identification accuracy, but jurors were unaware of the effects associated with weapon visibility. As we have seen before, jurors felt that witness confidence was an important determinant of identification accuracy. The presence of expert testimony improved juror knowledge of the effects of weapon visibility and witness confidence. If jurors were actually making use of their knowledge about the effects of disguise, retention interval, and biased lineup instructions, we would expect this knowledge to be reflected in their estimates of the likelihood that the eyewitness in their case made a correct identification (and in other dependent measures such as evaluations of the prosecution and defense evidence, witness credibility, and verdicts).

Indeed, because the knowledge questions were geared precisely to the eyewitness evidence in the cases the mock-jurors were presented (the knowledge ds in Table 15.3) it might be argued that even without expert testimony the differences on these dependent measures ought to equal at least the magnitude of the largest knowledge difference (the $d = 2.26$ for disguise effects) and should perhaps be even larger due to the fact that there was a large knowledge difference associated with lineup instructions and a moderate-sized difference associated with retention interval. This critical point can be put another way: The *knowledge* measures tell us that jurors in poor witnessing conditions believed that disguise (and lineup bias, as well) would seriously undercut the accuracy of an eyewitness like the one they heard testify, whereas jurors in the good witnessing conditions logically believed that their eyewitness (who saw an undisguised perpetrator and received no biased instructions) would not be impaired by such problems. Because the trial they saw was a pure eyewitness identification, case logic would dictate that evaluations of the accuracy of the eyewitness identification in the poor and good witnessing conditions ought to reflect and possibly even closely parallel the magnitude of differences reflected in the *knowledge* measures.

Integration of knowledge into decisions

Of course, possession of knowledge about an eyewitness factor does not guarantee that the knowledge will be successfully employed when jurors make judgments about the trial evidence and formulate verdicts. Indeed, we know from our earlier discussion of these results that, in the absence of expert testimony, knowledge was *not* translated into differential judgments about the eyewitness, the evidence, or verdicts. Jurors did not make systematic use of their purported knowledge – in the absence of expert testimony there is little evidence that their knowledge (other than their beliefs about the diagnostic value of eyewitness confidence) had any impact on their decisions. The following details the relationship between the *knowledge* measures and the other judgments made by the mock-jurors who provided the *knowledge* ratings.

Juror inferences. Inferences refer to the jurors' perceptions of the credibility of the eyewitness and the strengths of the prosecution's and defense's cases. Ratings of credibility varied directly with the witness's confidence level (d = .37 overall), but as shown in the middle section of Table 15.3, confidence was given less weight in determining witness credibility if the expert testified (d = .11) than if no expert testified (d = .52). WIC also affected eyewitness credibility ratings to a greater extent if the expert testified (d = .34) than if no expert testified (d = -.01), indicating that expert testimony improved juror sensitivity to WIC effects. The prosecution's case was perceived as being stronger in the good WIC (d = .30), but WIC had more of an effect on the perceived strength of the prosecution's case if the expert testified (d = .54) than if no expert testified (d = .15). The prosecution's case was perceived as stronger if the witness was 100% confident (d = .20). The defense case was perceived as being stronger in the poor WIC (d = -.30) and if the expert testified (d = .23). WIC had a stronger influence on defense case strength ratings if the expert testified (d = -.53) than if no expert

Table 15.3. *Influence of WIC and witness confidence on juror knowledge, inference, and judgments*

| | WIC (Witnessing and Identification Conditions) | | Confidence | |
	No expert	expert	No expert	expert
Juror knowledge				
Disguise	2.26	2.36		
Weapon presence	-.03	.41		
Retention interval	.74	.83		
Lineup instructions	1.79	1.60		
Witness confidence			.84	.52
Average	1.21	1.30	.84	.52
Juror Inference				
Credibility of eyewitness	-.01	.34	.52	.11
Strength of prosec. case	.15	.54	.24	.14
Strength of the def. case	-.13	-.53	-.21	.08
Average	.10	.47	.32	.11
Juror judgments				
Probability of correct identification	.12	.53	.53	.16
Verdict	.20	.45	.20	-.08
Average	.16	.49	.37	.12

Note: Values are *d*s. Averages ignore the direction of the correlations

testified (d = -.13). Note that in all instances, the WIC and confidence manipulations produced far smaller effects on inferences than one would expect given the magnitude of the knowledge differences reported in the top portion of Table 15.3 and that in the no-expert conditions confidence had a larger, sometimes much larger, effect on inferences than the combined influence of the WIC factors.

Juror decision making. Overall, WIC had an appreciable effect on jurors' judgments about the *accuracy of the identification* (d = .30). Jurors were more likely to judge the identification accurate in the good WIC rather than in the poor WIC. However, as shown in Table 15.3, WIC had a large influence on jurors' judgments if the expert testified (d = .53) but a negligible effect if no expert testified (d = .12). Expert testimony produced trivial main effects on probability ratings. Thus, there was no evidence for a skepticism effect.

WIC had a main effect on *verdict* such that more convictions were obtained with good WIC ($d = .29$). Once again, WIC had a stronger influence on verdicts if the expert gave testimony ($d = .45$) than if no expert testified ($d = .20$). Expert testimony and form of expert testimony produced trivial main effects on verdicts, again indicating no skepticism effect. Note, once again, that in all instances, the WIC and confidence manipulations produced far smaller effects on decisions than one would expect given the magnitude of the knowledge differences reported in the top portion of Table 15.3, and that in the no-expert conditions confidence had a larger, sometimes much larger, effect on decisions than the combined influence of the WIC factors.

In sum, although jurors indicated that they believed several of the factors included in the WIC manipulation would have a (sometimes very strong) influence on eyewitness performance, without expert testimony, WIC had negligible effects on juror inferences about the eyewitness and the strength of the defense and prosecution cases. In short, without the benefit of expert testimony jurors failed to make even minimal use of their knowledge of eyewitnessing factors and relied heavily on witness confidence in forming their judgments. However, when the expert testified jurors demonstrated significant sensitivity to WIC when drawing inferences . about the credibility of the eyewitness and about the strength of the prosecution's and defense's cases – though still not of a magnitude that matched the effects jurors claimed for these factors in the *knowledge* measures. The presence of expert testimony also reduced jurors' heavy reliance on witness confidence. The presence of expert testimony also increased the apparent strength of the defense's case but did not increase juror skepticism about the eyewitness's credibility. In fact, overall, the conviction rate for jurors in the no-expert condition was .38 under poor WIC and .48 under good WIC. The conviction rate for jurors in the expert condition was .36 under poor WIC and .58 under good WIC. As the full report of this study indicates (Cutler, Penrod, & Dexter, 1989), some forms of defense-called expert testimony proved more helpful to the defense and others actually proved more helpful to the prosecution (in the sense that more convictions were obtained in good WIC condition).

Knowledge versus integration

It is clear from the previous analyses that jurors do indeed possess some knowledge of the effects of disguise, retention interval, and suggestive lineup instructions. However, jurors are unaware of the influence of weapon visibility and are unaware that confidence is not a powerful predictor of identification accuracy. Thus, poor knowledge is partly responsible for the lack of juror sensitivity. Evidence for problems of integration skills emerges from the findings that WIC, without expert testimony, had a trivial influence on inferences and decisions (all d's were less than .20). Thus, it is both lack of appropriate knowledge and poor integration skills that jointly contribute to produce poor juror sensitivity to eyewitness evidence.

This experiment indicates that expert testimony improved juror knowledge. Expert testimony also increased the juror reliance on witnessing and identification conditions and reduced juror reliance on witness confidence when drawing inferences about the credibility of the eyewitness and the strength of the prosecution's case. There was no evidence to suggest that expert testimony promoted indiscriminant skepticism about the eyewitness's credibility, the accuracy of the identification, or the defendant's culpability (all d's were less than .10), which means that the general impact of expert testimony was to produce less favorable ratings on these variables when WIC was poor, but more favorable ratings when WIC was good. These results indicate that it would be a bad idea for a defendant to call an eyewitness expert when witnessing and identification conditions are favorable to a correct identification.

General summary

There was little evidence for expert-induced skepticism in these studies (Cutler, Dexter, & Penrod, 1989; Cutler, Penrod, & Dexter, 1989). Expert testimony produced nonsignificant main effects on eyewitness credibility ratings, prosecution case strength ratings, and verdicts. Inclusion of the expert testimony did influence jurors' perceptions of the strength of the defense case and in the expected direction. This effect was greater among eligible jurors than it was among undergraduate jurors.

Expert testimony sensitized both groups of jurors to witnessing and identification conditions and to witness confidence. Jurors who heard expert testimony gave less weight to witness confidence when rating the credibility of the eyewitness and the defense's case strength than did jurors who heard no expert testimony. In rating the strength of both the prosecution and defense's cases, jurors who heard expert testimony gave more weight to the witnessing and identification conditions than did jurors who heard no expert testimony. Higher order interactions involving juror type were almost uniformly nonsignificant. Only 1 out of the 16 interactions was significant (only slightly more than one would expect by chance alone), and this interaction showed that eligible jurors relied more on the witness's confidence than did undergraduate jurors in rating the strength of the defense's case.   Thus, eligible jurors and undergraduates performed comparably. The nonsignificant differences observed in the studies should be considered in light of their design and the very large sample sizes, both of which increase the likelihood of detecting significant differences ($N = 538$ in the undergraduate study, $N = 96$ in the experienced jury sample, and $N = 634$ for the combined samples).

The results provide support for the use of expert psychological testimony in eyewitness cases. Without such testimony, jurors appear insensitive to the factors that influence eyewitness identification accuracy. Expert testimony improved sensitivity without affecting jurors' overall level of skepticism about the identification.

Other research on expert sensitization

Our framework for analyzing the effects of expert testimony can be also be applied to an experiment conducted by Wells and Wright (1983; cited in Wells, 1986). They exposed 90 students to individually staged thefts. Witnesses later attempted identifications from thief-present or thief-absent photoarrays. The quality of viewing conditions was manipulated (poor, moderate, and good) by simultaneously varying exposure time, distance to perpetrator, and the extent to which the witness's view of the thief's face was obstructed. This manipulation was successful. Among the 75 subjects who made positive identifications, 69% in the good, 52% in the moderate, and 38% in the poor viewing conditions were accurate.

A random sample of eight accurate and eight inaccurate witnesses were then cross-examined. The videotaped cross-examinations were shown to 300 students who played the roles of jurors and evaluated the accuracy of the identifications. Half of the mock-jurors were exposed to expert testimony, which, presented on videotape, encouraged subjects to pay attention to the witnessing conditions, discussed several factors including opportunity to view, exposure time, and the weak relation between memory for trivial details and identification accuracy. Results are displayed in Figure 15.3.

Mock-jurors not exposed to expert testimony showed little sensitivity to the influence of witnessing conditions. Their judgments simply did not vary substantially or systematically with the witnessing and identification conditions. In contrast, among subjects exposed to expert testimony, mock-juror beliefs reflected sensitivity to the witnessing conditions. Accurate eyewitnesses were most likely to be believed in the good, less likely to be believed in the moderate, and least likely to be believed in the poor

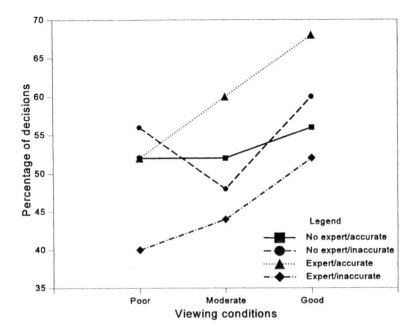

Figure 15.3. The sensitizing effects of expert testimony

witnessing conditions. This finding indicates that the expert testimony enhanced juror sensitivity. When there was no expert testimony the jurors could not differentiate accurate from inaccurate witnesses. With expert testimony the jurors could differentiate (and with equal success at all three condition levels). In addition the expert testimony made jurors sensitive to witnessing condition effects.

These results are consistent with the findings from a growing body of research on expert psychological testimony which indicate that expert testimony has a salutary effect on juror decision processes. In this respect, we are optimistic about its value as a safeguard, especially in light of the more dismal findings for cross-examination.

Assessing the impact of court-appointed and opposing experts

Two additional themes have emerged in the debate over the admissibility of expert psychological testimony. First, some psychologists and legal scholars have raised the question of whether expert psychological testimony is more appropriately offered by an expert procured by the courtroom adversaries (most often the defendant) or by the court. Second, in the case of the adversarial witness, both psychologists and legal scholars have recognized the increasingly common presence of *opposing* experts in court and raised questions about the likely effects on jurors of opposing testimony. Both issues can be illuminated by data.

16 Court-appointed and opposing experts: Better alternatives?

A concern often raised by psychologists is the difficulty of playing the role of advocate for the defendant while simultaneously maintaining the dispassionate objectivity of a scientist (Hastie, 1986; Loftus, 1986; McCloskey, Egeth, & McKenna, 1986). It is not uncommon for expert psychologists to feel pressured to misrepresent the psychological literature – for example, by not discussing specific findings; by not acknowledging limitations of research such as small numbers of studies, conflicting findings, weak theories, and factors that make generalizability of results questionable; or by not developing factors that might operate to increase the likelihood of a correct identification. These pressures emanate from attorneys who are attempting to put on the strongest case possible, have no interest in eliciting potentially damaging testimony from their own witness, and recognize that in an adversarial system the responsibility for attacking helpful witnesses rests with the other side. Many psychologists and other experts feel uncomfortable being thrust into a role where they may not have an opportunity to present a fully balanced overview of research findings and theories.

One possible solution to the adversarialization of expert testimony is to have an expert testify not on behalf of one side but as a friend of the court. Judges may use their discretion to invite independently expert testimony on behalf of the court, though they rarely do so. A recent survey of 431 federal judges (Cecil & Willging, 1994) reveals that only 20% have ever made such an appointment (more than half had done so only once), and few (8%) thought that such experts would be helpful in criminal cases. Three-quarters of the judges cited a faith in the adversarial system as one factor weighing against court-appointed experts. Although from the psychologist's perspective a court appointment may be preferred to being hired by one side for the reasons just described, the federal judge's faith in the adversarial system raises the question of whether it is reasonable to believe that a court-appointed expert will have the same effect as an adversarial expert will.

We (Cutler, Dexter, & Penrod, 1990) conducted an experiment to examine the influence of court-appointed expert testimony. The expert testimony was identical to the defense-hired expert testimony in Cutler,

Table 16.1. *Skepticism effects and expert testimony*

Dependent Variable	No Expert Advice M	Court Appointed Expert M	d
(1) Verdict	.57	.30	-.55**
(2) Culpability	.63	.59	-.16
(3) Accuracy of Witness's Identification	.67	.57	-.40*
(4) General Accuracy of Identifications	.73	.61	-.59***
(5) Strength of Prosecution's Case	6.58	5.83	-.45**
(6) Strength of Defense's Case	4.76	4.72	-.02
(7) Eyewitness Credibility	6.19	5.58	-.33

Note. $N = 144$. $* = p < .10$; $** = p < .05$; $*** = p < .01$.

Penrod, and Dexter (1990; see also Cutler, Dexter, & Penrod, 1989) – in fact it was the same videotaped footage. The only difference was that the expert was introduced by the judge as having been court-appointed and, through editing, questions were put to the witness by the judge. As in the other Cutler et al. studies witnessing and identification conditions (WIC: good vs. poor; see Chapter 15) and witness confidence (80% vs. 100%) were manipulated. In addition, jurors heard either court-appointed expert testimony, no expert testimony, or judges' instructions (and no expert testimony). The results concerning judges' instructions are described in Chapter 17. Subjects were 144 students who watched the trial, rendered verdicts, and completed various rating scales.

Overall WIC did not significantly influence verdicts. The conviction rates were 44% in the poor WIC and 43% in the good WIC conditions. Witness confidence produced a marginally significant effect, with jurors convicting more frequently if they viewed a 100% confident witness (49% v. 39%; $d = .18$). In this instance one form of expert testimony did produce skepticism effects, which are displayed in Table 16.1. Jurors exposed to court-appointed expert testimony were significantly less likely to convict, perceived the identification as significantly less likely to be accurate and the prosecution's case as significantly stronger. They also perceived the defendant as less culpable and the eyewitness as less credible, although these differences were not statistically significant.

None of the interactions was significant (or even marginally significant), indicating that court-appointed expert testimony did not sensitize jurors to the influences of WIC and witness confidence on eyewitness accuracy.

In short, the court-appointed witness produced skepticism and not sensitivity – hardly desirable results. That a court-appointed expert would produce a less desirable effect than an adversarial expert is somewhat surprising. It is reasonable to expect that the court-appointed expert would be perceived as more credible than the adversarial expert. Ratings of credibility did in fact differ significantly in this direction. But what effect does enhanced credibility have on persuasiveness? According to contemporary persuasion theorists (for example, Petty & Cacioppo, 1986), the effects of credibility can be complex. One possibility is that, as credibility increases, motivation to process the testimony also increases. Thus, the content of the testimony from a more credible expert might be given greater weight than that from a less credible expert. In contrast, when credibility reaches a certain point, perhaps motivation to process the testimony declines (especially if the testimony is complex and requires considerable cognitive effort). This could explain the results of our experiment. The adversarial expert could have been perceived as being of moderate credibility (the credibility ratings suggest that this is so), so mock-jurors might have been motivated to analyze critically (and subsequently decided to use) the content of his testimony. In contrast, the court-appointed expert was viewed as more credible. Perhaps the mock-jurors thought it sufficient to grasp the gist of his testimony (e.g., that eyewitness identifications are often unreliable) and did not carefully process and employ his description of the factors that influence identification accuracy. Another possibility is that the defense-hired expert was attended to to a greater extent than the court-appointed expert because the defense-hired expert's testimony was expected to rebut the prosecution's case. These explanations could account for why the expert testimony would lead to enhanced sensitivity in the adversarial expert condition but enhanced skepticism in the court-appointed expert. Only future research can test these hypotheses.

Opposing experts

With increasing frequency, expert psychological testimony on any subject is met with expert psychological testimony contradicting the proffered conclusions. A compelling example of this phenomenon is the trial of John Hinckley, Jr., who was accused of attempting to assassinate President Reagan. Hinckley's defense team employed the insanity defense. At trial, six psychologists and psychiatrists hired by the prosecution concluded that Hinckley was not insane at the time of the crime whereas a half-dozen hired by the defense concluded that he was insane. This widely publicized trial raised serious doubts in the public's mind about the reputation and value of expert psychological testimony (Rogers & Ewing, 1989).

Much less commonly (but with increasing frequency), expert psychological testimony on eyewitness memory is met with opposing-expert testimony (e.g., *United States v. Downing*, 1985). Unlike opposing clinical testimony, in which a conclusion is in debate (e.g., whether or not a defendant is competent to stand trial or was insane at the time the crime was committed), opposing-eyewitness expert testimony more typically debates the value and relevance of research on eyewitness memory. To illustrate, the defense expert is likely to discuss some general principle of how memory works and how some factors (relevant to the case) influence eyewitness memory. The prosecution expert, in opposition, does not offer alternative theories of memory or conclusions about the research, but instead argues that limitations associated with the research (e.g., unrealistic simulations of crimes and identification procedures and nonrepresentative subjects) are so severe as to render it irrelevant. They are also likely to argue that the research findings are often so unreliable as to be inconclusive. Depending on the content of the defense-hired expert's testimony, opposing-expert testimony may be accurate and important. But what effect does this "battle of the experts" have on jury decisions?

We conducted two experiments using variations of the trial materials in Cutler, Dexter, & Penrod (1989) to examine the influence of opposing-expert testimony. Experiment 1 studied the impact of opposing-expert testimony on juror predeliberation verdicts. Experiment 2 also examined the expert's influence on predeliberation verdicts but additionally addressed the question of whether deliberation has any further influence on mock jurors' reactions to opposing-expert testimony. Although the two experiments were conducted separately, results of the experiments were combined to maximize statistical power. This combination was justified given that (a) the videotaped trial materials were identical; (b) the subject pools were comparable; and (c) tests revealed no differences between the two samples. Witnessing and identification conditions (WIC), witness confidence, and defense-hired versus no-expert testimony were manipulated as in the Cutler et al. studies already described. The opposing-expert testimony was added as a third level to the expert testimony condition.

The opposing-expert first established his credentials in a manner similar to that of the defense-hired expert. Educational history, research activity, and employment were comparable for the two experts. The opposing-expert raised the following points (drawn from a mixture of critical writings and actual testimony): (a) the research techniques employed in eyewitness research are not always reliable; (b) many cognitive and experimental psychologists agree that the research techniques adopted for most studies do not generalize to actual crime settings; (c) no specific conclusions can be drawn about the manner in which stress and violence affects eyewitness memory and there is no way of knowing whether the stress experienced by the witness was of sufficient magnitude to impair memory; (d) the few (at the time) published studies of weapon focus yield inconsistent findings concerning the manner in which a weapon affects recognition memory; (e) even though it is possible to assess the fairness of lineups in eyewitness research, there is no way to assess the fairness of a lineup in an actual crime situation; (f) the findings concerning confidence and accuracy are highly inconsistent and no one knows how strong the confidence-accuracy relation actually is; (g) although memory declines over time there is no way of knowing if a given witness is accurate or inaccurate after a specific time delay; and, (h) in general, the research and theory about human memory do not allow us to determine the accuracy or inaccuracy of witnesses.

During the defense's cross-examination of the opposing-expert the following points were brought out: (a) psychologists' criticisms of the eyewitness literature are primarily directed toward the applicability of the research to criminal settings and not toward the quality of the research; (b) the general quality of eyewitness research meets the standards set by research psychologists (as evidenced by publications in refereed journals); and (c) the views held by the opposing-expert are more characteristic of the minority of experimental psychologists, whereas the views of the defense-hired expert are more characteristic of the majority of experimental psychologists.

Subjects were 616 undergraduates who viewed the videotaped trials and rendered verdicts. Other dependent variables were assessed, as in the previous experiments, but given that the pattern of results was comparable, only verdict analyses will be presented here.

Jurors were significantly more likely to convict under good WIC than under poor WIC ($d = .32$; 52% vs. 36%). Although jurors who heard the highly confident witness were more likely to convict than jurors who heard the less confident witness ($d = .08$, 44% vs. 40%), the difference was small and nonsignificant. Of course, because these results are averaged across the three expert witness conditions, they conceal some additional and meaningful differences.

Mean conviction rates were 52%, 49%, and 29% in the no-expert, defense-hired expert, and opposing-expert conditions, respectively. Jurors in the opposing-expert condition were significantly less likely to convict than subjects in both the defense-hired expert condition ($d = .40$) and the no-expert condition ($d = .60$). Thus, only the opposing-expert condition produced a significant skepticism effect.

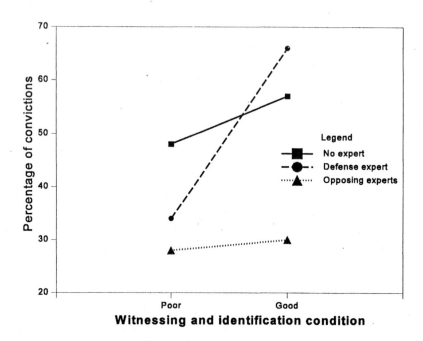

Figure 16.1. Effects of expert testimony on juror sensitivity to witnessing conditions

The sensitization effect for WIC is displayed in Figure 16.1. The defense-hired expert produced the largest sensitization effect – an effect that differed significantly from both the no-expert and opposing-expert conditions. In other words, among jurors exposed to defense-hired expert testimony, WIC had a significantly larger effect on verdicts ($d = .64$) than it did among jurors exposed to no expert testimony ($d = .26$) and jurors exposed to opposing-experts ($d = .04$). The weak sensitization effect for the opposing-expert condition and the virtually nonexistent effect in the no-expert condition did not differ significantly.

The sensitization effect for witness confidence is shown in Figure 16.2. Jurors exposed to the defense-hired expert and jurors exposed to no expert were comparably affected by witness confidence (ds = .24 for the no-expert condition and .16 for the defense-hired expert condition). The interaction tests indicated that sensitization did not differ significantly for these two groups. The opposing-experts condition, on the other hand, produced a reversal effect, with subjects convicting more often when the witness was

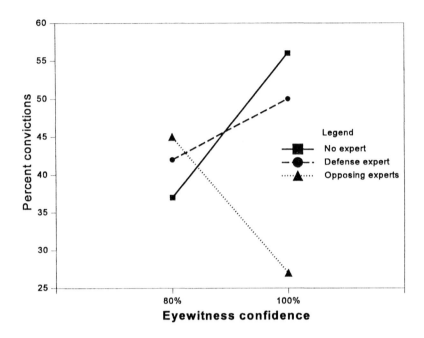

Figure 16.2. Effects of expert testimony on juror sensitivity to witness confidence

80% confident than if the witness was 100% confident ($d = -.36$). This effect differs (marginally significant) from the no-expert condition.

In sum, these results are consistent with the those of experiments just reviewed in which the defense-hired expert produced enhanced sensitivity to witnessing and identification conditions. Witness confidence did not significantly influence verdicts in this experiment (in contrast to the previous research), so the lack of a sensitization effect on witness confidence is understandable. The opposing experts, on the other hand, did not enhance sensitivity but produced considerable skepticism. We speculate, but cannot prove with these data, that the skepticism effects produced by the opposing expert might arise because so much of the (conflicting) trial evidence concerns the eyewitness identification and may prompt jurors to infer that there is a problem with eyewitness evidence – hence the skepticism effect. And, although jurors might be inclined to scrutinize carefully the eyewitness evidence, the battle of the experts may persuade them that there is no reliable basis for such scrutiny – hence the lack of any sensitizing effect. Further research will undoubtedly shed light on these effects. Additional analyses indicated that the results cannot be attributed to different levels of credibility attributed to or liking for the experts.

Conclusions

Taken together, the studies reviewed in this chapter indicate that expert psychological testimony can serve as a safeguard against mistaken identification. There is substantial evidence that jurors are insensitive to eyewitnessing and identification factors that influence eyewitness performance. Part of the problem is that laypersons are not aware of the variety of factors that have such influences, but a significant part of the problem is that jurors simply do not make use of the knowledge they do possess. Even when jurors appear to believe that a particular eyewitnessing factor is relevant in the case they are deciding and believe that the factor substantially reduces the likelihood their eyewitness has made an accurate identification, the latter belief does not significantly influence their evaluations of witness credibility or their verdicts. Instead, jurors rely almost exclusively on witness confidence as a guide to witness accuracy – and in doing so, choose one of the less reliable indicators of eyewitness accuracy.

The general picture changes when expert testimony about eyewitnesses is presented to the jury. There is little empirical evidence that jurors are confused by the testimony or are prejudiced by it (especially insofar as skepticism is an index of prejudice). Expert testimony appears to have the beneficial effect of educating jurors about factors that influence eyewitness identification and enhancing their reliance on those factors when rendering decisions in eyewitness cases. Indeed, results from our research indicate that expert testimony on eyewitness memory can work on behalf of the prosecution as well as the defense. Note in Figure 16.1 that the combination of good witnessing and identification conditions and expert testimony increased the strength of the prosecution's case relative to the no-expert condition. As a possible mechanism for increasing the likelihood of appropriate convictions, prosecutors may wish to introduce expert testimony in cases where witnessing and identification conditions would tend to facilitate an accurate identification.

The concerns over the format in which expert psychological testimony is presented appear to be warranted. Based on the experiments we have reviewed, court-appointed expert testimony produces a qualitatively different impact than does adversarial expert testimony. Likewise, opposing expert testimony significantly alters the manner in which expert testimony impacts jury decision making. Based on the available data, adversarial, unopposed expert testimony produces the greatest degree of sensitivity and the least amount of skepticism. This conclusion, of course, must be considered in light of the limited quantity of research conducted to date. Nevertheless, these initial findings clearly support the contention that the effects of expert testimony are not straightforward and that speculation about such effects can be substantially refined with data.

Part VI

Is the judge an effective safeguard against mistaken identification?

17 Instructing the jury about problems of mistaken identification

Some courts have gravitated to the use of special judicial instructions pertaining to eyewitness identification in an effort to safeguard defendants from erroneous conviction. Judges' instructions have some distinct advantages over cross-examination: Unlike cross-examination, they may go beyond the scope of the direct examination and they reduce the adversarial flavor of comments that might be made by the counsel.

One of the leading cases involving judicial instructions is *United States v. Telfaire* (1972). In this case the United States Court of Appeals for the District of Columbia endorsed the use of a cautionary eyewitness instruction. The instruction adopted by the Court of Appeals was designed to direct the attention of the jury to specific factors associated with the crime that might influence the accuracy of an identification. Here is the instruction:

One of the most important issues in this case is the identification of the defendant as the perpetrator of the crime. The Government has the burden of proving identity, beyond a reasonable doubt. It is not essential that the witness himself be free from doubt as to the correctness of the witness's statement. However, you, the jury, must be satisfied beyond a reasonable doubt of the accuracy of the identification of the defendant before you may convict. If you are not convinced beyond a reasonable doubt that the defendant was the person who committed the crime, you must find the defendant not guilty.

Identification testimony is an expression of belief or impression by the witness. Its value depends on the opportunity the witness had to observe the offender at the time of the offense and to make a reliable identification later.

In appraising the identification testimony of a witness, you should consider the following:

(a) Are you convinced that the witness had the capacity and an adequate opportunity to observe the defender?

255

Whether the witness had an adequate opportunity to observe the offender at the time of the offense will be affected by such matters as how long or short a time was available, how far or close the witness was, how good were the lighting conditions, whether the witness had an occasion to see or know the person in the past.

(b) Are you satisfied that the identification made by the witness subsequent to the offense was the product of his own recollection? You may take into account both the strength of the identification and the circumstances under which the identification was made.

If the identification by the witness may have been influenced by the circumstances under which the defendant was presented to him for identification, you should scrutinize the identification with great care. You may also consider the length of time that lapsed between the occurrence of the crime and the next opportunity of the witness to see the defendant, as a factor bearing on the reliability of the identification.

(c) Finally, you must consider the credibility of each identification witness in the same way as any other witness, consider whether the witness is truthful, and consider whether the witness had the capacity and opportunity to make a reliable observation of the matter covered in his testimony.

I again emphasize that the burden of proof on the prosecutor extends to every element of the crime charged, and this specifically includes the burden of proving beyond a reasonable doubt that the identity of the defendant as the perpetrator of the crime with which the defendant stands charged. If after examining the testimony, you have a reasonable doubt as to the accuracy of the identification, you must find the defendant not guilty.

Although the *Telfaire* instruction appears to be a step in the appropriate direction, there are reasons to believe that the instruction will be only minimally effective.

First, the instruction points to a limited number of eyewitnessing factors without explaining how the factors influence memory or identifying the magnitude of their effects. Second, the factors to which the *Telfaire* instructions allude are based on legal precedents (e.g., *Neil v. Biggers*, 1972) rather than psychological research; consequently, the accuracy of the assumptions embodied in the instruction can be questioned. Third, although the court correctly identified a number of factors that influence identification accuracy (exposure duration, lighting, proximity, prior acquaintance, retention interval, repeated observation), it also identified one ("strength of identification" or eyewitness confidence) which is not a strong predictor, and is overrelied upon by jurors (see Chapters 11–14). Fourth, the court also failed to identify many other predictors of identification accuracy (e.g., disguise, weapon focus, cross-race recognition, and specific factors affecting suggestiveness – see Chapters 6 and 7). Finally, these instructions are likely to be of assistance to the jury only to the extent that the factors mentioned in the instruction are raised during trial and made the subject of direct and cross-examination.

Several experiments have examined the effects of judges' instructions on mock-juror decisions. In Katzev and Wishart's (1985) experiment, 108 subjects (comprising 30 juries) watched a 40-minute videotaped trial involving an eyewitnessed incident. There were three conditions of judicial commentary: (a) a control condition in which the judge delivered standard instructions regarding issues of reasonable doubt; (b) a condition in which the judge delivered standard instructions plus a summary of the witnessing conditions (instruction + summary); and (c) a condition in which the judge delivered standard instructions, the summary, and a commentary on the psychological findings regarding eyewitness identification (instruction + summary + commentary). Results indicated that the instruction + summary + commentary condition yielded significantly fewer predeliberation guilty verdicts (12%) and shorter deliberation times (9.6 min.) than did the control condition (28%, 23 min.), with the instruction + summary condition falling in between on both measures (20%, 16.5 min.). Thus, this experiment produced evidence that judges' instructions produce skepticism. It might also be the case that the instructions improved sensitivity, but there is no way to tell given the design of the experiment.

Our (Cutler, Dexter, & Penrod, 1990; see Chapter 16) experiment on court-appointed experts also contained a judge's instruction condition together with manipulations of witnessing and identification conditions (WIC) and witness confidence. The instructions employed in the study were based on those developed in *Telfaire* (1972). We will now compare the results from a trial condition using *Telfaire* instructions with results obtained in a no-expert/no instruction control condition.

As we mentioned in Chapters 13 and 14, in the absence of expert testimony, WIC produced a nonsignificant effect and witness confidence produced a marginally significant effect on juror verdicts. The instruction effects are summarized in Table 17.1. The *Telfaire* instructions (vs. the no-expert control) produced nonsignificant main effects on all dependent variables. Not only were the magnitudes of the effects small, but the directions were inconsistent. Most important, no significant interactions emerged between the *Telfaire* variable and either WIC or witness confidence. These findings indicate that the *Telfaire* instruction did not influence the manner in which jurors evaluated the eyewitness identification evidence – there were neither skepticism effects nor sensitizing effects.

Table 17.1. *Effects of Telfaire instruction*

Dependent variable	No expert M	Telfaire instructions M	d
Proportion convictions	.57	.50	-.14
Culpability[a]	.63	.68	.20
Accuracy of identification[b]	.67	.64	-.12
Prosecution's Case strength[c]	6.58	6.32	-.16
Defense's case strength[c]	4.76	4.37	-.21
Eyewitness's credibility[c]	6.19	6.00	-.10

[a]Probability that the defendant is guilty.
[b]Probability that the identification is correct.
[c]Rated on 7-point scales.

Zemba and Geiselman (1993) examined whether the time at which the *Telfaire* instruction is delivered qualifies its effect on jury decision processes. They hypothesized that providing the *Telfaire* instructions both before and after the presentation of identification testimony would enhance its effect in comparison to presenting the instruction only after identification testimony. Subjects were 200 undergraduates. Each subject watched one version of the videotaped trial used by Cutler, Dexter, and Penrod (1990). Zemba and Geiselman manipulated the witnessing and identification conditions (WIC: good vs. poor) and the timing/frequency of the *Telfaire* instructions. In one condition the instructions were not presented at all. In another condition the *Telfaire* instructions were read just prior to the testimony of the eyewitness and again after the standard judges' instructions. In a third condition the *Telfaire* instructions were read only after the standard judges' instructions at the end of the trial. After the trial each subject completed a questionnaire containing a verdict form and other items.

Mock-jurors who heard the *Telfaire* instructions both before and after the eyewitness testimony were significantly more likely to convict (54%) than were mock-jurors who heard the *Telfaire* instructions only after the eyewitness testimony (27%) and mock-jurors who did not hear *Telfaire* instructions (39%). The difference between the latter two conditions is marginally significant. Witnessing and identification conditions did not significantly influence verdicts. The proportions of convictions were 49% in the good and 40% in the poor viewing conditions (a nonsignificant difference). Among subjects who heard *Telfaire* instructions both before and after the eyewitness testimony, the percentages of convictions did not differ significantly as a function of good (56%) versus poor (53%) witnessing and identification conditions. Neither was this difference significant among subjects who heard *Telfaire* instructions only after the eyewitness testimony (28% vs. 26%, respectively). In contrast, among subjects who did not hear *Telfaire* instructions the difference in conviction rate was much larger (50% in the good vs. 28% in the poor witnessing identification conditions), but the two-way interaction between witnessing/identification conditions and instructions was not statistically significant.

In sum, timing of the instructions significantly influenced verdicts, with subjects hearing the instructions both before and after trial convicting *more* often, regardless of witnessing and identification conditions. Clearly, the instructions did not improve sensitivity in this experiment. Indeed, subjects who did not hear the instruction appeared to have the most sensitivity.

Greene (1988) examined the influence of the Telfaire instructions in two experiments. In Experiment 1, each of 127 undergraduates viewed one of two videotaped, 90-minute simulations of an assault trial concerning an incident in a tavern. The defendant was charged with throwing a bottle that struck and partially wounded another person in the tavern. In the "strong identification" version, the barmaid, who identified the defendant as the person who threw the bottle, testified that the defendant was seated directly below a light, his table was near her in the bar, and she had an unobstructed view of him. In the "weak identification" version, the barmaid testified that the defendant was sitting in a dimly lit area, not close to the bar, and that her view was partially obstructed. Half of the subjects who viewed each version also heard the *Telfaire* instructions as part of the judge's charge; the other half did not hear the *Telfaire* instructions but did hear instructions relating to the charge. After viewing the trial, jurors deliberated for 30 minutes, during which time they had access to a written copy of the judge's instructions. After deliberation subjects completed questionnaires that required them to render verdicts (guilty, not guilty, or hung) and answer additional questions about the trial and deliberation.

Greene found that, overall, the percentage of hung juries was comparable in the *Telfaire* and no-*Telfaire* instruction conditions. With respect to juries that did reach verdicts, those who heard weak identification evidence were unlikely to convict (3% in both instruction conditions). Among those who heard strong identification evidence, in contrast, 42% of those who did not hear *Telfaire* instructions convicted whereas only 6.5% of those who did hear *Telfaire* instructions convicted. Thus, in contrast to Cutler, Dexter, and Penrod (1990) and Zemba and Geiselman (1993), it appears that the *Telfaire* instructions may have *desensitized* jurors to eyewitness evidence in Greene's Experiment 1. Two questions remain, however. First, the low conviction rate in the weak identification condition may have created what is termed a *floor effect*. If the evidence had not been so weak, the *Telfaire* instructions may have reduced the convictionrate in that condition as well; thus, the results would show a skepticism effect rather than a desensitization effect. Second, Greene's Experiment 1 differed from the Cutler, Dexter, and Penrod and Zemba and Geiselman experiments in that her subjects were permitted to use written copies of the instructions during deliberation. It is conceivable that the instructions have more of a skepticizing effect when subjects can refer back to them during deliberation. It is also possible that deliberation further qualifies effects of both evidence and instructions. This possibility is tested in this chapter.

In Greene's second experiment, she revised the *Telfaire* instructions in several ways. She eliminated legal terminology, uncommon words, passive constructions, embedded phrases, and compound sentences. She reorganized the instructions into a more logical, hierarchical order. In addition, she made some changes to the content of the instructions to reflect contemporary eyewitness findings; specifically, the instructions were altered to include discussions of the confidence-accuracy relation, the influence of stress at the time of the crime, and fairness of lineup procedures on identification accuracy. The revised instruction was as follows:

One of the major issues in this case is the identification of the defendant as the person accused of committing a crime. The prosecution has the burden of proving beyond a reasonable doubt, not only that a crime was committed, but that the defendant was the person who committed it.

Identification testimony is an expression of belief by an eyewitness about a person who may have committed a crime. You should keep in mind that identifying a person who committed a crime may be very different from recognizing a friend you see repeatedly. In evaluating the testimony of any eyewitness, you should consider two sets of factors: first, factors present when the incident occurred; second, factors affecting the later identifications.

Factors present when the incident occurred are:

(a) how much time was available for observation;

(b) how well the scene was lit;

(c) how far the eyewitness was from the incident.

You should also consider how well the eyewitness could see and hear at the time. For example, if a witness is afraid or distracted, his or her capacity to perceive and remember is reduced.

A second set of factors affect later identification. You should consider how much time passed between the incident and the identification. For example, identification errors increase as time passes. You should also consider the circumstances surrounding the identification. For example, an identification made from a fair lineup of similar individuals is more reliable than other forms of identification such as viewing a suspect alone. You should also consider how certain the eyewitness was in making an identification. Certainty may or may not mean that the identification is accurate.

If, after considering all these factors, you have a reasonable doubt about the accuracy of the eyewitness's identification of the defendant as the person who may have committed a crime, then you must find the defendant not guilty.

Subjects in this experiment were 139 community residents who were called for jury duty in King County, Washington. They participated at the courthouse while waiting to be called to serve on a jury. Each juror watched one version of the trial used in Experiment 1, completed a predeliberation questionnaire, deliberated with other subjects for 30 minutes, and completed a postdeliberation questionnaire. Strength of the identification evidence was manipulated. In addition, subjects either heard no eyewitness instruction, the Telfaire instruction, or the revised instruction.

With respect to predeliberation verdicts, jurors who heard the strong identification testimony were significantly more likely to convict than were jurors who heard the weak identification testimony (50% vs. 34%). In addition, jurors who heard the revised instruction were less likely to convict (23%) than subjects who heard the standard *Telfaire* instructions (53%) or no eyewitness instruction (45%).

The postdeliberation verdicts are summarized in Table 17.2. The revised instruction led to the lowest percentages of convictions, the highest percentages of acquittals, and the lowest percentages of hung juries. Data from the no-instruction and standard *Telfaire* instruction conditions were nearly identical.

Thus, with respect to postdeliberation data, the revised instructions appear to produce skepticism and reduced sensitivity. In contrast, the unrevised *Telfaire* instructions had no notable effect – the pattern of results was very similar to the no-instruction condition. Greene reports that jurors who heard the revised instructions spent less time discussing the instructions and referred to a copy of the instructions less often during deliberations. The results of Greene's experiments raise serious concerns' about the viability of instructions as a safeguard against mistaken identification – only in the crude sense that the revised instructions increased general skepticism about eyewitness identifications is there reason to think that these instructions would reduce conviction errors.

Table 17.2. *Postdeliberation verdicts (in percentages)*

Condition	Guilty	Not guilty	Hung
Telfaire			
Weak ID	0.0	41.4	58.6
Strong ID	35.0	35.0	30.0
Revised Telfaire			
Weak ID	0.0	73.2	26.8
Strong ID	0.0	75.0	25.0
No Instruction			
Weak ID	0.0	42.3	57.7
Strong ID	34.8	21.7	43.5

In a third study Greene conducted a nationwide survey of reactions to the *Telfaire* and revised *Telfaire* instructions. Of the 300 judges who received a survey, 102 (34%) responded, and 89 (30%) provided completed questionnaires. The *Telfaire* instructions were evaluated by 52 judges and the revised *Telfaire* instructions by 37 judges. In response to the question: "How effective do you think this instruction will be in conveying the intended legal concepts to the jury?" the revised instruction was rated as significantly more effective than the original: Among those who evaluated the revised instruction 62.5% thought it was extremely or very effective, whereas 23.4% who evaluated the original instruction thought it was extremely or very effective. In response to the question: "Overall, would you consider this a proper instruction to give to the jury?" 78% of the judges who evaluated the original instruction and 53% who evaluated the revised instruction responded "no"; the respective percentages of "yes" responses were 12% and 37%. These differences in percentages between the revised and original instructions were statistically significant. Last, in response to the question: "Do you perceive bias favoring either party in the language of the instruction?" (responses were provided on a scale from -3 = bias in favor of the defense to +3 = bias in favor of the prosecution),61% of the judges who received the revised instruction and 34% who received the original instruction thought the instruction carried a strong defense bias (a significant difference). In summary, judges thought that the revised instruction was more effective, more proper, but more defense-biased than the original instruction.

Table 17.3. *Telfaire instructions and juror skepticism*

| Study | N | Proportion of guilt judgments | | |
		No Telfaire	Telfaire	Revised
Katzev & Wishart	108	.28	.16[a]	
Cutler et al.	144	.57	.50	
Zemba & Geiselman	200	.39	.41[a]	
Greene (Study 1)	127	.23	.05	
Greene (Study 2)	139	.17	.17	.00[b]
Unweighted means		.33	.26	

a: combines two instruction conditions, *b*: postdeliberation

Although the judges appear to be correct in thinking that the revised instruction might favor the defendant (as reflected in the skepticism effect in Study 2 above), they were in error in gauging that the revised instruction would be more effective than the original – at least insofar as increased sensitivity to eyewitness factors is used as the criterion of effectiveness.

Taken together, Greene's studies raise serious questions about the effectiveness of *Telfaire*-like instructions.

In summary, the experiments we have reviewed here provide little evidence that judges' instructions concerning the reliability of eyewitness identification enhance juror sensitivity to eyewitness identification evidence. Manipulations of timing and content of the instructions did not improve the impact of the instructions. In a couple of instances there was increased skepticism following instructions (see Table 17.3), but the effect is not systematic. And, there is no substantial evidence for enhanced sensitivity among jurors who received *Telfaire* instructions in these studies (see Table 17.4). Rather, the evidence indicates that the *Telfaire* instructions – perhaps because they confuse jurors – actually reduced juror sensitivity to witnessing and identification conditions compared to uninstructed jurors. Indeed, to the cynical reader, careful scrutiny of these results – especially a comparison of conviction rates in good eyewitnessing conditions for uninstructed versus instructed jurors (Table 17.4) – will suggest that the defense should be especially eager to request *Telfaire* instructions when an identification has been made under good witnessing conditions!

Table 17.4. *Juror sensitivity to witnessing conditions with and without Telfaire instructions*

Study	N	No *Telfaire* Instructions		*Telfaire* Instructed	
		Poor conditions	Good conditions	Poor conditions	Good conditions
Cutler et al.	144	.57	.57	.50	.50
Zemba & Geiselman	200	.28	.50	.40	.42[a]
Greene (Study 1)	127	.03	.42	.03	.07
Greene (Study 2)	139	.00	.35	.00	.17[b]
Unweighted means		.22	.46	.23	.29

a: combines two instruction conditions, *b*: post-deliberation

On the whole we are forced to conclude that the judges' instructions do not serve as an effective safeguard against mistaken identifications and convictions and that expert testimony is therefore more effective than judges' instructions as a safeguard.

18 A postscript

During the week in which this book was receiving final edits in preparation for publication, there were two stories in the news that touched upon a number of the issues raised in this volume.

The first story concerned the release from a Jackson, Mississippi prison of Melissa Gammill. Ms. Gammill had served ten months of in prison following her conviction and ten year sentence for burglary. She was arrested after being identified from a mugshot by Darron Terry as the woman he encountered burglarizing his home in December 1993. Ms. Gammill was unable to offer an alibi for the night of the burglary – which had been committed three months before her arrest – and was convicted on the basis of Mr. Terry's identification. ("Look-Alike. . .", 1995). She joins a growing list of individuals convicted on the basis of mistaken eyewitness identifications.

The second story in the news concerned the O.J. Simpson trial and the lengthy and aggressive cross-examination by defense attorneys Barry Scheck and Peter Neufeld of prosecution forensic experts. Scheck, a law professor at the Benjamin A. Cardozo School of Law of Yeshiva University in New York, and Peter Neufeld, a New York lawyer are both securing publicity for their work on the Simpson defense team. They were brought onto the defense team because they have experience in handling cases involving DNA evidence. Indeed, in recent months both men have also been front page news as a result of their work on an entirely different DNA-related undertaking ("Imprisoned Man . . .", 1995; Kolata, 1994). The Innocence Project is a two-year-old program run by Scheck and Neufeld with the assistance of law students at Cardozo. The Project that has been using DNA testing to secure the release of individuals erroneously convicted of a variety of crimes. As of the fall of 1994 they had secured the release of eight prisoners including one mentally retarded man who was on death row and several more appeared likely to be released as a result of DNA tests.

One factor that motivated the creation of the Project was the revelation that in one-third of the criminal cases in which DNA tests are run by the FBI, the suspect does not match the DNA sample from the crime scene – a result that suggested to Neufeld and Scheck that DNA testing might be used to establish the innocence of falsely convicted individuals. Scheck and Neufeld arrange tests of DNA crime scene samples in cases where there is some reason to believe the convicted party might be innocent. These tend to be older cases for which DNA tests simply were not available or more recent cases in which the defendant was unable to secure the $2,000 required for the test.

How do there erroneous convictions arise? The stories behind these convictions are not unlike the stories recounted in chapter 1 and are detailed in several newspaper accounts (English, 1995; "Imprisoned Man . . .", 1995; Kolata, 1994; "Look-Alike. . .", 1995; Span, 1995). For example, Edward Honaker was accused of rape and sodomy in the summer of 1984 before DNA testing had been developed. The crime was committed in the middle of the night in June of 1984 when a young couple, sleeping in their car, was awakened by a man who claimed he was a police officer and requested that they get out of their car. When they exited the car the man brandished a gun in his left hand, chased the man off run, and drove the woman to a cabin, where he raped and sodomized her. During the assault he complained to her about his experiences in Vietnam.

Honaker was arrested on October 1984 and the main evidence against him was that the couple had identified his picture out of a set of six photographs and later identified him in court. A hair found on the woman's shorts was also characterized as just like Honaker's head hair . He was convicted in February 1985 and given three life sentences for the rape and sodomy and two additional two-year sentences for using a gun while committing the crime

At trial Honaker noted he was right-handed and had never been in Vietnam. His alibi was that he was was sleeping in his mother's house 80 miles away on the night of the crime. Furthermore, he testified that he had had a vasectomy in 1977 and therefore could be the source of the sperm on the victim. The prosecutor argued that the vasectomy might have failed.

Tests by two different labs have shown that the semen was not Honaker's and he was eventually released from prison late in 1994 – seven months after the DNA results were placed before Virginia governor George Allen.

DNA tests similarly proved that Brian Piszczek, was not guilty of a rape and assault committed in 1990 in Cleveland. Piszczek's photograph was picked out of a display by the victim who identified him as the rapist. In addition, hair collected from the crime scene was said to be consistent with Piszczek's hair.

At his trial Piszczek argued that he did not match the description of the rapist given by the victim. A former girlfriend testified that he was with her – six miles from the scene of the crime – the night of the crime and that he did not have access to a car. Piszczek requested DNA tests, but they were not done because he could not afford them. In September 1994 Piszczek was released from an Ohio penitentiary after having served four years of a 15- to 25-year sentence.

Neufeld and Scheck also obtained DNA test results which indicate that Terry Chalmers, who served nine years for a rape committed at knifepoint in Mount Vernon, N.Y. in 1986. Chalmers was arrested the day after the assualt. The victim identified him from a photograph and two subsequent lineups. He was convicted by a jury and sentenced to 12 to 24 years in prison – a sentence that was compounded because he had a prior conviction for sexual abuse and attempted robbery in 1985.

In January 1995 the District Attorney decided to seek dismissal of the charges against Chalmers as a result of the DNA tests.

Neufeld concludes: "Eyewitness identifications are not very reliable, and when an eyewitness who is sincere but mistaken takes the stand and says, 'I'll never forget that face,' that leads to more unjust convictions than any other Factor." (Span, 1995, p. E1). Scheck has expressed particular concern about the implications of the fact that a high percentage of the FBI DNA tests do not produce matches to suspects and the fact that so many of the DNA tests handled by the Innocence Project reveal false convictions: "If we are going to acknowledge that the system is so imperfect that innocent people are convicted, it is inevitable to conclude that innocent people will be executed. It is the most powerful argument against the death penalty that I know of." (English, 1995, p. 38).

Of course, if you have traversed the full length of this book, you will not be surprised to learn about even more erroneous convictions based wholly or in part on mistaken eyewitness identifications. As we saw in Chapter 1 there is an abundance of such cases. We hope, however, that you share our dismay with these facts. Close inspection of the cases mentioned in this *New York Times* article would undoubtedly reveal a variety of factors that could have contributed to these identification errors, including witness (Chapter 6), perpetrator, and event factors (Chapter 7), and suggestiveness in identification procedures (Chapter 8). Who can be blamed for these errors? In some respects the fault can be placed at the feet of attorneys who cannot conduct effective cross-examination of witnesses because these attorneys do not have adequate opportunities to develop the facts underlying identifications and are not adequately informed about threats to eyewitness reliability (Chapters 9 and 10).

Some of the fault might be placed at the feet of jurors who are not equipped to evaluate systematically eyewitness identifications (Chapters 11, 12, and 13). Perhaps most of the fault should be placed at the feet of the judiciary, which has remained resistant to the introduction of expert psychological testimony about factors that influence eyewitness performance (Chapters 2 and 3). There are now sound reasons to believe that jurors not only need such testimony but also benefit from it (Chapters 14, 15, and 16). Judges and attorneys who cling to traditional methods of instructing jurors (Chapter 17) are not serving well the interests of jurors, innocent defendants, or the public.

References

Adams-Price, C. (1991). Eyewitness memory and aging: Predictors of accuracy in recall and person recognition. Unpublished manuscript. Institute of Gerontology, University of Michigan.

Anthony, T., Cooper, C., & Mullen, B. (1992). Cross-racial facial identification: A social cognitive integration. *Personality and Social Psychology Bulletin, 18,* 296–301.

Bailey, F. L., & Rothblatt, H. B. (1985). *Successful techniques for criminal trials.* Rochester, NY: Lawyers Co-operative.

Baltes, P. B., & Schaie, K. W. (1976). On the plasticity of intelligence in adulthood and old age. *American Psychologist, 31,* 720–725.

Bangert-Drowns, R. L. (1986). Review of developments in meta-analytic method. *Psychological Bulletin, 99,* 388–399.

Bartlett, J. C., & Fulton, A. (1991). Familiarity and recognition of faces in old age. *Memory and Cognition, 19,* 229–238.

Beaman, A. L. (1991). An empirical comparison of meta-analytic and traditional reviews. *Personality and Social Psychology Bulletin, 17,* 252–257.

Bell, B. E., & Loftus, E. F. (1988). Degree of detail of eyewitness testimony and mock-juror judgment. *Journal of Applied Social Psychology, 18,* 1171–1192.

Bell, B. E., & Loftus, E. F. (1989). Trivial persuasion in the courtroom: The power of (a few) minor details. *Journal of Personality and Social Psychology, 56,* 669–679.

Berman, G. L., Narby, D. J., & Cutler, B. L. (1994). Effects of inconsistent eyewitness statements on mock-jurors' evaluations of the eyewitness, perceptions of defendant culpability and verdicts. *Law and Human Behavior. 19,* 79-88.

Borchard, E. M. (1932). *Convicting the innocent: Errors of criminal justice.* New Haven: Yale University Press.

Bothwell, R. K., Brigham, J. C., & Malpass, R. S. (1989). Cross-racial identification. *Personality and Social Psychology Bulletin, 15,* 19–25.

Bothwell, R. K., Deffenbacher, K. A., & Brigham, J. C. (1987). Correlation of eyewitness accuracy and confidence: Optimality hypothesis revisited. *Journal of Applied Psychology, 72,* 691–695.

Brandon, R., & Davies, C. (1973). *Wrongful imprisonment.* London: Allen & Unwin.

Brigham, J. C., & Bothwell, R.K. (1983). The ability of prospective jurors to estimate the accuracy of eyewitness identifications. *Law and Human Behaviour, 7,* 19–30

Brigham, J. C., & Cairns, D.L. (1988). The effect of mugshot inspections on eyewitness identification accuracy. *Journal of Applied Social Psychology, 18,* 1394–1410.

Brigham, J. C., Maass, A., Snyder, L. D., & Spaulding K. (1982). Accuracy of eyewitness identifications in a field setting. *Journal of Personality and Social Psychology, 42,* 673–680.

Brigham, J. C., and Pfeifer, J. E. (1994). Evaluating the fairness of lineups. In D. F. Ross, J. D. Read, & M. P. Toglia, (Eds.), *Adult eyewitness testimony: Current trends and developments* (pp. 223–244). New York: Cambridge University Press.

Brigham, J. C., & Ready, D. J. (1985). Own-race bias in lineup construction. *Law and Human Behaviour, 9*, 415–424.

Brigham, J. C., Ready, D. J., & Spier, S. A. (1990). Standards for evaluating the fairness of photograph lineups. *Basic and Applied Social Psychology, 11,* 149–163.

Brigham, J. C., Van Verst, M., & Bothwell, R. K. (1986). Accuracy of children's eyewitness identifications in a field setting. *Basic and Applied Social Psychology, 7,* 295–306.

Brigham, J. C., & Wolfskiel, M. P. (1983). Opinions of attorneys and law enforcement personnel on the accuracy of eyewitness identification. *Law and Human Behavior, 7,* 337–349.

Brown, E., Deffenbacher, K., & Sturgill, W. (1977). Memory for faces and the circumstances of encounter. *Journal of Applied Psychology, 62,* 311–318.

Buckhout, R. (1974). Eyewitness testimony. *Scientific American, 231,* 23–31.

Buckhout, R., Figueroa, D., & Hoff, E. (1975). Eyewitness identification: Effects of suggestion and bias in identification from photographs. *Bulletin of the Psychonomic Society, 6,* 71–74.

Cassell, P. G. (1992). 200-year-old tradition of peremptory challenges fades away. *The Review (July 31),* A17, A21.

Cavoukian, A. (1980, September). *Eyewitness testimony: The ineffectiveness of discrediting information.* Paper presented at the meeting of the American Psychological Association Meeting, Montreal.

Cecil, J. S., & Willging, T. E. (1994). The use of court-appointed experts in federal courts. *Judicature, 78,* 41–46.

Chance, J. E., & Goldstein, A. G. (1984). Face-recognition memory: Implications for children's eyewitness testimony. *Journal of Social Issues, 40,* 69–85.

Christiaanson, S. (1992). Emotional stress and eyewitness memory: A critical review. *Psychological Bulletin, 112,* 284–309.

Clifford, B. R., & Bull, R. (1978). *The psychology of person identification.* Boston: Routledge & Kegan.

Clifford, B. R., & Hollin, C. R. (1981). Effects of the type of incident and the number of perpetrators on eyewitness memory. *Journal of Applied Psychology, 66,* 364–370.

Clifford, B. R., & Scott, J. (1978). Individual and situational factors in eyewitness testimony. *Journal of Applied Psychology, 63,* 352–359.

Cohen, J. (1962). The statistical power of abnormal-social psychological research: A review. *Journal of Abnormal and Social Psychology, 65,* 145–153.

Cohen, J. (1977). *Statistical power analysis for the behavioral sciences* (rev. ed.). New York: Academic Press.

Cohen, M. E., & Carr, W. J. (1975). Facial recognition and the von Restorff effect. *Bulletin of the Psychonomic Society, 6,* 383–384.

Commonwealth v. Jones, 287 N.E. 2d 599 (Mass., 1972).

Cooper, H. M., & Lemke, K. M. (1991). On the role of meta-analysis in personality and social psychology. *Personality and Social Psychology Bulletin, 17,* 245–251.

Criglow v. State, 36 S.W.2d 400 (1931).

Cutler, B. L., Dexter, H. R., & Penrod, S. D. (1989). Expert testimony and jury decision making: An empirical analysis. *Behavioral Sciences and Law, 7,* 215–225.

Cutler, B. L., Dexter, H. R., & Penrod, S. D. (1990). Nonadversarial methods for improving juror sensitivity to eyewitness evidence. *Journal of Applied Social Psychology, 20,* 1197–1207.

Cutler, B. L., & Fisher, R. P. (1990). Live lineups, videotaped lineups, and photoarrays. *Forensic Reports, 3,* 439–448.

Cutler, B. L., Moran, G., & Narby, D. J. (1992). Jury selection in insanity defense cases. *Journal of Research in Personality, 26,* 165–182.

Cutler, B. L., & Penrod, S. D. (1988a). Improving the reliability of eyewitness identification: Lineup construction and presentation. *Journal of Applied Psychology, 73,* 281–290.

Cutler, B. L. & Penrod, S. (1988b). Context reinstatement and eyewitness identification. In G. Davies & D. Thomson (Eds.), *Memory in context: Context in memory.* Chichester: Wiley.

Cutler, B. L., & Penrod, S. D. (1989). Forensically relevant moderators of the relation between eyewitness identification accuracy and confidence. *Journal of Applied Psychology, 74,* 650–652.

Cutler, B. L., Penrod, S. D., & Dexter, H. R. (1989). The eyewitness, the expert psychologist, and the jury. *Law and Human Behavior, 13,* 311–332.

Cutler, B. L., Penrod, S. D., & Dexter, H. R. (1990a). Juror sensitivity to eyewitness identification evidence. *Law and Human Behavior, 14,* 185–191.

Cutler, B. L., Penrod, S. D., & Dexter, H. R. (1990b). Nonadversarial methods for sensitizing jurors to eyewitness evidence. *Journal of Applied Social Psychology, 20,* 1197–1207.

Cutler, B. L., Penrod, S. D., & Martens, T. K. (1987a). The reliability of eyewitness identifications: The role of system and estimator variables. *Law and Human Behavior, 11,* 223–258.

Cutler, B. L., Penrod, S. D., & Martens, T. K. (1987b). Improving the reliability of eyewitness identifications: Putting context into context. *Journal of Applied Psychology, 72,* 629–637.

Cutler, B. L., Penrod, S. D., O'Rourke, T. E., & Martens, T. K. (1986). Unconfounding the effects of contextual cues on eyewitness identification accuracy. *Social Behaviour, 1,* 113–134.

Cutler, B. L., Penrod, S. D., & Stuve, T. E. (1988). Juror decision making in eyewitness identification cases. *Law and Human Behavior, 12,* 41–55.

Daubert v. Merrell Dow Pharmaceuticals, Inc., 125 L. Ed. 2d 469, 113 S. Ct. 2786 (1993).

Davies, G. M., Ellis, H. D., & Shepherd, J. (1978). Face recognition accuracy as a function of mode of representation. *Journal of Applied Psychology, 63,* 180–187.

Davies, G. M., Shepherd, J. W., & Ellis, H. D. (1979). Effects of interpolated mugshot exposure on accuracy of eyewitness identification. *Journal of Applied Psychology, 64,* 232–237.

Deffenbacher, K. A. (1983). Eyewitness accuracy and confidence: Can we infer anything about their relationship? *Law and Human Behavior, 4,* 243–260.

Deffenbacher, K. A. (1991). A maturing of research on the behavior of eyewitnesses. *Applied Cognitive Psychology, 5,* 377–402.

Deffenbacher, K. A., & Loftus, E. F. (1982). Do jurors share a common understanding concerning eyewitness behavior? *Law and Human Behavior, 6,*

15–30.

Devine, P. G., & Malpass, R. S. (1985). Orienting strategies in differential face recognition. *Personality and Social Psychology Bulletin, 11*, 33–40.

Doob, A. N., & Kirshenbaum, H. M. (1973). Bias in police lineups: Partial remembering. *Journal of Police Science and Administration, 1*, 287–293.

Eagly, A. H., & Carli, L. L. (1981). Sex of researchers and sex-typed communications as determinants of sex differences in influenceability: A meta-analysis of social influence studies. *Psychological Bulletin, 90*, 1–20.

Easter v. Stainer, 1994 U.S. Dist. LEXIS 5668 (1994).

Echavarria v. State, 839 P.2D 589 (1992).

Elliott, R. (1993). Expert testimony about eyewitness identification: A critique. *Law and Human Behavior, 17*, 423–437.

Ellis, H. D., Davies, G. M., & Shepherd, J. W. (1977). Experimental studies of face identification. *Journal of Criminal Defense, 3*, 219–234.

Ellison, K. W., & Buckhout, R. (1981). *Psychology and criminal justice.* New York: Harper & Row.

English, T.J. (1995, January 2). On the defensive: as the leading legal experts in DNA testing, Peter Neufeld and Barry Scheck specialize in freeing the wrongfully convicted. *New York Magazine*, p. 38.

Erlenmeyer-Kimling, L., & Jarvik, L. F. (1963). Genetics and intelligence: A review. *Science, 142*, 1477–1479.

Farrell v. State, 612 N.E.2d 124 (1993)

Fazio, R. H., & Zanna, M. P. (1981). Direct experience and attitude-behavior consistency. In L. Berkowitz (Ed.), *Advances in experimental social psychology (Vol. 14)*. New York, NY: Academic Press.

Federal Rules of Evidence for United States Courts and Magistrates (1975). St. Paul, MN: West Publishing Company.

Feinman, S., & Entwistle, D. R. (1976). Children's ability to recognize other children's faces. *Child Development, 47*, 506–510.

Fisher, R. P., & Cutler, B. L. (in press). Relation between consistency and accuracy of eyewitness testimony. In G. M. Davies, S. Lloyd-Bostock, M. McMurran, & C. Wilson (Eds.), *Psychology and law: Advances in research*. Berlin: De Gruyter.

Fisher, R. P., & Geiselman, R. E. (1992). *Memory-enhancing techniques for investigative interviewing.* Springfield, IL: Charles C. Thomas.

Fleishman, J. J., Buckley, M. L., Klosinsky, M. J., Smith, N., & Tuck, B. (1976). Judged attractiveness in recognition memory of women's faces. *Perceptual and Motor Skills, 43*, 709–710.

Florida Standard Jury Instructions in Criminal Cases (1994). Tallahassee, FL: The Florida Bar.

Fox, S. G., & Walters, H. A. (1986). The impact of general versus specific expert testimony and eyewitness confidence upon mock-juror judgment. *Law and Human Behavior, 10*, 215–228.

Frank, J., & Frank, B. (1957). *Not guilty.* London: Gallancz.

Friedman, H. (1982). Simplified determinations of statistical power, magnitude of effect and research sample sizes. *Educational and Psychological Measurement, 42*, 521–526.

Frye v. United States, 293 F. 1013 (D.C. Cir. 1923).

Fulero, S. M. (1993). Eyewitness expert testimony: An overview and annotated bibliography, 1931–1988. Unpublished manuscript, Sinclair College.

Fulero, S. M., & Penrod, S. D. (1990). Attorney jury selection folklore: What do they think and how can psychologists help? *Forensic Reports, 3*, 233–259.

George, R. (1991). A field and experimental evaluation of three methods of interviewing witnesses/victims of crime. Unpublished manuscript. Polytechnic of East London.

Gilbert v. California, 388 U.S. 263, 87 S.Ct. 1951, 18 L.Ed.2d 1178 (1967).

Glass, G. V., McGaw, B., & Smith, M. L. (1981). *Meta-analysis in social research.* Beverly Hills, CA: Sage.

Going, M., & Read, J. D. (1974). Effects of uniqueness, sex of subject, and sex of photograph on facial recognition. *Perceptual and Motor Skills, 39*, 109–110.

Goldberg, L. R. (1968). Simple models or simple processes? Some research on clinical judgments. *American Psychologist, 23*, 483–496.

Goldstein, A. G., Chance, J. E., & Schneller, G. R. (1989). Frequency of eyewitness identification in criminal cases: A survey of prosecutors. *Bulletin of the Psychonomic Society, 27*, 71–74.

Goldstein, A. G., Chance, J. E., & Schneller, G. R. (1991). Frequency of eyewitness identifications in criminal cases: A survey of prosecutors. *Bulletin of the Psychonomic Society, 27*, 71–74.

Gorenstein, G. W., & Ellsworth, P. (1980). Effect of choosing an incorrect photograph on a later identification by an eyewitness. *Journal of Applied Psychology, 65*, 616–622.

Greene, E. (1988). Judge's instruction on eyewitness testimony: Evaluation and revision. *Journal of Applied Social Psychology, 18*, 252–276.

Hall, D. F. (1980, May). Memory for faces and words: Effects of stimulus presentation interval and depth of processing. Paper presented at the meeting of the Midwestern Psychological Association, St. Louis.

Hamling v. United States, 418 United States 87, 135, 94 S.Ct. 2887, 2916, 41 L.Ed.2d 590 (1974).

Harris, M. J. (1991). Controversy and cumulation: Meta-analysis and research on interpersonal expectancy effects. *Personality and Social Psychology Bulletin, 17*, 316–322.

Hastie, R. (1986). Notes on the psychologist expert witness. *Law and Human Behavior, 10*, 79–82.

Hastie, R., Landsman, R., & Loftus, E. F. (1978). Eyewitness testimony: The dangers of guessing. *Jurimetrics Journal, 19*, 1-8.

Hedges, L.V. (1982). Estimation of effect size from a series of independent experiments. *Psychological Bulletin, 92*, 490–499.

Hedges, L. V., & Olkin, I. (1985). *Statistical methods for meta-analysis.* San Diego, CA: Academic Press.

Heller, B. L. (1993). Twenty-second annual review of criminal procedure: United States Supreme Court and Courts of Appeals 1991–1992 I. Investigation and police Practices: Identifications, *Georgetown Law Journal, 81.*

Hosch, H. H. (1994). Individual differences in personality and eyewitness identification. *Adult eyewitness testimony: Current trends and developments* (pp. 328–347). New York: Cambridge University Press.

Hosch, H. M., Beck, E. L., & McIntyre, P. (1980). Influence of expert testimony regarding eyewitness accuracy on jury decisions. *Law and Human Behavior, 4*, 287–296.

Hosch, H. M., & Cooper, S. D. (1982). Victimization as a determinant of eyewitness accuracy. *Journal of Applied Psychology, 67*, 649–652.

Hosch, H. M., Leippe, M. R., Marchioni, P. M., & Cooper, D. S. (1984). Victimization, self-monitoring, and eyewitness identification. *Journal of Applied Psychology, 69,* 280–288.

Hosch, H. M., & Platz, S. J. (1984). Self-monitoring and eyewitness accuracy. *Personality and Social Psychology Bulletin, 10,* 289–292.

Howells, T. H. (1938). A study of ability to recognize faces. *Journal of Abnormal Social Psychology, 33,* 124–127.

Huff, C. R. (1987). Wrongful conviction: Societal tolerance of injustice. *Research in Social Problems and Public Policy, 4,* 99–115.

Huff, R., Rattner, A., & Sagarin, E. (1986). Guilty until proven innocent. *Crime and Delinquency, 32,* 518–544.

Imprisoned man is cleared in rape. (1995, January 31). *Bergen Record,* p. A5.

Johnson, C., & Scott, B. (1976, September). Eyewitness testimony and suspect identification as a function of arousal, sex of witness, and scheduling of interrogation. Paper presented at the meeting of the American Psychological Association, Washington, D.C.

Johnson v. Wainwright, 806 F.2D 1479 (1986).

Jordan v. State, 1994 Tex. App. LEXIS 1477 (1994).

Kassin, S. (1979). Personal communication cited by Wells, G. L. (1984). How adequate is human intuition for judging eyewitness testimony. In G. L. Wells & E. F. Loftus (Eds.), *Eyewitness testimony: Psychological perspectives* (pp. 256–272). New York: Cambridge University Press.

Kassin, S. M., Ellsworth, P. C., & Smith, V. L. (1989). The "general acceptance" of psychological research on eyewitness testimony: A survey of the experts. *American Psychologist, 44,* 1089–1098.

Kassin, S. M., Ellsworth, P. C., & Smith, V. L. (1994). *Deja vu* all over again: Elliott's critique of eyewitness experts. *Law and Human Behavior, 18,* 203–210.

Katzev, R. D., & Wishart, S. S. (1985). The impact of judicial commentary concerning eyewitness identifications on jury decision making. *The Journal of Criminal Law and Criminology, 76,* 733–745.

Kennedy, T. D., & Haygood, R. C. (1992). The discrediting effect in eyewitness testimony. *Journal of Applied Social Psychology, 22,* 70–82.

Kirby v. Illinois, 406 United States 682, 689 (1972).

Kohnken, G., & Maass. A. (1988). Eyewitness testimony: False alarms on biased instructions? *Journal of Applied Psychology, 73,* 363–370.

Kolata, G. (August 5, 1994). Advocates use DNA defense to unlock prison doors. *New York Times,* 1.

Konecni, V. J., & Ebbesen, E. B. (1979). External validity of research in legal psychology. *Law and Human Behavior, 3,* 39–70.

Konecni, V. J., & Ebbesen, E. B. (1986). Courtroom testimony by psychologists on eyewitness identification issues: Critical notes and reflections. *Law and Human Behavior, 10,* 117–126.

Krafka, C., & Penrod, S. (1985). Reinstatement of context in a field experiment on eyewitness identification. *Journal of Personality and Social Psychology, 49,* 58–69.

Krist v. Eli Lilly and Co., 897 F.2d 293 (7th Cir. 1990).

Laughery, K. R., Alexander, J. F., & Lane, A. B. (1971). Recognition of human faces: Effects of target exposure time, target position, and type of photograph. *Journal of Applied Psychology, 59,* 490–496.

Leippe, M.R., Manion, A.P., & Romanczyk, A. (1992). Eyewitness persuasion: How and how well do fact finders judge the accuracy of adults' and children's memory reports? *Journal of Personality and Social Psychology, 63,* 181-197.

Leippe, M. R., Wells, G. L., & Ostrom, T. M. (1978). Crime seriousness as a determinant of accuracy in eyewitness identification. *Journal of Applied Psychology, 63,* 345-351.

Light, L., Kayra-Stuart, F., & Hollander, S. (1979). Recognition memory for typical and unusual faces. *Journal of Experimental Psychology, 5,* 212-228.

Lindsay, R. C. L. (1994). Biased lineups: Where do they come from? In D. F. Ross, J. D. Read, & M. P. Toglia (Eds.), *Adult eyewitness testimony: Current trends and developments* (pp. 182-200). New York: Cambridge University Press.

Lindsay, R. C. L., Lea, J. A,. & Fulford, J. A. (1991). Sequential lineup presentation: Technique matters. *Journal of Applied Psychology, 76,* 741-745.

Lindsay, R. C. L., Lea, J. A., Nosworthy, G. J., & Fulford, J. A. (1991). Biased lineups: Sequential presentation reduces the problem. *Journal of Applied Psychology, 76,* 796-802.

Lindsay, R. C. L., Lim, R., Marando, L., & Cully, D. (1986). Mock-juror evaluations of eyewitness testimony: A test of metamemory hypotheses. *Journal of Applied Social Psychology,* 16, 447-459.

Lindsay, R. C. L., Wallbridge, H., & Drennan, D. (1987). Do the clothes make the man? An exploration of the effect of lineup attire on eyewitness identification accuracy. *Canadian Journal of Behavioural Science, 19,* 463-478.

Lindsay, R. C. L., & Wells, G. L. (1980). What price justice? Exploring the relationship of lineup fairness to identification accuracy. *Law and Human Behavior, 4,* 303-314.

Lindsay, R. C. L., & Wells, G. L. (1983). What do we really know about cross-race eyewitness identification? In S. M. A. Lloyd-Bostock & B. R. Clifford (Eds.), *Evaluating witness evidence: Recent psychological research and new perspectives* (pp. 219-234). New York: Wiley.

Lindsay, R. C. L., & Wells, G. L. (1985). Improving eyewitness identifications from lineups: Simultaneous versus sequential lineup presentation. *Journal of Applied Psychology, 70,* 556-564.

Lindsay, R. C. L., Wells, G. L., & O'Connor, F. J. (1989). Mock juror belief of accurate and inaccurate eyewitnesses: A replication and extension. *Law and Human Behavior, 13,* 333-339.

Lindsay, R. C. L., Wells, G. L., & Rumpel, C. M. (1981). Can people detect eyewitness identification accuracy within and across situations? *Journal of Applied Psychology, 66,* 79-89.

Lloyd-Bostock, S., & Clifford, B. R. (1983). *Evaluating witness evidence.* London: Wiley.

Loftus, E. F. (1974). Reconstructive memory: The incredible eyewitness. *Psychology Today, 8,* 116-119.

Loftus, E. F. (1979). *Eyewitness testimony.* Cambridge, MA: Harvard University Press.

Loftus, E. F. (1980). Impact of expert psychological testimony on the unreliability of eyewitness identification. *Journal of Applied Psychology, 65,* 9-15.

Loftus, E. F. (1986a). Experimental psychologist as advocate or impartial educator. *Law and Human Behavior, 10,* 63-78.

Loftus, E. F. (1986b). Ten years in the life of an expert witness. *Law and Human Behavior, 10,* 241-263.

Loftus, E. F., Loftus, G. R., & Messo, J. (1987). Some facts about "weapon focus." *Law and Human Behavior, 11,* 55-62.

Loh, W. D. (1981). Psycholegal research: Past and present. *Michigan Law Review, 79,* 659–707.

Look-alike named a suspect, and a woman leaves prison. (1995, April 17). *New York Times, p.* 13.

Luus, C. E. (1991). *Eyewitness confidence: Social influence and belief perseverance.* Unpublished doctoral dissertation, Iowa State University.

Luus, C. E., & Wells, G. L. (1991). Eyewitness identification and the selection of distracters for lineups. *Law and Human Behavior, 15,* 43–57.

Luus, C. A. E., & Wells, G. L. (1994). The malleability of eyewitness confidence: Co-witness and perseverance effects. *Journal of Applied Psychology, 79,* 714–723.

Maass, A., Brigham, J. C., & West, S. G. (1985). Testifying on eyewitness reliability: Expert advice is not always persuasive. *Journal of Applied Social Psychology, 15,* 207–229.

Maass, A., & Kohnken, G. (1989). Eyewitness identification: Simulating the "weapon effect." *Law and Human Behavior, 13,* 397–409.

McCloskey, M., & Egeth, H. (1983). Eyewitness identification: What can a psychologist tell a jury? *American Psychologist, 38,* 550–563.

McCloskey, M., Egeth, H., & McKenna, J. (1986). The experimental psychologist in court: The ethics of expert testimony. *Law and Human Behavior, 10,* 1–13.

McCloskey, M., Egeth, H., Webb, E., Washburn, A., & McKenna, J. (1981). Eyewitnesses, jurors and the issue of overbelief. Unpublished manuscript, Johns Hopkins University.

McConkey, K. M., & Roche, S. M. (1989). Knowledge of eyewitness memory. *Australian Psychologist, 24,* 377–384.

Malpass, R. S., & Devine, P. G. (1981). Eyewitness Identification: Lineup instructions and the absence of the offender. *Journal of Applied Psychology, 66,* 482–489.

Malpass, R. S., & Devine, P. G. (1983). Measuring the fairness of eyewitness identification lineups. In S. M. A. Lloyd-Bostock and B. R. Clifford (Eds.), *Evaluating witness evidence* (pp. 81–102). Chichester, Great Britain: John Wiley & Sons.

Manson v. Brathwaite, 432 U.S. 98, 112, 97 S.Ct. 2243, 2252, 53 L.Ed.2d 140 (1977).

Moore v. Tate, 882 F.2D 1107 (1989).

Moran, G., & Comfort, J. C. (1986). Neither "tentative" or "fragmentary": Verdict preference of impaneled felony jurors as a function of attitude toward capital punishment. *Journal of Applied Psychology, 71,* 146–155.

Moran, G., Cutler, B. L., & Loftus, E. F. (1990). Jury selection in major controlled substance trials: the need for extended voir dire. *Forensic Reports, 3,* 331–348.

Narby, D. J. (1993). *The effectiveness of voir dire as a safeguard against erroneous conviction resulting from mistaken eyewitness identification.* Unpublished doctoral dissertation, Florida International University, Miami.

Narby, D. J., & Cutler, B. L. (1994). Effectiveness of voir dire as a safeguard in eyewitness cases. *Journal of Applied Psychology, 79,* 274–279.

Narby, D. J., Cutler, B. L., & Moran, G. (1993). A meta-analysis of the association between authoritarianism and jurors' perceptions of defendant culpability. *Journal of Applied Psychology, 78,* 34–42.

Neil v. Biggers, 409 U.S. 188, 34 L.Ed.2d 401 (1972)), cert. denied, 444 U.S. 909, 100 S.Ct. 221, 62 L.Ed.2d 144 (1979).

Noon, E., & Hollin, C. R. (1987). Lay knowledge of eyewitness behaviour: A British survey. *Applied Cognitive Psychology, 1,* 143–153.

Oakes, L. (1993). A miscarriage of justice. *Star Tribune,* October 17, 18A.

O'Rourke, T. E., Penrod, S. D., & Cutler, B. L. (1989). The external validity of eyewitness identification research: Generalizing across subject populations. *Law and Human Behavior, 13,* 385–397.

Pachella, R. G. (1986). Personal values and the values of expert testimony. *Law and Human Behavior, 10,* 145–150.

Paley, B., & Geiselman, R. E. (1989). The effects of alternative photospread instructions on suspect identification performance. *American Journal of Forensic Psychology, 7,* 3–13.

Pankey v. Commonwealth, 485 S.W.2d 513 (KY. 1972).

Parker, J. F., Haverfield, E., & Baker-Thomas, S. (1986). Eyewitness testimony of children. *Journal of Applied Social Psychology, 16,* 287–302.

Parker, J. F., & Ryan, V. (1993). An attempt to reduce guessing behavior in children's and adults' eyewitness identifications. *Law and Human Behavior, 17,* 11–26.

Patterson, K. E., & Baddeley, A. D. (1977). When face recognition fails. Journal of Experimental Psychology: *Human Learning and Memory, 3,* 406–407.

Penrod, S. D., & Cutler, B. L. (1987). Assessing the competency of juries. In I. Weiner & A. Hess (Eds.), *The handbook of forensic psychology.* New York: Wiley.

Penrod, S., Loftus, E. F., & Winkler, J. D. (1982). Eyewitness reliability. In R. Bray & N. Kerr (Eds.), *The psychology of the courtroom.* New York: Academic Press.

Penry, J. (1971). *Looking at faces and remembering them: A guide to facial identification.* London: Elek Books.

People v. Brooks, 490 N.Y.S.2d 692 (1985).

People v. Campbell, 847 P.2D 228 (Co, 1992).

People v. Collier, 249 P.2d 72 (Cal. 1952).

People v. Contreras, 17 Cal.App.4th 813, 21 Cal.Rptr.2d 496 (1993).

People v. Johnson, 38 Cal. App. 3d 1, 112 Cal. Rptr. 834 (1974).

People v. Kurylczyk, 443 Mich. 289, 505 N.W.2d 528 (1993).

People v. Lewis, 520 N.Y.S.2d 125 (1987).

People v. McDonald, 37 Cal.3d 351, 690 P.2d 709, 716, 208 Cal.Rptr. 236, 245 (1984)

People v. Russell, 69 Cal.2d 187, 443 P.2d 794, 70 Cal. Rptr. 210, cert. denied, 393 United States 864 (1968).

Petty, R. E., & Cacioppo, J. T. (1986). The elaboration likelihood model of persuasion. In L. Berkowitz (Ed.), *Advances in experimental social psychology Vol. 19,* (pp. 123–205). New York: Academic Press.

Pigott, M. A., Brigham, J. C., & Bothwell, R. K. (1990). A field study of the relationship between quality of eyewitnesses' descriptions and identification accuracy. *Journal of Police Science and Administration, 17,* 84–88.

Platz, S. J., & Hosch, H. M. (1988). Cross racial/ethnic eyewitness identification: A field study. *Journal of Applied Social Psychology, 18,* 972–984.

Powers, T., & Luginbuhl, J. (1987, August). *Jurors' death penalty support and conviction proneness.* Paper presented at the 95th annual meeting of the American Psychological Association, New York.

Prager, I. R., Moran, G., & Sanchez, J. (1992). Assistant public defenders: Job analysis project. Unpublished manuscript. Florida International University, Miami.

Rahaim, G. L., & Brodsky, S. L. (1982). Empirical evidence versus common sense: Juror and lawyer knowledge of eyewitness accuracy. *Law and Psychology Review, 7,* 1–15.

Read, J. D. (1994). Understanding bystander misidentifications: The role of familiarity and contextual knowledge. In D. F. Ross, J. D., Read, & M. P. Toglia (Eds.), *Adult eyewitness testimony: Current trends and developments* (pp. 56–79). New York: Cambridge University Press.

Read, J. D., Vokey, J. R., & Hammersley, R. (in press). Changing photos of faces: Effects of duration and photo similarity on recognition and the accuracy-confidence relationship. *Journal of Experimental Psychology: Learning, Memory and Cognition.*

Read, J. D., Yuille, J. C., & Tollestrup, P. (in press). Recollections of a robbery: Effects of arousal and alcohol upon recall and person identification. *Law and Human Behavior.*

Rincon v. United States, 114 S. Ct. 41 (1993).

Rogers, R., & Ewing, C. P. (1989). Ultimate opinion proscriptions: A cosmetic fix and a plea for empiricism. *Law and Human Behavior, 13,* 357–374.

Rosenthal, R. (1976). *Experimenter effects in behavioral research.* New York: Irvington Press.

Rosenthal, R. (1978). Combining results of independent studies. *Psychological Bulletin, 85,* 185–193.

Rosenthal, R. (1979). The "file drawer problem" and tolerance for null results. *Psychological Bulletin, 86,* 638–641.

Rosenthal, R. (1991). *Meta-analytic procedures for social research.* Beverly Hills: Sage.

Rosenthal, R., & Rubin, D. (1982). A simple, general purpose display of magnitude of experimental effect. *Journal of Educational Psychology, 74,* 166–169.

Ross, D. F., Ceci, S. J., Dunning, D., & Toglia, M. P. (1991). Unconscious transference and mistaken identity: When a witness misidentifies a familiar but innocent person from a lineup . Paper presented at the American Psychological Society, Washington, D. C., June.

Ross, D. F., Read, J. D., & Toglia, M. P. (Eds.) (1994). *Adult eyewitness testimony: Current trends and developments* (pp. 80–100). New York: Cambridge University Press.

Sanders, G . S., & Warnick, D. H. (1980). Some conditions maximizing eyewitness accuracy: A learning memory model. *Journal of Criminal Justice, 8,* 395–403.

Saunders, D. M., Vidmar, N., & Hewitt, E. C. (1983). Eyewitness testimony and the discrediting effect. In S. M. A. Lloyd-Bostock and B. R. Clifford (Eds.), *Evaluating witness evidence* (pp. 57–78). New York: Wiley.

Shapiro, P. N., & Penrod, S. D. (1986). Meta-analysis of facial identification studies. *Psychological Bulletin, 100,* 139–156.

Shepherd, J. W. (1983). Identification after long delays. In S. M. A. Lloyd-Bostock & B. R. Clifford (Eds.), *Evaluating witness evidence* (pp. 173–187). Chichester: Wiley.

Shepherd, J. W., Ellis, H. D., & Davies, G. M. (1982). *Identification evidence.* Great Britain: Aberdeen University Press.

Skamarocius v. State 1987, 731 P.2d 63 (Alaska App. 1987).

Smith, A. D., & Winograd, E. (1978). Age differences in remembering face. *Developmental Psychology, 14,* 443–444.

Smith, S. M., & Vela, E. (1990). Environmental context-dependent eyewitness recognition. *Applied Cognitive Psychology, 6*, 125–139.

Snyder, M. (1979). Self-monitoring processes. In L. Berkowitz (Ed.), *Advances in experimental social psychology, Vol. 12* (pp. 85–128). New York: Academic Press.

Span, P. (1995, January 2). 'No higher calling'; Long before O.J., Barry Scheck and Peter Neufeld were at the forefront of applying dna tests to unravel criminal cases. *Los Angeles Times*, p. E1.

Sporer, S. (in press). Person descriptions in an archival analysis of criminal cases. *Journal of Applied Psychology*.

State v. Buell, 22 Ohio St.3d 124, 489 N.E. 2D 795, cert. denied, 479 U.S. 871, 107 S.Ct. 240, 93 L.Ed.2d 165 (1986).

State v. Chapple, 135 Ariz. 281, 660 P.2d 1208, 1221 (1983).

State v. Dillon, Ohio App. LEXIS 38 1994 .

State v. Johnson, 743 P.2d 290 (Wash. App. 1987).

State v. Johnson, 227 Conn. 611; 630 A.2d 69 (1993).

State v. Malarney, 18 Fla. L. Week. D906 (1993).

State v. McCord, 505 N.W.2d 388 (1993).

State v. Miller, 1994 WL 79292 (1994).

State v. Moon, 45 Wash. App. 692, 726 P.2d 1263 (1986).

Steblay, N. M. (1992). A meta-analytic review of the weapon focus effect. *Law and Human Behavior, 16*, 413–424.

Stovall vs. Denno (1967). 388 U.S. 293.

Sussman, E. D., & Sugarman, R. C. (1972). The effect of certain distractions on identification by witnesses. In A. Zavala, J. J. Paley, & R. R. J. Gallati (Eds.), *Personal appearance identification*. Springfield, IL: Charles Thomas.

Tollestrup, P. A., Turtle, J. W., & Yuille, J. C. (1994). Actual victims and witnesses to robbery and fraud: An archival analysis. *Adult eyewitness testimony: Current trends and developments* (pp. 144–160). New York: Cambridge University Press.

Tooley, V., Brigham, J. C., Maas, A., & Bothwell, R. K. (1986). Facial recognition: Weapon effect and attentional focus. *Journal of Applied Social Psychology, 17*, 845–859.

Tversky, A., & Kahneman, D. (1974). Judgment under uncertainty: Heuristics and biases. *Science, 185*, 1124–1131.

United States v. Amador-Galvan, 9 F.3d 1414 (9th Cir. 1993).

United States v. Amaral, 488 F.2d 1148 (9th Cir. 1973).

United States v. Ash, 413 United States 300 (1973).

United States v. Benitez, 741 F.2d 1312 (11th Cir. 1984).

United States v. Brewer, 783 F.2d 841 (9th Cir.), cert. denied, 479 U.S. 831 (1986).

United States v. Brown, 540 F.2d 1048, (10th Cir. 1976), cert. denied, 429 U.S. 1100, 97 S.Ct. 1122, 51 L.Ed.2d 549 (1977).

United States v. Brown, 501 F.2d 146 (9th Cir. 1974), rev'd on other grounds sub nom.

United States v. Brown, 557 F.2d 541 (6th Cir. 1977).

United States v. Christophe, 833 F.2d 1296, 1300 (9th Cir. 1987).

United States v. Collins, 837 F.2d 477 (6th Cir. 1988).

United States v. Curry, 977 F.2d 1042, 1052 (7th Cir. 1992), cert. denied, --- U.S. ----, 113 S.Ct. 1357, 122 L.Ed.2d 737 (1993).

United States v. Dowling, 855 F.2d 114, 118 (3d Cir. 1988), aff'd on other grounds, 493 U.S. 342, 110 S.Ct. 668, 107 L.Ed.2d 708 (1990).

United States v. Downing, 753 F.2d 1224 (3d Cir. 1985).

United States v. Fosher, 590 F.2d 381, 382–84 (1st Cir. 1979).

United States v. Gates, 20 F.3d 1550 (11th Cir. 1994).

United States v. George, 975 F.2D 1431 (9th Cir. 1992).

United States v. Green, 548 F.2d 1261 (6th Cir. 1977).

United States v. Harris, 995 F.2d 532 (4th Cir. 1993).

United States v. Holloway, 971 F.2d 675, 679 (11th Cir. 1992).

United States v. Hudson and Smith, 884 F.2D 1016 (7th Cir. 1989).

United States v. Langford, 802 F.2D 1176 (1986).

United States v. Little, U.S. App. LEXIS 2617 (1994).

United States v. Moore, 786 F.2d 1308 (5th Cir. 1986).

United States v. Nobles, 422 U.S. 225, 95 S.Ct. 2160, 45 L.Ed.2d 141 (1975).

United States v. Poole, 794 F.2d 462, 468 (9th Cir. 1986) (amended on other grounds, 806 F.2d 853 [9th Cir. 1986]).

United States v. Rasheed, 663 F.2d 843 (9th Cir.) cert. denied, 454 United States 1157, 102 S.Ct. 1031, 71 L.Ed.2d 315 (1982).

United States v. Rincon, 984 F.2d 1003 (9th Cir. 1993).

United States v. Rincon, 11 F.3d 922 (9th Cir. 1993).

United States v. Rincon, 1994 WL 265047 (9th Cir. 1994).

United States v. Russell, 532 F.2d 1063 (6th Cir. 1976).

United States v. Sebetich, 776 F.2d 412, 419 (3d Cir. 1985), cert. denied, --- U.S. ---, 108 S.Ct. 725, 98 L.Ed.2d 673 (1988).

United States v. Sims, 617 F.2d 1371, 1375 (9th Cir. 1980).

United States v. Smith, 736 F.2d 1103, 1105–06 (6th Cir. 1984), cert. denied, 469 U.S. 868, 105 S.Ct. 213, 83 L.Ed.2d 143 (1984).

United States v. Stevens, 935 F.2d 1380, 1400–01 (3d Cir. 1991).

United States v. Telfaire, 469 F.2d 552, 558–59 (D. C. Cir.1979).

United States v. Thevis, 665 F.2d 616 (5th Cir.), cert. denied, 456 U.S. 1008, 102 S.Ct. 2300, 73 L.Ed.2d 1303 (1982).

United States v. Tyler, 714 F.2d 664 (1983).

United States v. Wade, 388 U.S. 218 (1967).

United States v. Watson, 587 F.2d 365, 368–69 (7th Cir. 1978), cert. denied, 439 U.S. 1132, 99 S.Ct. 1055, 59 L.Ed.2d 95 (1979).

Wall, P. C. (1965). *Eyewitness identification in criminal cases.* Springfield, IL: Charles C. Thomas.

Walters, C. M. (1985). Admission of expert testimony on eyewitness identification. *California Law Review, 73,* 1402–1430.

Watkins v. Sowders, 449 U.S. 341 (1981).

Weinberg, H. I., & Baron, R. S. (1982). The discredible eyewitness. *Personality and Social Psychology Bulletin, 8,* 60–67.

Weiten, W., & Diamond, S. S. (1979). A critical review of the jury simulation paradigm: The case of defendant characteristics. *Law and Human Behavior, 3,* 71–93.

Wells, G. L. (1986). Expert psychological testimony: Empirical and conceptual analyses of effects. *Law and Human Behavior, 10,* 83–95.

Wells, G. L. (1984). How adequate is human intuition for judging eyewitness testimony. In G. L. Wells & E. F. Loftus (Eds.), *Eyewitness testimony: Psychological perspectives* (pp. 256–272). New York: Cambridge University Press.

Wells, G. L. (1985). Verbal descriptions of faces from memory: Are they diagnostic of identification accuracy? *Journal of Applied Psychology, 70,* 619–626.

Wells, G. L. (1993). What do we know about eyewitness identification? *American Psychologist, 48,* 553–571.

Wells, G. L., & Leippe, M. R. (1981). How do triers of fact infer the accuracy of eyewitness identifications? Using memory for peripheral detail can be misleading. *Journal of Applied Psychology, 66,* 682–687.

Wells, G. L., Leippe, M. R., & Ostrom, T. M. (1979). Guidelines for empirically assessing the fairness of a lineup. *Law and Human Behavior, 3,* 285–293.

Wells, G. L., Lindsay, R. C. L., & Ferguson, T. J. (1979). Accuracy, confidence, and juror perceptions in eyewitness identification. *Journal of Applied Psychology, 64,* 440–448.

Wells, G. L., Lindsay, R. C. L., & Tousignant, J. P. (1980). Effects of expert psychological advice on human performance in judging the validity of eyewitness testimony. *Law and Human Behavior, 4,* 275–285.

Wells, G. L., & Luus, C. E. (1990). Police lineups as experiments: Social methodology as a framework for properly conducted lineups. *Personality and Social Psychology Bulletin, 16,* 106–117.

Wells, G. L., Seelau, E. P., Rydell, S. M., & Luus, C. A. (1994). Recommendations for properly conducted lineup identification tasks. In D.F. Ross, J.D. Read, & M.P. Toglia, (Eds.), *Adult eyewitness testimony: Current trends and developments* (pp. 223–244). New York: Cambridge University Press.

Whitener, E. M. (1990). Confusion of confidence intervals and credibility intervals in meta-analyses. *Journal of Applied Psychology, 75,* 315–321.

Wier, J. A., & Wrightsman, L. S. (1990). The determinants of mock-jurors' verdicts in a rape case. *Journal of Applied Social Psychology, 20,* 901–919.

Williams, K .D., Loftus, E. F., & Deffenbacher, K. A. (1992). Eyewitness evidence and testimony. In D. K., Kagehiro, & W. S. Laufer, (Eds.) *Handbook of psychology and law.* New York: Springer-Verlag.

Witryol, S., & Kaess, W. (1957). Sex differences in social memory tasks. *Journal of Abnormal and Social Psychology, 54,* 343–346.

Woodhead, M. M., Baddeley, A. D., & Simmonds, D. C. (1979). On training people to recognize faces. *Ergonomics, 22,* 333–343.

Wrightsman, L. S., Nietzel, M. T., & Fortune, W. H. (1993). *Psychology and the legal system (third edition).* Pacific Grove, CA: Brooks/Cole Publishing Company.

Yarmey, A. D., & Jones, H. P. T. (1983a). Accuracy of memory of male and female eyewitnesses to criminal assault and rape. *Bulletin of the Psychonomic Society, 2,* 89–92.

Yarmey, A. D., & Jones, H. P. T. (1983b). Is the psychology of eyewitness identification a matter of common sense? In S. Lloyd-Bostock and B. R. Clifford (Eds.), *Evaluating witness evidence: Recent psychological research and new perspectives.* Chichester, England: Wiley.

Yarmey, A. D., & Kent, J. (1980). Eyewitness identification by elderly and young adults. Unpublished manuscript, University of Guelph.

Yuille, J. C., & Tollestrup, P. A. (1990). Some effects of alcohol on eyewitness memory. *Journal of Applied Psychology, 75,* 268–273.

Zemba, D. J., & Geiselman, R. E. (1993). *Eyewitness identification instructions to the jury: Help or hindrance in the decision-making process?* Manuscript under review.

Name index

Subject index

Printed in the United Kingdom
by Lightning Source UK Ltd.
9711000001B/163-168